TARGUM AND TESTAMENT

Aramaic Paraphrases of the Hebrew Bible:
A Light on the New Testament

Martin McNamara MSC

TARGUM
AND TESTAMENT

Aramaic Paraphrases of the Hebrew Bible :
A Light on the New Testament

IRISH UNIVERSITY PRESS

Shannon · Ireland

Imprimatur: ✠ Josephus,
Archiepiscopus Tuamensis
Die ix mense Augusto A.D. 1968

ISBN 0 7165 0619 X

Microfilm, microfiche and other forms of micro-publishing
© Irish University Microforms   Shannon   Ireland

Irish University Press Shannon Ireland

DUBLIN   CORK   BELFAST   LONDON   NEW YORK

T M MacGlinchey publisher
Robert Hogg printer

FILMSET AND PRINTED IN THE REPUBLIC OF IRELAND AT THE
IRISH UNIVERSITY PRESS, SHANNON

Contents

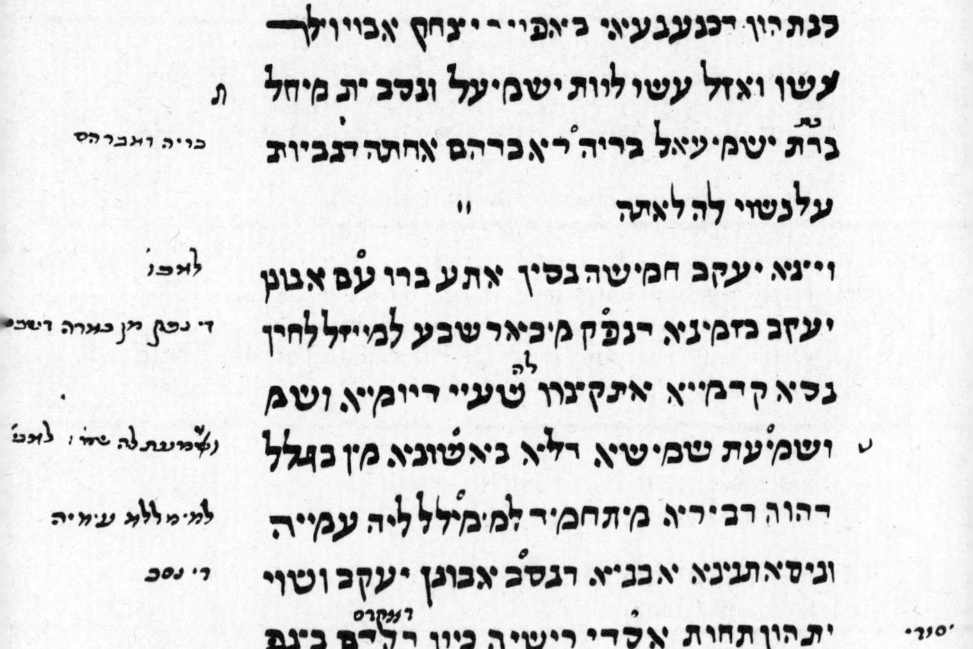

כנת הון דכנענעאי באפי׳ דיצחק אביו׳ ל־

עשו ואזל עשו לוות ישמיעאל ונסב ית מחל ת

ברת ישמיעאל בריה דאברהם אחתה דנביות

עלנשוי לה לאתה ײ

ויינא יעקב חמישה בסין אתע ברו עם אבון

יעקב בזמינא דנפק מיבאר שבע למיזל לחרן

נסא קדמיא אתקצור טעי דיומיא ושם

ושמיעת שמישיא דלא באשונא מן בגלל

דהוה דבירא מתחמיד למ מללה ליה עמיה

וניסא תנינא אבניא דנסב אבונן יעקב וטוי

יתהון תחות אסדי רישיה כיון דלרס כנב

ביגפרא ואשתכח כלהון לאבן חדא היא אבנא

ראקים קיימ יאו אריך משח על ראשה

וניסא תליתאה כיון דנטל אבונן יעקב יגלוי

למיזל לחרן כפינת ארעא קדמוי ואשתכח

יתיב בחרן ונסא רביעאה אבנא דהוון כל

רעיא מתכנשין למגללה יתה מעלוי פומיה

יבארה ולא הוון יכלין כיון דאתא אבונן יעק ב

Marginal notes (right side, top to bottom):

ת

כריה ואברהם

לאבוי

די נסב מן כאורה ושב

ונלשמעתה שמ. לאבוי

למ מלל עמיה

ר׳ נסב

דמקרס

סורי

דמקיס

תליתי־ע

ותקפת

שעה ונצרא

דעבדה

ב טפרוטאיה ולא

The Palestinian Targum as found in Codex Neofiti 1 (Apostolic Vatican Library), folio 56a, with midrash on the Well of Jacob (Genesis 28:10); translation on pp. 145 f., below. Reproduction of Targum by kind permission of the Biblioteca Apostolica.

The Targum of Pseudo-Jonathan (British Museum MS. Addit. 27031, folio 55b; courtesy of the Trustees of the British Museum) with paraphrase of the opening words of the Blessing of Jacob (Genesis 49:1–7); translation on p. 140, below.

Abbreviations

Frag. Targ.	Fragment Targum
HT	Hebrew Text
Meg.	*Megillah*
MT	Masoretic Text
Onk.	Onkelos
Pal. Targ.	Palestinian Targum(s)
Ps.-Jon.	Pseudo-Jonathan
RSV	The Holy Bible, Revised Standard Version
Targ. Proph.	Targum to the Prophets
TJ I	Targum Jerushalmi 1 = Pseudo-Jonathan
TJ 2	Targum Jerushalmi 2 = Fragment Targum
Tos.	Tosephta

I

Ancient Jewish Writings

Over the past century scholars have turned to the literatures of many nations in their effort to elucidate problems arising from the writings of the New Testament. Egyptian, Babylonian and Iranian traditions have by some been considered to have influenced the New Testament, as have also Greek and Jewish traditions.

The arguments for Egyptian or Babylonian influences were at best weak. What slight evidence for Babylonian contacts there may be would at most indicate an indirect and remote influence, that is, through a prior influence on Jewish religion and thought. And the same can be said for the parallels brought forward from Iranian religion and civilization.

A much stronger case can be advanced for Hellenistic Greek influence on the New Testament writers. Paul was a Roman citizen from Tarsus who expressly declares he became Greek to the Greeks. The entire johannine tradition (the Fourth Gospel, the three Letters and the Apocalypse of John) was probably formed in Asia Minor. Luke was a well-educated Greek and the First Gospel, as well as the Gospel of Mark, were first written in Greek. The gospel tradition may well have adopted Greek ways of thought in an effort to make it meaningful to the Greek-speaking world. There are many who maintain that such in fact was the case and that in the New Testament we find many concepts taken over from Hellenistic civilization, such as saviour, redemption, liberty, freedom of speech (*parrhêsia*), and Lord (in speaking of Christ as Lord, Kyrios).

There is, of course, no *a priori* reason why such should not have been the case. In matters of this nature we must go on the available evidence alone. Yet we can never lose sight of the fact that the preaching of the gospel had its origins within Judaism. Christ and the Apostles were Jews. The gospel tradition, too, was formed in a Jewish atmosphere within Palestine during the early years of the nascent Church. And this tradition was formed by men who for the greater part were themselves Jews. And even when Christianity moved beyond Palestine to the Greek world, it was brought there by Jews. They may preach to Greeks but they would naturally have thought as Hebrews.

While Hellenistic influence can by no means be excluded *a priori,* its importance should not be exaggerated. It may well be that what at first sight appears Greek may on more detailed analysis be shown as typically Jewish. And in point of fact such has often been the case, at least as far as the *immediate* source of the concepts in question go. In some cases there may be a remote Greek influence, in so far as Judaism had already assimilated a number of Greek ideas. It is natural, in any event, that we should explore Judaism to the full to see what light it has to shed on the New Testament. It is the most likely source for immediate influence on the New Testament writers, and so far it has proved by far the richest source for New Testament parallels.[1]

It is not sufficient, however, to say that parallels to New Testament texts, to passages from the Gospels in particular, are to be sought in Judaism rather than in Hellenism. Judaism in the New Testament period had a variety of currents within it. One must also seek to determine to what particular form of Judaism the New Testament writings are most closely related, to see which form has influenced these writings the most. This approach will have a bearing not merely on the interpretation of individual texts but on our overall view of the New Testament and its relation to the Jewish religion. Before this can be done, however, the relation of the New Testament to the individual forms of Jewish religion must first be considered.

Jewish Apocalyptic

Apocalyptic writings were composed in Judaism from the second century B.C. to the second century A.D. The best-known

1. Among the more recent studies to bring out the Jewish background of the Fourth Gospel we may instance I. de la Potterie's *Alètheia. La notion johannique de vérité et ses antécédents historiques,* a doctoral dissertation presented at the Pontifical Biblical Institute, Rome. Chapter 3 of this work has been published: ' "Je suis la Voie, la Vérité et la Vie" (Jn 14,6)' in *Nouvelle revue théologique* 38 (1966) 907–42.

works in this class of literature are the book of Daniel and the Apocalypse—the former from the Old Testament, the latter from the New. (How far the Apocalypse of John can really be styled apocalyptic need not trouble us here.) But apart from these two canonical writings we have a number of apocryphal apocalyptic books, such as the Book of Jubilees, the Book of Henoch, the Testaments of the Twelve Patriarchs, Fourth Esdras and Second Baruch. While the apocalyptic writings differ considerably among themselves, they have in common that, by a literary device, history up to the time of the apocalyptic writer (and original reader) is presented as revelation made to some prominent figure of Israel's past (Henoch, Moses, Esdras, Baruch, *et al.*), a revelation supposedly to be kept secret until later times, generally that of the actual authors of the works themselves. In these writings revelation (in Greek *apokalypsis,* whence the name 'apocalyptic') plays a major role and comes to the 'seer' through the opening of the heavens, visions, communications through angels, etc. Apocalyptic also indulges in 'revelations' on the messianic age and on the end of the world.

The importance of Jewish apocalyptic for an understanding of certain sections of the New Testament cannot be denied. But neither should the influence of this form of literature on the New Testament be exaggerated. The apocalyptic writers were somewhat off the mainstream of Judaism and they cannot be taken to represent the normal religious teaching of their age. Their religious ideas were peculiar to themselves rather than the common beliefs of the people within which, according to our evidence, Christianity arose. Sometimes the presence of certain apocalyptic teaching in the New Testament may be explained by the presence of apocalyptic elements in general Jewish culture rather than by a direct dependence of the New Testament on the works of the apocalyptic writers.

A certain caution is also necessary in the use of some of those apocalyptic works which show the most marked resemblance to the New Testament, a caution due to the uncertainty of the date to be ascribed to these works or to the relevant sections of them. This is particularly true of the parable section of the Book of Henoch (chapters 37–71) with its speculations on the Son of Man. The same holds for much of the Testaments of the Twelve Patriarchs. It is not in the least certain whether the

close relationship between these works and the New Testament
is to be explained through dependence of the New Testament
on them or through dependence of the relevant sections of the
works in question on the text of the New Testament. It is quite
possible that the works in question are really Christian com-
positions on the basis of Jewish documents or traditions. An
argument in favour of this latter viewpoint comes from Qumrân
where fragments of all sections of the Book of Henoch have been
found, except that of the parables, and where fragments of a
Testament of Levi and of a Testament of Naphthali have
shown up, but no evidence whatever of Testaments for all
Twelve Patriarchs. The Testaments of the Twelve Patriarchs
may then very well be a Christian composition, as it certainly
has at least a number of Christian interpolations.

In comparing the Gospels, or the New Testament in general,
with any given form of Judaism we must consider the points in
which the two differ as well as those in which they agree. And
from this point of view we can say that much of the language
and many of the concepts of the New Testament are nowhere
found in the apocalyptic writings. We fail to find in them, for
instance, such expressions as 'Father in heaven', 'merit before
your Father in heaven', etc. In this, Christ does not use the
language of apocalyptic. We must turn elsewhere for a literature
which will use this language.

The Dead Sea Scrolls

The Dead Sea Scrolls, discovered in the caves around Qumrân
from 1947 onwards, have thrown a flood of light on one section
of Judaism for the period about the turn of the era. To these
scrolls we can also add the texts from Murabba'at and neighbouring areas, coming in the main from the fourth decade of
the second century A.D.

These new manuscripts and fragments are of immense
importance for the history of the text of the Hebrew Bible. They
are likewise of prime importance for a study of first-century
Aramaic. These two aspects of the importance of the new finds
need not detain us here; we shall return to them later. What is
more important from our point of view is the strictly sectarian
writings of the Qumrân community which tell us of the religious
beliefs and messianic expectations of the monks of Qumrân.

One great advantage of these documents is that a definite date can be affixed to them; the latest text was written before A.D. 70. They are then roughly contemporary with the Gospels and a good part of the New Testament.

In view of the novelty and of the nature of the material, it is only natural that over the past two decades scholars have devoted their attention to the bearing of the Qumrân texts on the New Testament. While admitting the positive contributions these texts have to make in the field of Jewish-New Testament relationships, one should not forget the limitations inherent in this new corpus of literature. It was produced by Jews who had voluntarily cut themselves off from the main body of their people, from official Jewry which they considered to be in error in the matter of the calendar. Christ and his apostles, on the other hand, as far as we know followed the official calendar, visiting the temple and observing the regular Jewish feasts at the set time.

Then again, while the Scrolls elucidate certain aspects of the vocabulary of the New Testament, in other respects the language of the Qumrân manuscripts is as alien to that of the Gospels as the language of the apocalyptic writings is. This fact must be borne in mind when one compares the writings of the Qumrân sectaries with the New Testament. It indicates that there is a difference of background between the two, that other influences have been operative in the formation of the New Testament than the form of Judaism represented by the Qumrân community.

Rabbinic Judaism

The favourite source of parallels for the New Testament has long been rabbinic writings such as the Mishnah, the Tosephta, the Talmud and the midrashim. How rich these are in illustrative material is clear from the four dense volumes of H. L. Strack and P. Billerbeck (actually almost entirely the work of Billerbeck alone): *Kommentar zum Neuen Testament aus Talmud und Midrasch*. Since rabbinic writings are closely related to the targums—to which the present work is entirely devoted—and seeing that in the course of this work occasional reference will be made to midrash and to the rabbinic writings, a few words on the nature of these rabbinic works will not be out of place here.

Present-day Judaism is the continuation of the religion of the scribes and the Pharisees who are so often mentioned in the Gospels. With the fall of Jerusalem and the destruction of the Temple in A.D. 70, the Sadducees and the Essenes practically pass from the scene, and of the three major Jewish religious groups the Pharisees alone remain. The rabbis, the religious teachers of this class, immediately set themselves the task of reorganizing Judaism for the future. The outcome of this work, and the culmination of a process that had been operative for some centuries before the Christian era, can be seen in the works already referred to: the Mishnah, Tosephta, Talmud and midrashim.

Characteristic of the scribes and Pharisees, as of their successors the rabbis, was their insistence on the oral law. This embraced an entire complex of new legislation which had developed over a long period in an effort to keep men from transgressing the letter of the written Law of Moses. This oral law they themselves refer to as 'tradition', 'the tradition (or 'traditions') of the elders'. It is the 'traditions of the scribes and Pharisees' referred to in the Gospels (see Mark 7:5; Matthew 15:2,6). It was their way of life; the way in which they set themselves to walk. Since the Hebrew word for 'to go', 'to walk', is *halak*, custom, traditional law, or the traditional interpretation of a written law is known as *halakah* (plural: *halakoth*).

The main preoccupation of the rabbis was with the legalistic side of their tradition. During the New Testament period the understanding of it was very much debated among them. The development went on after the fall of Jerusalem and the long process finally resulted in a multiplicity of enactments on every aspect of Jewish life. The need for some form of codification was evident. Preliminary collections of laws finally led to an authoritative text by Rabbi Judah the Patriarch (R. Judah *ha-nasi*) about A.D. 180. This authoritative code of Jewish law, which will serve as the basis of still later development, is known as the *Mishnah*. In it all the laws are brought under six heads, constituting six large divisions, called *orders*: 1, *Zeraʿim* ('Seeds'); 2, *Moʿed* ('Set Feasts'); 3, *Nashim* ('Women'); 4, *Nezikin* ('Damages'); 5, *Kodashim* ('Holy Things'); 6, *Toharoth* ('Cleanlinesses'). Within each of these orders there are minor divisions, called *tractates*, dealing with specific subjects. Thus, for instance, within the second major division we find among others the tractates *Shabbath* ('The Sabbath') and *Megillah* ('The Scroll' [of Esther]). The Mishnah is cited according to tractate, not order; e.g. *Meg.* (*Megillah*) 4,2.

Generally the Mishnah restricts itself to a concise formulation of halakah with little preoccupation to found the laws on Scripture or to connect them with biblical texts. The ultimate formulations found in the Mishnah are presumably the outcome of many discussions. Yet we find relatively few records of debates in its text and very few anecdotes are given. The Mishnah is evidently designed as an authoritative code of laws, a good amount of earlier halakah and halakic opinions being purposely omitted.

Such material omitted from the Mishnah is called *Baraita* ('external' or 'excluded'). Sometimes it consisted of abstract halakoth; at other times it was in the nature of exposition, illustration, scriptural explanation, or discussion bearing on the laws which in the Mishnah are recorded without comment. The *Tosephta* ('Supplement')—more or less contemporary with the Mishnah—is a work in which this second class of material is preserved. It has the same divisions into orders and tractates as R. Judah's Mishnah, but the tractates do not always follow the same sequence. What relation the Tosephta bears to the Mishnah is not altogether certain. Sometimes its text is verbally identical with that of the Mishnah; much found in the Mishnah is omitted in the Tosephta or is found there in a brief and obscure fashion. It seems to presuppose the Mishnah and intends to preserve material omitted from it.

The following example will illustrate the relation of the two works. Mishnah *Sukkah* ('The Feast of Tabernacles') 4,9, when speaking of the rite of the pouring out of water which took place every day for seven days during the festival, tells us that when the procession carrying the water arrived from the Pool of Shiloah at the Water Gate of the Temple a plain note was sounded on the shofar. The Tosephta (*Sukkah* 3,3–14) takes occasion of mention of the Water Gate to recall the various biblical references to wells and to water; the prophecies of the rivers of water to flow from the Temple in messianic times (Ezek 47:3–16; Is 33:21; Zech 13:1; 14:8); the well that followed the Israelites during their desert wanderings

(Num 21:17–18; cf. 1 Cor 10:4).[2] All these texts were probably recalled during the ceremony. Their use in the liturgy explains how on the occasion of this feast Christ said in the Temple: 'If anyone thirsts let him come to me, and let him who believes in me drink. As the Scripture has said: Out of his heart shall flow rivers of living water' (John 7:37–38).

Jewish teachers of the age which produced the Mishnah (*ca.* A.D. 10–220) are known as *Tannaim* ('Traditionists' or generally 'Teachers'), those of the period following on it as *Amoraim* ('Expositors'). During this latter period (*ca.* A.D. 250–420) the Mishnah of R. Judah was expounded in the Jewish schools of Palestine and Babylonia. This later exposition of the Mishnah—known as *Gemara*—together with the Mishnah itself is known as the Talmud. As we have an exposition (Gemara) from Palestine and another from Babylonia, so, too, have we two talmuds: the Babylonian Talmud and the Palestinian Talmud (the latter also known as the Talmud of Jerusalem). The Gemara studies the Mishnah text in detail, and on the occasion of the discussions a host of Baraita and legendary material was introduced. The Babylonian Talmud is cited according to the Mishnah tractate commented on, and the folio of the Hebrew printed text; e.g. *Shabbath* 118b. The Palestinian Talmud is cited according to the Mishnah tractate, preceded by Jer. (i.e. Jerusalem) or Pal. (Palestine) and followed by chapter and paragraph of the Mishnah tractate commented on, plus folio of printed edition, or by one of these only; e.g. Jer. (or Pal.) *Yoma* 3,6,40c; Jer. (Pal.) *Yoma* 3,6; or Jer. (Pal.) *Yoma* 40c.

The following example will give some idea of the relation of the Gemara to the Mishnah and will illustrate how the material of both can be of importance for an understanding of the New Testament. In Matthew 12:1–8 (cf. Mark 2:23–28; Luke 6:1–5) we read of Jesus's disciples being censured by the Pharisees for plucking ears of corn on the Sabbath and (according to Luke 6:1) rubbing them with their hands. The Mishnah tractate *Shabbath* lists thirty-nine main classes of work which are prohibited on the Sabbath and the greater part of

2. See text of Tosephta in A. W. Greenup, *Sukka, Mishnah and Tosefta with Introduction, Translation and Short Notes* (London: S.P.C.K., 1925; *Translation of Early Documents. Series III: Rabbinic Texts*), pp. 73–77.

this tractate is taken up with the various actions which come under these thirty-nine headings. These various actions are given in the Palestinian Talmud (Jer. *Shabbath* 7,2) as $39 \times 39 = 1,521$. Plucking ears of corn is not explicitly condemned in the Mishnah, although one of the thirty-nine primary acts of labour listed there is winnowing and grinding (Mishnah, *Shabbath* 7,2). A more detailed discussion in the Babylonian Talmud (*Shabbath* 128ab) shows that opinion was divided on the permissiveness of the act of rubbing ears of corn and eating it. 'One may pluck with the hand and eat [on the Sabbath], but one may not pluck with an implement; and one may rub and eat [on the Sabbath], but one may not rub with an implement. These are the words of Rabbi Akiba, but other sages say that one may rub with one's finger-tips and eat, but one may not rub a quantity with the hand (and eat).'[3] There was then a difference of opinion on the point among second-century rabbis. The Pharisees of the first century followed a ruling later mitigated. They were probably of the strict school of Shammai.[4] The Mishnah tends to follow in general the more lenient laws of Hillel.

Rabbinic Midrash must now be considered.[5] We have seen how the Mishnah makes no attempt to base its laws on the Bible. This enunciation of halakah without reference to scriptural foundation is often referred to as the mishnah method. The rabbis, nonetheless, were keenly interested in the Bible and in its interpretation. Any rabbinic interpretation of the Bible could be called *midrash* (a word coming from the Hebrew verb *darash*, 'to seek', 'to search out', 'to interpret Scripture'). In rabbinic Judaism two forms of biblical interpretation are known. The first is *peshat* ('simple'), i.e. the simple or literal sense of Scripture, the determination of what the plain sense of a biblical text is. The other is *derash* which sought to go

3. See W. O. E. Oesterley, *Tractate Shabbath. Mishnah. Translated from the Hebrew with introductory Notes* (London: S.P.C.K., 1929), pp. xix–xx.
4. It appears that towards the middle decades of the first century A.D. the Shammaites were more numerous and aggressive than the Hillelites; see G. F. Moore, *Judaism in the First Centuries of the Christian Era. The Age of the Tannaim*, vol. 1 (Cambridge: Harvard University Press, 1927), p. 81.
5. On the entire question of midrash see Addison G. Wright, 'The Literary Genre Midrash' in *Catholic Biblical Quarterly* 28 (1966) 105–38, 417–57, and separately (same title) in book-form (Staten Island: Alba House, 1967).

beyond the plain sense to find hidden meanings in the text. *Derash* can also be called *midrash*. Midrash properly so called is, however, any consideration of the biblical text with a view to rendering its message alive and meaningful for later generations. Its point of departure is the text of Scripture which it seeks to actualize in various ways. This it can do in two distinct manners: in a legalistic and non-legalistic fashion. We thus have two kinds of midrash: *midrash halakah* and *midrash haggadah*. Midrash halakah is the derivation from, or confirmation by, Scripture of the rules of the oral unwritten law. Midrash haggadah is the non-juristic interpretation of Scripture.

Haggadah in this sense is the non-juristic teaching of Scripture as brought out in the profounder study of its religious, moral and historical teaching. It was held in high regard in Judaism; in a rabbinic work (*Sifrè* Deut 11:22) we read: 'Those who interpret the implications of Scripture say: If you wish to know the Creator of the world, learn Haggadah; from it you will come to know God and cleave to his ways.' With a view to rendering the religious message of the Bible clearer, this form of interpretation tends to indulge in anecdotes and in the use of legendary material. These non-historical elements are often referred to as *haggadoth* (the plural of haggadah).

This midrashic interpretation (both halakic and haggadic) was in time consigned to writing in works known as *midrashim* (the plural of midrash). We find the halakic midrash in the Mekilta (on the book of Exodus) and in other midrashim. We have the haggadic midrash in expositional and homiletic commentaries. As an example of this type of haggadic midrash we cite the exposition of Gen 11:2 as found in *Genesis Rabba* 38, 7–8:

> *And it came to pass, as they journeyed from the East* [Hebrew: *Miḳḳedem*] (Gen 11:2). They travelled from further east to nearer east. R. Leazar and b. R. Simeon interpreted: They betook themselves away from the Ancient (*ḳadmon*) of the world, saying, 'We refuse to accept either Him or His divinity'.
>
> *That they found a plain.* R. Judah said: All the nations of the world assembled to discover which plain would hold them all, and eventually they found it. R. Nehemiah observed:

They found: thus it is written, *If it concerneth the scorners, He permits them to scorn* (Job 3:34).

And they dwelt there. R. Isaac said: Wherever you find dwelling mentioned, Satan becomes active. R. Helbo said: Wherever you find contentment, Satan brings accusations. R. Levi said: Wherever you find eating and drinking, the arch-robber [Satan] cuts his capers.[6]

The importance of all this rabbinical material for an understanding of the New Testament is undoubtedly immense. While receiving its final redaction in the Christian era, much of it can be presumed to go back to pre-Christian times. A large element of uncertainty remains, nonetheless, with regard to the dating of any particular passage. As we have it, it came from Judaism as reorganized or in the process of reorganization, after the fall of Jerusalem in A.D. 70. The rabbis cited as authorities, or as the source of individual interpretations, are almost entirely from this later period. The actual interpretation they give is doubtless very often much older than their own day. Still we would like some proof that such is the case. We shall see later that much of it probably depends on older tradition found in the Palestinian Targum to the Pentateuch. Another difficulty with rabbinic material is that it is linked with the Jewish *schools*; it need not necessarily have been known to the masses of the Jewish people, or if it was, this was probably from sources other than the scholastic discussions in which we now find it. There still remains for us to enquire whether there is such a further source within Judaism.

Liturgical Judaism

In the present work we devote our attention exclusively to this other brand of Jewish literature, i.e. the targums, or more specifically the Palestinian Targum to the Pentateuch. A *targum* is an Aramaic translation of a book or books of the Old Testament, Aramaic being the language spoken rather generally in Palestine in the time of Christ, and indeed for some centuries preceding it. In the regular synagogue service sections of the Pentateuch and of the Prophets were read out

6. As translated in *Midrash Rabbah*, ed. H. Freedman and M. Simon, vol. I (London: Soncino Press, 1939), pp. 306–7.

in Hebrew and were immediately translated into Aramaic. It is for this reason that we refer to these translations as liturgical renderings.

There are still extant two distinct Jewish targums of the Pentateuch. The first is a rather-literal rendering and is known as the Targum of Onkelos. The other, an extremely paraphrastic version, is called the Palestinian Targum of the Pentateuch. This Palestinian targum is now found in its entirety in Codex Neofiti, and in part in the texts of Pseudo-Jonathan, the Fragment Targum and in fragments from the Cairo Geniza. Being a paraphrase rather than a translation proper, this targum contains much additional material and consequently gives us a good idea of the religious concepts current when it was composed. This latter targum is written in the language known as Palestinian Aramaic.

Targums, standing as they do at the very heart of Jewish religion, would at first sight appear to be of prime importance to any study of the Jewish religion of Christ's day. One may legitimately ask why more use is not made of the Palestinian Targum to the Pentateuch and the Targum to the Prophets in New Testament studies. The difficulty one has to face immediately here is the date to be assigned to these targums as we now have them. The earliest *written texts* of these targums is rather recent when compared with the Dead Sea Scrolls or with most of the apocryphal writings. Yet, despite this rather late date of our present texts, the targums were considered quite important for New Testament studies until the opening years of the present century. This held also for the Palestinian Targum of the Pentateuch in which we are here chiefly interested. The view then gained currency that the texts of this targum are more recent than the Targum of Onkelos, and that it consequently cannot be used with any degree of certainty in the field of Jewish-New Testament relationships. The Targum of Onkelos was considered much more important than the Palestinian Targum in any study of the form of Aramaic spoken by Christ.

This situation continued until 1930 when Paul Kahle published texts of the Palestinian Targum found in the Cairo Geniza. These texts, the oldest of which he dated as A.D. 600–800, agree in the main with the texts of this targum already known, differing from them in no greater degree than do the known texts of the targum among themselves. If texts of the Palestinian Targum were being consigned to writing in the seventh or eighth century, the tradition which they enshrine must have been formed much earlier. These newly-published texts led to a fresh interest in the Palestinian Targum to the Pentateuch. A new approach to Jewish studies introduced about the same time also led to greater reverence for the antiquity of the tradition found in the Palestinian Targum. Interest in its bearing on the New Testament was also reawakened, and the more it was compared with the New Testament the greater was its relevance in this field perceived.

I have elsewhere gone in some detail into the history of targumic studies in the West from the sixteenth century down as far as 1965.[7] The dissertation in question attempted to put forward an argument for the pre-Christian date of the Palestinian Targum as a whole, and this from the manifold relationship it appears to bear to the New Testament. Since that work was written Roger Le Déaut, professor of targumic studies at the Biblical Institute, Rome, has given us a further work on the relation of Jewish liturgy and the targums to the New Testament.[8] He has also published a study on the targums themselves, placing them within the development of Judaism,[9] and has likewise brought out the first part of an introduction to targumic literature.[10] In 1967 P. Nickels O.F.M.CAP., a student of Le Déaut, gave us a rather complete bibliography of recent works on the bearing of various texts of the targums on New Testament studies.[11] The new approach to the targums, and to the Palestinian Targum to the Pentateuch in particular, is evidently bearing fruit.

It is only to be expected that a number of scholars should have remained sceptical of this new approach and unconvinced by the arguments put forward for the importance of the

7. *The New Testament and the Palestinian Targum to the Pentateuch* (Rome: Biblical Institute Press, 1966), pp. 5–35; 'Targumic Studies' in *The Catholic Biblical Quarterly* 28 (1966) 1–19.

8. *Liturgie juive et Nouveau Testament* (Rome: Biblical Institute Press, 1965).

9. 'Les études targumiques. État de la recherche et perspective pour l'éxégèse de l'Ancien Testament' in *Ephemerides theologicae lovanienses* 44 (1968) 5–34.

10. *Introduction à la littérature targumique* (Rome: Biblical Institute Press, 1966).

11. *Targum and New Testament. A Bibliography together with a New Testament Index* (Rome: Biblical Institute Press, 1967).

Palestinian Targum for New Testament studies. Few, however, spoke out openly against it. This was somewhat unfortunate. Any new approach needs criticism. Only in this way can technique be perfected.

One is glad to see that criticism has finally come. Joseph Fitzmyer has taken occasion of the third edition of Matthew Black's *An Aramaic Approach to the Gospel and Acts*[12] and of the present writer's *The New Testament and the Palestinian Targum to the Pentateuch*[13] to query the validity of the basis of this new approach. In particular he questions the assumption of an early, and even pre-Christian, date for the Palestinian Targum. He considers it quite illegitimate to use the Aramaic language of this targum as a witness of the Aramaic of first-century Palestine, and in general objects to the mode of argumentation used by writers in this field of research.

The present work was entirely composed before Fr. Fitzmyer's criticisms appeared. His objections do not appear to be well-founded, nor have they required any change in what had already been written. They merit serious consideration, none-theless, as they have to do with the validity of the method used in this new field of research.

The objections raised against Black's use of the Aramaic of the Palestinian Targum in New Testament studies will be considered later.[14] It does not interest us here, for we have purposely avoided this particular approach to the subject.

In his review of both works Fitzmyer objects to the designa-tion of the sources used as *the* Palestinian Targum. The complexity of the material, he maintains, makes it clear that one should really reckon with Palestinian Targums (of the Pentateuch) in order to avoid over-simplification.[15] Here there is merely a question of nomenclature. Every student of this material is, of course, acutely conscious of the complexity to which Fitzmyer refers. No two texts of the Palestinian Targum (Targums?) are verbally identical over very many verses. The complexity is, in fact, generally noted by students in this branch of Jewish studies. But it is equally clear that, despite these differences, all the texts in question represent the same

---

12. Published in 1967; reviewed in *Catholic Biblical Quarterly* 30 (1968) 417–28.
13. Reviewed in *Theological Studies* 29 (1968) 321–26.
14. Below, pp. 164f.
15. Pages 426 and 323 of reviews given in notes 12 and 13 above.

tradition of translation. There is a certain family unity among them. To speak of each individual text as a distinct Palestinian targum would be to ignore this close and evident relationship. I believe, then, that it is still better to abide by the traditional name 'Palestinian Targum'.[15a] We can refer to the extant texts of this as representative of the Palestinian Targum.

A further objection raised against the new targumic approach is that it indulges in circular reasoning, i.e. it 'proves' the early date of passages in the Palestinian Targum from the relation these bear to New Testament texts and uses them in New Testament studies because of the presumption that they pre-date the Christian era. 'Until we have at our disposal', writes Fitzmyer, 'critical editions of the various Palestinian Targums and a mode of dating them independently of New Testament material, comparison of such material with the New Testament will continue to repeat the arguments of circular reasoning that one meets all too frequently in this field of research.'[16]

Two assertions are made here, each of which can be objected to: first that the reasoning is circular, and secondly that we rely solely on the New Testament for the early dating of the Palestinian Targum to the Pentateuch.[17]

First, the accusation of circular reasoning. The phenomenon thus described I would prefer to call an argument from the convergence of evidence. Presuming that a manifold relation is shown to exist between the New Testament and the Palestinian Targum, we have in this a strong indication that the Palestinian Targum tradition existed when the New Testament was being composed, and that it influenced the New Testament writers. This manifold relationship, already established, invites one to turn to the Palestinian Targum in elucidating other difficult passages of the New Testament.[18]

To say that the only indications of an early date for the Palestinian Targum we have are drawn from the New Testament is quite inexact. There are, in fact, a host of indications from a number of sources apart from the New Testament that

---

15a. G. F. Moore (*Judaism* I, p. 304) and A. G. Wright (*art. cit.*, note 5 above, p. 422) use the designation desired by Fitzmyer.

16. Review in *Theological Studies*, p. 324.

17. We can speak of a targum *to, on* or *of* a book or books of the Old Testament; usage varies.

18. See M. McNamara, *The New Testament and the Palestinian Targum to the Pentateuch*, pp. 35f.

in the Palestinian Targum we have a very ancient and possibly, if not probably, pre-Christian work.[19] We have the arguments from its form of halakah, from its relation to early midrash and others besides. Above all there is the convergence of all the arguments, both those from the New Testament and those from other sources, indicating that in this work we have a very ancient source which merits the attention of students of the New Testament.

Fully conscious of the need to place the Palestinian Targum within what we consider its true setting in Judaism, the present work will first of all speak at some length of the development of doctrine and law in Israel, particularly in the post-exilic period. What is said in the first part on the formation of the targumic tradition is intended to give some idea of the situation within which the targums actually arose. Having treated of these matters we shall then turn to the question of the origin and date of the Palestinian Targum to the Pentateuch as we now have it.

In the second part of the work—on the relation of the Palestinian Targum to New Testament studies[20]—I avoid as far as possible those subjects treated of in the dissertation *The New Testament and the Palestinian Targum to the Pentateuch* (Rome, 1966). I have, however, taken this opportunity to go in greater detail into two questions already treated of there. The first is the text of 2 Cor 3:17—'The Lord is the Spirit'—illustrated in the dissertation through a text from the Targum of Pseudo-Jonathan. In the present work the interpretation given there is confirmed by texts from Tannaitic sources. What was said in the dissertation on the interpretation of Exodus 19:6 in later Judaism is here expanded in view of the importance of this later Jewish tradition for an understanding of the New Testament teaching of the universal priesthood of all believers.

An introduction to all extant targums has been added as an appendix. At some future date it may be possible to bring out the first part of the present work together with this appendix as a separate introduction to the targums.

---

19. These arguments are treated of below in chapter 8.
20. This second part was given in substance at a conference to the Irish Biblical Association, at Maynooth, in April 1968.

PART ONE:

Formation of Targumic Tradition

2

Development of Doctrine in Judaism

In the preceding chapter we have concentrated our attention on the targums and on the writings of rabbinic Judaism. Both of these represent normative Judaism as distinct from the sectarian or marginal form of Judaism represented by the Qumrân texts and the apocalyptic writings. Both the targums and the rabbinic writings belong to the oral law. They are the end product of a long period of development. Rightly to understand them we must consider them in their Jewish setting and within the development of doctrine and of law which is a feature of the Jewish religion of the Old Testament period. This is true in a particular way of the targums which alone interest us here. We shall better appreciate the arguments put forward in favour of an early date for the Palestinian Targum of the Pentateuch when we realize that the laws underlying the paraphrase were already operative within Judaism during the closing centuries of the pre-Christian era, and some of them, indeed, many centuries earlier.

Targums presuppose a text of Scripture. They come from a period when the sacred traditions of Israel had already been consigned to writing. Now, the Scriptures are a record of revelation. Before Israel's traditions came to be written down they first existed in oral form. And before receiving the form in which it was finally consigned to writing, the tradition had undergone a long process of development. This was more or less inevitable. Development in doctrine and in law is as natural and as necessary as the evolution of the human mind and of human society. It is likewise essential in any living religion. Revelation means a divine intervention in history, a communication of God with the human mind. The implications of the initial self-revelation of God, and of the truths which he has communicated, cannot immediately be grasped in their entirety by the human mind. There will remain in man's mind concepts which it had prior to the divine revelation. Time is required for man to purify his mind of false notions and to come to a clearer idea of God. Together with this, man who receives the divine revelation has the added difficulty of expressing ideas of a spiritual God in human language. All this leads to the formation of different theologies—that is, different ways of expressing revealed truths. Such theologies we have in point of fact in the Pentateuch, the five books of Moses known to the Jews as the Law (Torah).

Development in pre-exilic Jewish religion

When targums were first made, the inspired Scriptures had come to be accepted as the Word of God valid for all times. There was by then little or no memory of the complex tradition lying behind the accepted texts of Scripture. Where apparent (or real) contradictions appeared between different biblical texts, these had to be solved without recourse to the historical sciences now at our disposal.

All students of the Scriptures are well aware today that the Pentateuch is composed of four great sources, those of the Yahwist, the Elohist, the Deuteronomist and the Priestly Writer. Of these the Yahwist source is the oldest, having received its present form in the southern kingdom of Judah in the tenth or ninth century B.C. Next in time comes the Elohist, then the Deuteronomist, rewriting and retelling earlier traditions for a richer and more sophisticated society. The Priestly Source, in its present form, is the latest of the four. Each of these four sources has its own manner of presenting divine truths. By a comparison of their texts we can trace the development in theology and in law which took place in Israel from an early time down to the Exile (587–539 B.C.) and later.

A notable feature of the Yahwist source is the use of anthropomorphisms, i.e. the description of God in purely human form, the presentation of God as if he were a man. Yahweh acts as a potter, forming man out of the dust of the earth (Gen 2:7,19). He plants a garden in Eden (Gen 2:8); takes out one of Adam's ribs and closes up its place with flesh (Gen 2:21); he makes garments of skin for Adam and Eve (Gen 3:21); closes the door of the ark behind Noah (Gen 7:16) and comes down to see the tower of Babel (Gen 11:5).

The Yahwist well knew, of course, that God was spirit, not flesh. He uses anthropomorphisms with the intention of rendering his message the more vivid. Such a manner of speaking of God must, nonetheless, have appeared inappropriate to many. The Elohist presents a different picture of the deity. For him, God is the inaccessible who reveals himself in theophanies (i.e. divine apparitions; see Ex 3:1–6; 19:16,17,19; 33:9–11) and through the medium of dreams (Gen 28:12,17; 31:11–13). In the theology of the Priestly Writer, God is the omnipotent Creator who brings things into existence by a mere word.

The Yahwist has little scruple in recording actions of Abraham which to later generations must have appeared of dubious honesty. Thus, for instance, he tells us how, when in danger of death in Egypt because of his wife Sarai, Abraham tells her to say that she is really his sister, not his wife (Gen 12:11–19). The reader is left with the impression that Abraham is guilty of having Sarai tell a lie. We find a variant of this story in Gen 20, this time from the pen of the Elohist. But the point is now made that Sarai is really the sister (or rather the half-sister) of Abraham (Gen 20:12). The behaviour of the father of the race is justified. In this we have an example of the respect paid to the elders of Israel. It is a law found again in the Greek Septuagint rendering and in the targums and will be explicitly formulated as a law by the rabbis.

With regard to the development of law, we have many examples in the Pentateuch. In the earliest texts of the Passover ritual, for instance, the animal to be sacrificed is specified as a lamb (Ex 12:21). This represents a nomadic stage of Hebrew society when only small cattle (lambs and goats) were readily available. The Passover ritual as found in the book of Deuteronomy is intended for a society of landowners; and there it is specified (Deut 16:2) that the sacrificial animals can be taken from the herd (large animals) or from the flock (sheep and goats). A comparison of the texts of the Yahwist, the Deuteronomist (16:1–8) and the Priestly Writer (Ex 12:1–14; cf. Ezek 45:18–25) in fact shows us how much the doctrine and legislation on the Passover developed over the period covered by the Pentateuch. A similar evolution took place in the teaching and legislation concerning the Sabbath. The same holds true for the teaching on the Exodus, the chief event of Israelite history. In this we can trace a rich development from the earliest sources right down to New Testament times and later.

The Law of Moses in post-exilic Judaism

The exile in Babylon (587–539 B.C.) gave Israel an opportunity to reflect on the sins of her ancestors which had brought such disaster on her. The burden of the prophets' teaching for generations before was that infidelity to the Sinai covenant and to the law of God (given through Moses) spelt national disaster. Events had proved them right. Now as she pondered on all this in exile, her religious leaders resolved that never again would there be such unfaithfulness as brought about the dissolution of the nation at the fall of Jerusalem in 587.

During the exile in Babylon the Law of Moses became the conscious centre of the religious life of the Jews, a position it continued to occupy in the centuries to come. In the seventh year of the reign of the Persian king Artaxerxes (probably 458, but possibly 398 B.C.), Ezra the scribe came from the Persian court to Palestine with a mandate from the Persian monarch to reorganize Judaism in accordance with the Law of Moses, and to teach this law to those Jews who did not know it (Ezra 7:25–26). On the first day of the seventh month, on the occasion of the Feast of Tabernacles, the community of the returned exiles of Judah gathered together in a solemn convocation in Jerusalem to renew their allegiance to the Covenant. The solemn gathering is thus described in the book of Nehemiah (8:1–3,8):

And they told Ezra the scribe to bring the book of the Law of Moses which the Lord had given to Israel. And Ezra the scribe brought the Law before the assembly, both men and women and all who hear with understanding . . . And he read from it . . . from early morning until midday, in the presence of the men and women and those who could understand. And the ears of all the people were attentive to the book of the Law . . . And they read from the book, from the law of God, clearly [?; Hebrew: *mehporash*] and they gave the sense so that the people understood the reading.

We shall later consider the concluding section of this text in detail. For our purpose here it suffices to note that at this solemn assembly of that first day of the seventh month we have the birthday of Judaism, that is, the form of Hebrew religion which is to persist down to New Testament times. Judaism will not differ from earlier Hebrew religion in its creed but in the central role accorded to the Law of Moses. The 'book of the Law of Moses' spoken of in the citation given above is the Pentateuch in the form it had received by the time of Ezra, a form substantially that which it has today. The fundamental law of the Jewish people was henceforth to be the Law of Moses. Those who did not know this law were to be taught it. We should note, too, how at this assembly the people were made to hear the words of the Law and were given its meaning. Explanation accompanied reading. Knowledge of the Law of Moses was something held necessary for all Israel, not the privilege of any chosen few, such as scribes and priests. It will be the task of the religious leaders in the following centuries to see to it that all Israel will be acquainted with both the text and the meaning of the Law of Moses.

Text of the Pentateuch in post-exilic Judaism

Before we speak further of the position of the Law during this later period it will not be amiss to say a few words on the actual text of the Pentateuch during the centuries preceding the birth of Christ. We have said that the 'book of the Law of Moses' read and expounded by Ezra was fundamentally the same as the Pentateuch as we now know it. This should not lead us to believe that it was verbally identical with it. Our present Hebrew text of the Pentateuch (and of the entire Hebrew Bible) is known as the Masoretic Text (from the Hebrew word *Masorah*, meaning 'tradition') as it was given its final form, even as regards the correct reading of every word, by Jewish scholars called Masoretes in the eighth century A.D. or so. According to Jewish tradition this Masoretic text is the very same as that edited by the rabbis after the fall of Jerusalem in A.D. 70. The biblical texts from the Dead Sea area show that this tradition is quite exact. All the biblical texts from this area written after A.D. 100 are, in fact, identical with the Masoretic text.[1] According to the same rabbinic tradition the Masoretic text was edited by the rabbis from three biblical manuscripts saved from the Temple. In cases of divergence between these manuscripts in any given text, the majority rule was followed, the reading of two MSS. being taken against a reading represented by one MS. only.

We have here the recollection that before the editorial work of the rabbis a certain variety of biblical texts existed in Israel. The Qumrân finds bear abundant evidence of this. In the biblical texts written before A.D. 70 there are indications that at least three different forms of the Hebrew text of the Pentateuch were known.[2] To begin with there is a text differing but little from the later Masoretic text, and consequently known as the *Proto-Masoretic tradition*. This tradition, according to F. M. Cross, may go back to the fifth century B.C.

Scholars were long aware of the differences between the Masoretic text and the Greek Septuagint rendering made from an early Hebrew text. The Qumrân texts show us that this Hebrew text was used in Palestine side by side with the Proto-Masoretic text. Being the basis of the Septuagint translation made in Egypt, it is known as the *Egyptian tradition*. It is probably as old as the Proto-Masoretic tradition.

Before the Qumrân finds we also knew of the Samaritan Pentateuch, which differs in certain details from the Masoretic text. Among the biblical texts from Qumrân there are manuscripts with the Samaritan form of text, manuscripts representing the *Proto-Samaritan tradition*.

During the post-exilic period in Palestine, then, we have to reckon with three different forms of the Pentateuch, and perhaps more. An awareness of this variety of biblical texts is important for an understanding of the targums: the Aramaic rendering will reflect the Hebrew text used by the translator. Thus, for instance, in the Palestinian Targum (Gen 4:8) Cain says to Abel: 'Let us go out into the open field'; this represents

1. Cf. J. T. Milik, *Ten Years of Discovery in the Wilderness of Judaea* (London: S.C.M. Press, 1959), p. 29.
2. See F. Cross, *The Ancient Library of Qumran and Modern Biblical Studies* (New York: Anchor Books, 1961), pp. 168–94, esp. pp. 181–86.

the Samaritan and Septuagint tradition rather than that of the Masoretic text, in which these words are missing. In other passages as well, targumic renderings, particularly that of Pseudo-Jonathan, follow textual traditions other than that of the Masoretic text.

Scribes and the oral law

The written Law of Moses was not sufficient for everyday life in the new religious community of the Jews. Beside it there now began to develop a rich oral law, designed to explain and protect the Law of Moses. The men who developed this oral law from Ezra onwards were in rabbinic literature called 'the men of the Great Synagogue', the 'Great Synagogue' being a rather comprehensive title for a period of which later Jewish tradition knew few if any details.[3] The motto of these men was, according to the Mishnah tractate *Aboth* (1,1): 'Be deliberate in giving judgment, and raise up many disciples, and make a hedge [or 'barrier'] about the Law.' 'Making a hedge about the Law' meant introducing new ordinances in an effort to keep the people from infringing on the Law of Moses itself. We have a good example of what this meant in the opening words of the Mishnah (*Berakoth* 1,1), where we read that things which by the letter of the Law of Moses must be completed before morning (e.g. Lev 7:15; 22:30) must by rabbinical rule be done before midnight, 'to keep a man far removed from transgression'.

From Ezra onwards the Law of Moses was studied by the body of learned men known as scribes (*Sopherim*). To them also were entrusted the oral law and the task of making new decrees. We cannot say when this new body came into being. By 200 B.C., however, the scribes were an established institution in Israel. This we know from Sirach—himself a scribe—who in the book that bears his name (also known as Ecclesiasticus) gives us an admirable description of the scribe. 'The wisdom of the scribe depends on the opportunity for leisure; and he who has little business may become wise' (Sirach 38:24). While husbandmen and craftsmen are the mainstay of the social structure (38:25–32), their occupations give them no time for the wide range of

3. Cf. Moore, *Judaism* I, pp. 29–36.

studies required of the scholar and consequently 'they are not sought out in the council of the people, nor do they attain eminence in the public assembly. They do not sit in the judge's seat, nor do they understand the sentence of judgment; they cannot expound discipline or judgment, and they are not found using proverbs' (38:33). To all these things must the scribe address himself: to devote himself to the Law of the Most High, to seek out the wisdom of all the ancients, to be concerned with prophecies, to penetrate the subtleties of parables . . . (39:1ff).

It was these men who controlled the development of Judaism in the centuries preceding the birth of Christ. They are the scribes mentioned so often in the Gospels, generally in conjunction with the Pharisees. This latter group came into existence some time during the second century B.C. They differed from the scribes in that they were not of the learned class. Both, however, were of the same tradition, being passionately devoted to the oral law and to the 'tradition of the elders'.

The chief means of communicating a knowledge of the Pentateuch in New Testament times, and for long before, were the Sabbath synagogue assemblies. 'For from early generations Moses has had in every city those who preach him, for he is read every sabbath in the synagogues' (Acts 15:21). The Jewish historian Josephus (*Contra Apionem* II, 17[18] §175) is witness of the same: 'He [i.e. Moses] has proclaimed the Law to be the best and most necessary instruction of all; not once or twice or many times must one listen to it; for he has ordained that every week, other works being set aside, the people should come together to hear the Law and learn it exactly.'

How successful this work of the scribes and other religious teachers of Palestine was is vouched for by the acquaintance which such ordinary Jews as the Apostles and the writers who gave us the New Testament show with the sacred writings. 'That the synagogue gave opportunity to acquire such familiarity is sufficient testimony to the quality of its instruction. In the Hellenistic synagogues, the knowledge of Scripture which Paul assumes that his hearers possess gives similar witness.'[4]

4. *Ibid.*, p. 289.

Development of doctrine in post-exilic Judaism[5]

By the time of Ezra, as already noted, the Pentateuch existed in substantially the form it has today; this notwithstanding the variety in certain details which is evident from the three distinct textual traditions (Proto-Masoretic, Egyptian and Proto-Samaritan) known to have existed in Palestine before the Masoretic recension of *ca.* A.D. 100. The basic tradition of the teaching of the pre-exilic prophets was also fairly well established by the end of the Exile. Unlike the Pentateuch, the earlier prophetic tradition remained open to further development after the Exile. Some sections of the earlier prophetic writings were rewritten in the light of later development, earlier oracles were recast and new inspired additions were made to the body of prophetic teaching with the intent of having the Word of God given to Israel through the earlier prophets still resound and bear a message to later generations.

Fixing the tradition of the Law and the Prophets did not mean that development of doctrine or law had ended in Israel. This was far from the case. The centuries immediately preceding the birth of Christ were in fact years of intense evolution in both these fields. There is, however, one fundamental difference between this later development and that of the pre-exilic age. The later development is now bound by a written tradition and is altogether characterized by a reflection on this earlier inspired and written tradition. Its chief preoccupation seems to have been to develop and interpret this earlier tradition in an effort to bring out its meaning for later generations.

Sources of our information for this subsequent period of Jewish religion are the later books of the Old Testament itself (Chronicles, Maccabees, Wisdom, Sirach, Baruch, etc.), the additions made to the earlier prophetic works, and the re-reading and rewriting of earlier prophetic oracles—a rewriting that has been proven and clarified by modern critical studies. We have also the pre-Christian Jewish apocryphal works, and the early Qumrân writings. Then we have the Greek Septuagint translation of the Bible and the glosses added to the Hebrew

---

5. Cf. R. Le Déaut, 'Les études targumiques . . .' in *Ephemerides theologicae lovanienses* 44 (1968) 5–54 (with bibliography).

text of the Bible. Finally, we may list the earlier stage of rabbinic tradition in so far as this is known to us. These are our main sources, but there are others besides which do not concern us here.

The development that went on in Israel during this later period must have been very great. As yet, however, it has not been systematically studied from the point of view of development according to certain laws. As we have already noted, the Jewish religious mind of the period was centred on the earlier sacred tradition, on the written Word of God. Due to this reflection on the written Word, there grew up during this era a particular understanding of the sacred text, an exegetical tradition, which is seen in the later inspired additions of the Old Testament itself, in the glosses inserted into the Hebrew text of the Bible, and in occasional interpretative renderings found in the Greek translation of the Old Testament.

We should not conceive of this interpretation of Scripture as something entirely free, the outcome as it were of the untrammelled liberty of individual expositors. Because the exact meaning of the Pentateuch, particularly in legal matters, was of supreme importance for the Jews, we can legitimately presume that the teaching received in the schools and synagogues conformed to the teaching of the scribes. It is then a very legitimate presumption that during this period there was an authoritative interpretation of. the Scriptures, particularly of the Law of Moses. This seems to follow from what we have already said on the scribes and on the position of the Law of Moses in post-exilic Judaism. There must also have been a certain preoccupation to relate the oral to the written law. Seven rules of interpretation, bearing on this relationship, are attributed to Hillel (about 70 B.C. to A.D. 10). While some of these may have been formulated after Hillel's day, many of them probably antedate Hillel. The existence of standard commentary on the biblical text is evidenced also by scribal glosses, to a consideration of which we now turn.

Scribal glosses

The activity of the early scribes can be seen in the glosses whose presence critics have identified in the Hebrew text of the Bible. These glosses were, apparently, first of all written down on the margins of scrolls bearing texts of the Bible and were later incorporated by copyists into the biblical text itself. The glosses are evidence of a preoccupation to understand and explain the text of Scripture. In recent years a certain amount of attention has been devoted to such glosses, the diverse nature of which gives us an idea of the widespread interests of those whose task it was to comment on the sacred text. In the course of an important study on glosses G. R. Driver writes:

> The classification of glosses, too, can be fairly well defined according to their purpose. Their primary purpose is to obviate difficulties whether by simplifying the construction of the sentence or by interpreting obscure or unknown words; a secondary purpose is to present varying readings or draw attention to parallel passages. Glosses are also inserted in the text to explain historical allusions or even to put right what the glossator regards as false history. Others are added to enhance or mitigate the force of the original text or to give vent to feelings, chiefly of indignation, or to utter warnings which the reader or scribe may think appropriate. There are also glosses expressing theological opinions, and, what are exceptionally important, liturgical glosses . . . The subject is a large one and calls for investigation, especially liturgical glosses and the relation to Rabbinical canons of interpretation to additions of every kind to the Hebrew text.[6]

An examination of liturgical glosses would be of great interest for targumic studies. Professor J. Weingreen of Trinity College, Dublin, has devoted considerable attention to rabbinic-type glosses in the Hebrew text of the Bible and in the Greek Septuagint translation.[7] This he has done in an effort to bridge the gap between the Bible itself and the laws later formulated by the rabbis. The oral law which existed along with the Old

6. 'Glosses on the Hebrew Text of the Old Testament' in *L'Ancien Testament et l'Orient* (*Orientalia et Biblica Lovaniensia*, vol. I, 1 [57]), p. 160.

7. 'Rabbinic-Type Glosses in the Old Testament' in *Journal of Semitic Studies* 2 (1957) 149–62; 'A Rabbinic-Type Gloss in the LXX Version of 1 Samuel ii, 18' in *Vetus Testamentum* 14 (1964) 225–28; further studies, 16 (1966) 361–64; 518–22; 'Exposition in the Old Testament and in Rabbinic Writings' in *Promise and Fulfilment* (Hooke Festschrift, F. F. Bruce, ed., Edinburgh: T. & T. Clarke, 1963), pp. 187–201; 'Oral Torah and Written Records' in *Holy Book and Holy Tradition*, F. F. Bruce and E. G. Rupp ed. (Manchester University Press, 1968), pp. 54–67.

Testament during the latter's phases of development Professor Weingreen would define in broad terms as being 'a body of legalistic, historical, folkloreistic and expositional literature which was external to, but in effect supplemented and often modified, the basic biblical text'.[8] This oral law he considers to have existed in Israel even before the Exile. It is possible, he believes, that it was written down in summary fashion in later times. Thus, the official law would not have been passed on entirely by word of mouth, without the aid of written records.[9]

Turning from the oral law proper to rabbinic-type glosses, he considers that in these we find modes of interpretation which are the same as those of the Mishnah, and can therefore be described as rabbinic-type formulations.[10] One example of such a gloss he considers the italicized words of the following text of the book of Joshua (1:15): 'Then shall ye return to your inherited land *and ye shall take possession of it* which Moses, the servant of YHWH, gave unto you.' The words in italics break the continuity of Joshua's speech, constitute an obvious intrusion, are not found in the Greek Septuagint translation, and when they are removed the text flows freely. They are a brief note *on* the text, i.e. a gloss which some copyist inserted into the text.[11] We may note in passing that this phenomenon of 'interpolated passages' breaking the continuity of the text is very much a feature of the Palestinian Targum of the Pentateuch. We shall give examples of it later.

Another type of gloss is the variant reading. The scribe noted a different reading in another biblical manuscript and registered this variant above or next to the word in the text he was using. An example would be Ps 55:16: 'for there are evil things *in their dwelling place, in their midst*'. The italicized words are really a twofold statement of the same idea, one of the two groups probably a gloss.[12]

Professor Weingreen finds a pure Masoretic note in Ps 61:8b,[13] which is translated in the *Revised Standard Version* as: 'bid [Hebrew text: *mn*] love and faithfulness watch over him'

8. 'Oral Torah . . .', p. 60.
9. *Ibid.*, pp. 54f and *passim*.
10. 'A Rabbinic-Type Gloss in the LXX . . .', p. 227 and *passim*.
11. 'Rabbinic-Type Glosses in the Old Testament', pp. 150f.
12. *Ibid.*, p. 159.
13. *Ibid.*, p. 160. By a misprint the Psalm is wrongly given as 41 (*xli* instead of *lxi*).

[Hebrew: *ynṣrhw*], a somewhat awkward translation of the Hebrew text. The *n* (i.e. Nun) of the second Hebrew word given above, we may note, would ordinarily be assimilated to the following letter and the entire word written as *yṣrhw*. The two-lettered word *mn* has for long caused trouble. Weingreen sees in it an abbreviation in the pure Masoretic tradition: *mn = malê nun — Nun plene*, calling attention to the fact that, contrary to the usual rule, the *n* (Nun) of *ynṣrhw* is *not* assimilated. *Mn* is then a pure gloss, alien to the text. The text should be translated: 'may steadfast love and faithfulness watch over him.'

In all, Professor Weingreen finds four categories of such glosses: *a*) explanatory; *b*) extensions of themes; *c*) variant readings; *d*) Masoretic-type notes.[14] In his judgment these glosses represent official, standard commentary, expressed tersely. They may then be regarded as the literary prototypes of commentary with which we are familiar in rabbinic writings, both talmudic and medieval. He concludes that official expositional notes were written above the affected words in private manuscripts and that the continued association of these notes with the related words or phrases in the text led, ultimately, to their incorporation into the texts by copyists. Since such glosses appear in the Septuagint version, they point to an activity of authoritative exposition of biblical texts at least in post-exilic times.

The intention of these glossators, we may note, was that of the targumists: to give the sense of Scripture and help the people understand the reading.

Some laws underlying post-exilic exegesis

We now turn from the glosses to consider certain characteristic features of the Jewish approach to the Bible during the post-exilic age, characteristics found in later pre-Christian Jewish writings, both canonical and non-canonical.

1) *Free midrashic development*—Midrash, as we have seen, is a creative and actualizing rendition of the biblical text. It seeks to make the Scriptures understandable, relevant and useful

14. Cf. 'Rabbinic-Type Glosses in the Old Testament', summarized in 'A Rabbinic-Type Gloss in the LXX . . .', pp. 225f.

for a later generation. In our earlier treatment of the subject we spoke only of rabbinic midrash. The midrashic approach to the Scriptures is, however, well attested before the rabbinic and the Christian era. From the Old Testament period we have a clear example of it in chapters 10–19 of the book of Wisdom where early biblical history and the narrative of the Exodus are freely retold. Wis 10:21, in fact, has a midrashic paraphrase of Ex 15:2 found also in the Palestinian Targum to this same verse. We have further examples of pre-rabbinic midrash in the Passover Haggadah, the *Biblical Antiquities* of Pseudo-Philo, and possibly in the *Genesis Apocryphon* from Qumrân.

2) *Later theological views inserted into a biblical text or later translation*—The doctrine of messianism, the future life and other beliefs developed considerably after the Exile. R. Tournay has shown how ideas on the future life and angelology, developed in the later years of Old Testament Judaism, were inserted into the biblical text when the earlier tradition came to be re-edited.[15] This process of recasting earlier teaching in the light of later doctrine is known as rereading. At the end of his study Tournay remarks:

> It is interesting to see to what extent the Scriptures continued to live within the community of believers and how the faith of these believers poured itself into the very text of the ancient writings, thus registering the development of revelation for future generations. The forward thrust [*élan*] of this revelation went beyond the material content of the texts, and these latter were not considered as dead documents, fixed once for all; they always remained open to eventual enrichment. The Bible was already read and meditated on within a living tradition, a tradition anxious to answer the spiritual need of the Jewish people at every moment of its existence.[16]

It was within this same living tradition that the Aramaic paraphrases originated and Louis P. Smith justly compares the preoccupations of the final editor of Hosea with those of the targumists:

15. *Revue biblique* 69 (1962) pp. 481–505.
16. *Art. cit.*, pp. 504f.

The purpose of the edition was to present the teaching of the prophets in a form which would be understandable and edifying for the common people. So far as possible therefore ambiguities were made clear, contradictions were explained or removed, and teachings made applicable to the contemporary situation. Now this is exactly what the Aramaic paraphrase of the prophetic targum attempts to do a few centuries later with the Hebrew text.[17]

Later theological concepts have occasionally influenced the Greek Septuagint rendering. As an example we may take Jer 31:8 (Septuagint 38:8), where the Hebrew text, speaking of the return from Exile, says: 'Behold, I will bring them from the north country . . . among them the blind and the lame' (*bm 'wr wpsh*). This in the Septuagint becomes: 'Behold I will bring them from the north . . . *in a Passover feast*', reading the Hebrew words given above as *bmw'd psh*. The Greek rendering is partly due to a misreading of the Hebrew text. But its rendering is nonetheless influenced by the belief that the Messiah would come at the Passover, a belief found also in the Palestinian Targum (Ex 12:42) and commonly held by the Jews of St. Jerome's day.

3) *Avoidance of anthropomorphisms*—This tendency, found already in the Elohist source of the Pentateuch, became very pronounced in later Judaism. 'If one can judge by the tendencies manifested by the book of Chronicles and the ancient Septuagint, one can say that the preoccupation to eliminate from the Bible expressions injurious to the glory of God characterizes in a special manner the work of the scribes during the three centuries which preceded the capture of Jerusalem by Pompey'[18] (in 65 B.C.). All this is very much a feature of the targums.

4) *Respect due to Israel and the elders of Israel*—According to a later rabbinic dictum one should not speak disparagingly of the righteous, meaning by this the worthies of Israel.[19] We

---

17. 'The Prophetic Targum as Guide and Defence for the Higher Critic' in *Journal of Biblical Literature* 52 (1933) 122.

18. D. Barthélemy, 'Les tiqqune sopherim et la critique textuelle de l'A.T.' in *Vetus Testamentum, Suppléments*, vol. 9 (Leiden, 1963), p. 292.

19. Cf. M. McNamara, *The New Testament and the Palestinian Targum to the Pentateuch* (*Analecta Biblica* 27, Rome: Pontifical Institute, 1966), p. 54; see also D. Gooding, *Vetus Testamentum* 17 (1967) 188.

have seen how this maxim was probably shared already by the Elohist. The tendency to change the biblical text itself, or rewrite it in translation, in order to remove or tone down passages detrimental to the reputation of the elders of Israel is already attested in pre-Christian times. In Judges 18:30 we read of Gershom, the son of Moses, in a context speaking of idol worship in the tribe of Dan. The Masoretic Text changes 'Moses' of this text to 'Menasseh', doubtless out of respect for Moses. Professor David Gooding of Queen's University, Belfast, has shown how the law later formulated by the rabbis is operative already in the Septuagint translation, or in the Hebrew text on which this rendering is based.[20] There we have evidence of a 'whitewashing' tradition exculpating Jeroboam and Ahab. This tendency affects the targumic translation of certain passages both of the Pentateuch and of other books.

5) *Geography*—A natural tendency in any translation desirous of being meaningful to its readers is to replace ancient names with what the translator considers to be their contemporary equivalents. Thus we find that the Septuagint in Is 9:11 replaces the Aramaeans and Philistines of the Hebrew text with the Syrians and Greeks. Ancient translations such as the Septuagint and the Peshitta, however, differ here from the Aramaic targums in some respects. The former were for people living outside Palestine. On a number of occasions it was as well to leave the name of some ancient and unknown Palestinian site untranslated as to give a later equivalent, known in Palestine but unknown outside it. Renderings intended for Palestinian audiences, on the other hand, would be interested in giving the later name of the biblical site. And there was another factor which must have affected Aramaic renderings intended for Palestinian Jews. For official Judaism the exact identification of certain biblical sites was no mere matter of actualization or of exegetical curiosity. The location of certain biblical sites, such as the border towns of Israel, had a direct bearing on halakah, on whether the inhabitants were bound by the laws of the sabbatical year for instance. Hence we find

20. 'Ahab according to the Septuagint' in *Zeitschrift für die alttest. Wissensch.* 76 (1964) 269–80; 'The Septuagint's Rival Versions of Jeroboam's Rise to Power' in *Vetus Testamentum* 17 (1967) 173–89.

a certain preoccupation with the identification of the border towns of Israel in the Mishnah and Tosephta and in the Palestinian Talmud.[21] We may presume that there existed in Palestinian Judaism one or more traditions on the actual identification of biblical sites.

Conclusion

From all this we can see that in the centuries preceding the birth of Christ there came into existence in Judaism a tradition on the interpretation of the text of the Old Testament. The Scriptures were not transmitted as something without life or without a precise meaning for believers. The text was handed on together with its interpretation. It was on this tradition the scribes and translators drew in their explanation and rendering of the written Word of God. We must not consider the targumists outside this tradition. When these stood up in the synagogue to render the written Word in Aramaic, they spoke as heirs of a tradition.

21. See Tosephta, *Shebiith* 4, ed. Zuckermandel, p. 66, 10; Palestinian Talmud, *Shebith* 6,1,36c; *Sifre*, section *Ekeb*, at end; Mishna, *Shebi*, 6, 1; *Halla* 4,8; *Gittin* 1,1f; Tosephta, *Halla* 2,11(99), and below, pp. 190, 204f.

3

The Synagogue and Synagogue Worship

Because of the intimate relationship of synagogue worship and the Targums to the Pentateuch and to the Prophets, it is necessary to consider what form this worship took in pre-Christian times and in the days of our Lord.[1]

Authors are not agreed on the origins of the synagogue. The generally accepted view takes it that the later synagogue institution had its origins in the spontaneous meetings held by the Jews during the Exile for the purpose of praying, hearing their ancient traditions read and exhorting one another. Others see the origins of the synagogue within Palestine itself in the post-exilic period. Professor J. Weingreen has put forward the view that the ingredients of the synagogue—meetings with congregational prayer, the reading of sacred texts, the recital of psalm-like praises and the expository sermon—already existed in pre-exilic times. These traditions the Jews would have taken with them into exile and probably developed more thoroughly. What Ezra did when he had the Torah read and expounded to the assembled Jews (Neh 8:1ff) would then not have been something novel.[2]

What is important for our purpose, however, is that by New Testament times, and long before, the synagogue had become an established institution both in Palestine and in the Diaspora. Furthermore, the order of worship in the synagogue was by then fixed in its essentials.

1. For this chapter see E. Schürer, *A History of the Jewish People in the Time of Jesus Christ*, Eng. trans. of 2nd ed. by S. Taylor and P. Christie (Edinburgh: T. & T. Clarke, 1901), II,II, §27, pp. 52–89; G. Foot Moore, *Judaism* I, pp. 280–307; A. Edersheim, *Sketches of Jewish Social Life in the Days of Christ* (London, no date, preface 1876), pp. 249–80; P. Billerbeck, *Kommentar zum Neuen Testament aus Talmud und Midrasch*, vol. IV (Munich, 1928), pp. 115–88.

2. 'The Origin of the Synagogue' in *Hermathena* 98 (1964) 68–84; see p. 81 for summary.

Of course the Sabbath was the day *par excellence* for synagogue service. In Palestine, at least, there were also services on the second and fifth days of the week (Mónday and Thursday), the market days when the peasants came to the villages.

The synagogue was the centre of Jewish religious life. It was there the ordinary Jew worshipped and received instruction in the Law of Moses. It did not, however, displace the Temple. In fact it helped in its own way to foster love for God's House in Jerusalem. While the course[3] of priests and levites performed their sacred functions in the Temple, the (lay) Israelites of the course assembled in the local synagogue to show their solidarity with them and to manifest the connection of the synagogue with the Temple.[4] Throughout this week of service, the Israelites who assembled in the synagogues read the first chapter of Genesis. Each day of the week, for the six days from Sunday to Friday, they read in order the work of the six days of creation. 'On the first day they read from *In the beginning* . . . to *Let there be a firmament* [exclusive]; and on the second day, from *Let there be a firmament* [inclusive] to *waters be gathered together* [exclusive] etc.' (Mishnah, *Ta'anith* 4:3). We may remark that in the Palestinian Targum as found in Codex Neofiti the account of each of the six days of creation ends with the phrase: 'the order of the work of creation: the first (*resp.* second, etc.) day'.[5] This phrase may well be due to the synagogue custom just mentioned and may mark the conclusion of the daily readings for each of the six days.

Synagogue worship

The constant parts of the synagogue service were prayer, the reading of lessons from Scripture, followed where possible by a homily. The oldest Jewish prayer book (*Seder Amran Gaon*) we possess is from the ninth century. This, as one would expect, is based on older practice. With the aid of references in the

---

3. The 'course' (Hebrew *mishmar*, pl. *mismaroth*; literally 'guard[s]') was a division of priests and levites for duty in liturgical functions. For this duty priests and levites were divided into twenty-four courses or 'divisions', each course in its turn attending to the Temple liturgy. The Baptist's father, Zechariah, was of the 'division' or 'course' of Abijah (see Lk 1:5,8,23).

4. Cf. Schürer, *op. cit.*, II,I, pp. 275f, 291, note 249.

5. On other indications for the close connection of Neofiti with the Jewish liturgy see M. McNamara, *The New Testament and the Palestinian Targum* . . ., pp. 62f; *Rivista degli studi orientali* 41 (1966) 13.

Mishnah and other sources we can form a good idea of the prayers used in the synagogue during the early Christian centuries, and even in the time of Christ.

The Shema‘

The synagogue service began with the *Shema‘*, Israel's profession of faith in the One True God.[6] The Shema‘ consists of the following three passages: Deut 6:4–9, Deut 11:13–21, and Num 15:37–41—the text from Numbers probably being a later addition. It gets its name *Shema‘* ('Hear') from the opening section: 'Hear O Israel, the Lord our God, the Lord is One, and thou shalt love the Lord thy God with all thy heart, and with all thy soul, and with all thy might.' In Palestine the Shema‘ could be recited in Hebrew or in Aramaic.

The recitation of the Shema‘ was introduced and followed by short formulas blessing God and consequently known as *Berakoth* ('Blessings'). In the morning recitation two benedictions preceded it and one followed (Mishnah, *Berakoth* 1:4; 2:1f). Allowing for minor changes, the following can be taken as the benedictions recited before the Shema‘:

I. Blessed be Thou, O Lord, King of the world, Who formest the light and createst the darkness; Who makest peace and createst everything; Who in mercy givest light to the earth and to those who dwell upon it; and in Thy goodness day by day, renewest the works of creation. Blessed be the Lord our God for the Glory of His handiwork and for the light-giving lights which He has made for His praise. *Selah!* Blessed be the Lord our God, Who hath formed the lights.

II. With great love hast Thou loved us, O Lord our God, and with much overflowing pity hast Thou pitied us, our Father and our King. For the sake of our fathers who trusted in Thee, and Thou taughtest them the statutes of life, have mercy upon us and teach us. Enlighten our eyes to Thy commandments; unite our hearts to love and fear Thy name, and we shall not be put to shame, world without end. For

---

6. Cf. P. Billerbeck, *op. cit.*, IV, pp. 189–207; Moore, *Judaism* I, p. 291; I. Elbogen, *Der jüdische Gottesdienst in seiner geschichtlichen Entwicklung*, 2nd ed. (Frankfurt a. M., 1924; 4th ed. Hildesheim, 1962, §7); Schürer, *op. cit.*, II, II, pp. 84f.

Thou art a God who preparest salvation, and us hast Thou chosen from among all nations and tongues, and hast in truth brought us near to Thy great Name—*Selah*—that we may lovingly praise Thee and Thy Oneness. Blessed be the Lord Who in love chose His people Israel.[7]

Then came the Shema' proper, on the oneness of God and the love of him expressed through fidelity to the commandments. After this came the final benediction, a prayer for deliverance, which was basically as follows:

True it is that Thou art the Lord our God and the God of our fathers, our King and the King of our fathers, our Saviour, the Rock of our salvation, our Help and our Deliverer. Thy Name is from everlasting, and there is no god beside Thee. A new song did they that were delivered sing to Thy Name by the seashore; together did all praise and own Thee King, and say: The Lord shall reign forever and ever. Blessed be the Lord who saves Israel.

The Shema' and the commandments

The three biblical texts comprising the Shema' are so much part of tradition in the second century A.D. that one could speculate on the choice of the order in which they are given. R. Joshua ben Karha (*ca.* A.D. 140–165) says that Deut 6:4–9 preceded Deut 11:13–21, 'so that a man may first take upon him the yoke of the kingdom of heaven, and afterward take upon him the yoke of the commandments'. Again Deut 11:13–21 precedes Num 15:37–41, because the former applies both by day and night while the latter applies by day only (Mishnah, *Berakoth* 2,2).

Originally the commandments formed part of the Shema' (Mishnah, *Tamid*, 5,1), and there were, apparently, Hebrew manuscripts in circulation containing only the commandments and Israel's profession of faith. The Nash papyrus (*ca.* 150 B.C.) is an example, with the ten commandments and Deut 6:4–6.

---

7. Texts in Edersheim, *op. cit.*, pp. 269f; cf. also Billerbeck, *op. cit.*, pp. 192–94; J. Bonsirven, *Textes rabbiniques des deux premiers siècles chrétiens* (Rome: Biblical Institute Press, 1955), p. 2; Paul P. Levertoff, 'Synagogue Worship in the First Century' in *Liturgy and Worship*, W. K. Lowther Clarke and C. Harris eds. (London: S.P.C.K., 1932), pp. 67–70.

In Christ's day, too, the commandments would have been part of the Shema'. The former were later omitted 'to give no occasion to the cavils of heretics'; that these might not say: 'The Ten Commandments *only* were given to Moses on Sinai' (Jer. *Berakoth* 3c middle; Bab. *Berakoth* 12a). The 'heretics' in question were probably Christians.

Synagogue liturgy apparently affected the Palestinian Targum rendering, where a blessing on the divine name is inserted after the translation of the opening words of the Shema' (Deut 6:4; Gen 49:2). This is but another indication of the close connection of the Palestinian Targum and the liturgy of the synagogue. It is likewise a further argument for the venerable age of the former.

The bearing of the Shema' and of the targumic rendering of Deut 6:4f on certain New Testament texts, such as Mark 12:29f (and parallels) merits separate consideration, and will be treated of in the second part of this work.

The Eighteen Benedictions (Shemoneh Esreh)[8]

After the Shema' came the Prayer proper, the *Tephillah*. In the oldest form known to us this consisted in a series of 'Benedictions', so called because each ascription or petition ended with the words: 'Blessed art Thou, O Lord', etc. These prayers, apart from some reference to the fall of Jerusalem, are much earlier than Christian times. The arrangement of these Benedictions was made towards the end of the first century A.D. Their number was then eighteen, in Hebrew *Shemoneh Esreh*, whence the name. When a nineteenth prayer (i.e. no. 12) against the 'heretics' (i.e. Christians) was introduced at the end of the first century, the prayer continued to bear the same name: the Eighteen (Benedictions).

The prayer opens with the praise of God (nos. 1–3) and closes with thanksgiving to God (nos. 17–18[19]). In between (4–16) we have petitions. Rabbi Gamaliel II, under whose authority the arrangement of the Benedictions was made, made the daily recitation of the *Shemoneh Esreh* obligatory for every Jew. In the synagogue service for Sabbaths and festivals, however, only the first three and the last three, i.e. those on

8. Cf. Moore, *op. cit.*, pp. 291–96; Billerbeck, *op. cit.*, pp. 208–49; Schürer, *op. cit.*, II, II, pp. 85–89; Bonsirven, *op. cit.*, pp. 2–3; Levertoff, *op. cit.*, pp. 70–74.

praise and on thanksgiving, were recited. For the recitation Hebrew or Aramaic could be used. We have the *Shemoneh Esreh* in a Palestinian and Babylonian recension, the latter being considered a more developed form of the prayer than the former.

The language of the Benedictions draws heavily on the Scriptures, particularly on the Psalms. No. 2 expresses faith in the resurrection: 'Thou art mighty for ever, O Lord; . . . Thou restorest life to the dead (cf. 2 Cor 1 :9). Thou art mighty to save . . . Blessed art Thou, O Lord, who restorest the dead.' No. 14(15) looks forward to the Messiah. 'Have pity, O Lord our God, on Israel thy people, on Jerusalem thy city, and on Zion the dwelling-place of thy glory, and on thy altar, and on thy Palace and on the kingdom of the House of David, the Messiah [of] thy righteousness. Blessed art Thou, O Lord our God, the builder of Jerusalem.' Thus the Palestinian recension. The other is more explicit: 'The offspring of David, thy servant, speedily cause to flourish, and let his horn be exalted in thy salvation; for thy salvation do we hope daily. Blessed art thou, O Lord, who causest the horn of salvation to flourish.' No. 3 is on the sanctification of the divine Name: 'Thou art holy and fearsome is thy Name, and there is no God apart from Thee. Blessed art Thou, O Lord, the holy God.'

Sentiments expressed in these benedictions are found throughout the Palestinian Targum to the Pentateuch and the other liturgical paraphrases of the Old Testament as well. All originated at the very heart of Israelite piety.

The Kaddish[9]

After the Prayer (*Tephillah*) came the reading of the Scriptures, accompanied in Palestine by a rendering into Aramaic. Then came the homily which in Palestine was for the greater part in Aramaic. The preacher closed the homily with the following ascription in Aramaic: 'May his great name be blessed for-ever and for ever and ever.' In due time, and in the pre-Christian era, this developed into a longer Aramaic prayer known as the *Kaddish* which came to be used in other places of

9. Cf. Elbogen, *op. cit.*, §12a; David de Sola Pool, *The Old Jewish-Aramaic Prayer, the Kaddish*, 1909; Moore, *Judaism* I, p. 306; III, p. 101, note 84; Bonsirven, *op. cit.*, p. 3; Levertoff, *op. cit.*, pp. 74–75.

the liturgy as well. There are various forms of this extended prayer. It was also used in the Temple. The form of the Kaddish of New Testament times is hard to determine, but it must have been essentially the liturgical Kaddish, which we give here:

> Exalted and hallowed be His great name in the world, which He created according to His Will; and let His kingdom come in your lifetime and in the lifetime of the whole house of Israel, very speedily.
> ℞ Amen.
> Blessed be His great name, world without end. Blessed and praised, celebrated and exalted, extolled and adored, magnified and worshipped be Thy holy name. Blessed be He far above all benedictions, hymns, thanks, praises and consolations, which have been uttered in the world.
> ℞ Amen.
> May the prayers and supplications of all Israel be graciously received before their Father in heaven.
> ℞ Amen.
> May perfect peace descend from heaven, and life upon us and all Israel.
> ℞ Amen.
> May He who makes peace in His heaven confer peace upon us and upon all Israel.
> ℞ Amen.

Scripture readings[10]

Readings from the Scriptures, from the Pentateuch at any rate, are probably as old as the synagogue system itself. In Jewish sources of the early Christian period Moses is said to have prescribed the reading of the Law on Sabbaths, holy days, new moons and the intermediate days of festivals with octaves or such periods, while Ezra is said to have ordained the reading on the market days (Monday and Thursday) and at the afternoon service (the *minḥah*) of the Sabbath. This is another way of saying that the custom was then of immemorial antiquity.

10. Cf. Moore, *Judaism* I, pp. 296–303; Charles Perrot, '*Petuhot* et *Setumot*. Etude sur les alinéas du Pentateuque' in *Revue biblique* 76 (1969) 50–91: a study of the open (*petuhot*) and closed (*setumot*) *parashyot* or sections of the Pentateuch and of the bearing of this evidence on the history of the development of the readings of the Pentateuch in the synagogues. He believes Neofiti represents an old recension of the Palestinian Targum.

By New Testament times the reading consisted of passages from the Law and the Prophets. The lesson could be read by any male Jew, adult or minor, free from certain impediments. The reader was required to *read* from the scroll. He could not recite the passage from memory. And he stood as he read.

The Mishnah and Tosephta (tractate *Megillah*) give detailed instructions on this reading of the Scriptures. More than one reader was required: on a Monday, Thursday, and Sabbath afternoon three; on certain other days four; on a festival day five; on the Day of Atonement six; on the Sabbath morning service seven. There was no reading from the Prophets on the Monday, Thursday and Sabbath afternoon service, nor on the new moons and mid-festival services (Mishnah, *Meg.* 4,1–2). Each reader had to read a minimum of three verses from the Law (*Meg.* 4,4). As a general rule a Benediction was said by the first and last reader of the section from the Pentateuch.

Fixed readings

Certain days had fixed readings assigned to them. The list given by the Mishnah (*Meg.* 3,4–6) is as follows:

A. *The four Sabbaths of Adar (i.e. the month preceding Nisan)*

First Sabbath	(1)	Ex 30:11–16
Second Sabbath	(2)	Deut 25:17–19
Third Sabbath	(3)	Num 19:1–20
Fourth Sabbath	(4)	Ex 12:1–20

B. *Festivals*

Passover	(5)	Lev 23:1ff(section: 'The Set Feasts')
Pentecost	(6)	Deut 16:9–12 (section: 'Seven Weeks')
The New Year	(7)	Lev 23:23ff
Day of Atonement	(8)	Lev 16:1–34
First day of Tabernacles	(9)	Lev 23:1ff (as at Passover)
Other days of Tabernacles	(10)	Num 29:17ff
Feast of Dedication	(11)	Num 7:1–89
Purim	(12)	Ex 17:8–16

C. *Other festival days*

First days of the month (i.e. new moons)	(13)	Num 28:11–15
The Maamads (i.e. synagogue service while the course of priests and levites officiated in the temple)	(14)	Gen ch. 1
Fast days	(15)	Lev 26:3–46 ('The Blessing and the Curses')

The readings assigned to the four special Sabbaths are known from their opening Hebrew words as *Shekalim* ('Shekels'); *Zakor* ('Remember what Amalek did'); *Parah* ('The red heifer'); and *ha-Ḥodesh* ('This month'). Their choice for the season immediately preceding Nisan is obvious: they recall the duty of paying the temple tax and of performing the required preparations for Passover. Amalek, through Heman, is associated with the feast of Purim, held on Adar 14 (or 15). All these were probably fixed readings in pre-Christian times.

So too, probably, are the lessons assigned to the major festivals and the Day of Atonement. About the others G. F. Moore has serious doubts.[11] This mishnah prescription, he believes, has a systematic look about it and may be later than the fall of Jerusalem (A.D. 70).

Palestinian cycle of Scripture readings[12]

For the New Testament period and for some centuries later there appears to have been no *lectio continua* of the Prophets. This is implied by Mishnah, *Meg.* 4,4, which states that a reader may leave out verses in the Prophets, but not in the Law. The same tractate has repeated references to reading the Pentateuch 'in the fixed order', but never refers to such fixed order for the *Haftarah*. The choice of passage was probably left to the head of the synagogue or the reader himself. Luke 4:16ff tells us of Jesus's participation at a synagogue service at

Nazareth. The description corresponds exactly to what the Mishnah and later Jewish texts have on synagogue usage. It is not clear whether the Haftarah (Is 61:1ff) read by Jesus was chosen by himself or determined by the head of the synagogue. The former seems to have been the case.

Today the Jews and Samaritans complete the reading of the Pentateuch in a one-year cycle. The present-day Jewish annual cycle is that attested for Babylonian Judaism in the early centuries of the Christian era. With this annual cycle of Babylon the text of the Babylonian Talmud (*Meg.* 29b) contrasts the triennial cycle then in use in Palestine: 'Those [Jews] of the West [i.e. Palestine] complete the reading of the Pentateuch in three years.' This Palestinian cycle continued in use in Palestinian Judaism for a long time, until it was finally superseded by the Babylonian custom. It occasioned the division of the Pentateuch into 154 sections (*sedarim*) still found in Hebrew Bibles.

The text of the Babylonian Talmud shows that the triennial cycle was established throughout Palestine in the third century. How much older than this it is, we cannot say. From the evidence available to us from the Mishnah and Tosephta it seems to follow that it was not the established practice in the second century A.D. That the Pentateuch should be read consecutively, in a fixed order, seems to be a guiding principle. But in the middle of the second century R. Meir and R. Judah ben Ila'i held divergent views on what this order should be (Tos., *Meg.* 4,10). R. Meir maintained that the *lectio continua* should embrace all synagogue readings of the Pentateuch. 'At the place where they leave off at the Sabbath morning service, they begin at the afternoon service; where they leave off at that service, they begin on Monday; where they leave off on Monday, they begin on Thursday; and where they leave off on Thursday, they begin on the following Sabbath' (*ibid.*). His contemporary, R. Judah, was of the view that the *lectio continua* should only embrace the Sabbath morning service, and that the reading at each Sabbath morning service should commence where the reading of the preceding Sabbath morning service ended.

The system presumed by the Mishnah tractate *Megillah* appears to be that advocated by R. Judah ben Ila'i. The tractate speaks of reading according to the 'set order' (3,4.6; 4,4). This set order is put aside for the four special Sabbaths of Adar. 'On the fifth they revert to the set order' (3,4). The *lectio continua* is also broken by other days to which a special reading is assigned. 'At all those times they break off [from the set order in the reading of the Law]; on the first days of the months, at the [Feast of] Dedication, at Purim, on days of fasting, and at the Maamads and on the Day of Atonement' (3,4). 'On Mondays and Thursdays and on Sabbaths at the Afternoon Prayer [*minḥah*] they read according to the set order; and these are not taken into account' (3,6). Canon Danby is very probably right when he takes this to mean that on these days the lessons from the Pentateuch were from the section prescribed for the following Sabbath;[13] what was read during the week was read again the following Sabbath at the morning service.

In the rabbinic reckoning (noted at the end of the Hebrew Bible) there are 5,845 verses in the Pentateuch. Assuming the normal number of readers (seven) and the minimum number of verses (three) with a maximum number of forty-nine Sabbaths per year (i.e. fifty-three minus the four special Sabbaths), R. Judah's system, and that of the Mishnah, would take almost six years to go through. Add to this the Sabbath readings omitted by the concurrence of some of the other special days and the Sabbath, and the period will be longer. It has been reckoned that R. Meir's system would take about two years and four months for the reading of the Pentateuch.

There is clearly no evidence that in the Palestine of New Testament times or for some time later the Pentateuch was read in a cycle, beginning and ending on a given feast or date. G. F. Moore has serious doubts that there was even any *lectio continua* in mishnaic times. He takes the injunction of Mishnah, *Meg.* 4,4—not to skip from place to place in the Pentateuch—as an indication that in practice this was done.[14] He is likewise of the opinion that when readings on ordinary Sabbaths first became customary in the synagogue service, the passage to be read was freely chosen by the reader or by the head of the

---

13. *The Mishnah, translated from the Hebrew* . . . (Oxford University Press, 1933), p. 205.
14. *Op. cit.*, pp. 298f.

synagogue.[15] This was scarcely the procedure in New Testament times. Ezra had the commission of teaching the Law of Moses to the Jews, and the synagogue was the ideal place to do this. It was important that all Israel know the entire Law. This would indicate that the Pentateuch be read through consecutively at the regular Sabbath morning services. The evidence from New Testament times supports this. 'For from early generations Moses has had in every city those who preach him, for he is read every sabbath in the synagogues' (Acts 15:21). The text of Josephus already cited indicates the same.[16] Philo, too, informs us that Moses commanded that the Jews should assemble on the seventh day, and, being seated, should reverently and decorously listen to the Law, in order that no one might be ignorant of it.[17]

It would appear, then, that at least by New Testament times there was a *lectio continua* of the Pentateuch. The manner in which this was done does not then appear to have been determined. It was probably left to local custom. To postulate any cycle, be it annual, triennial or of some other sort, for Palestine goes beyond the evidence at our disposal. Theories based on any such cycle (and there are a number of them) are founded on very insecure premises.[18]

15. *Ibid.*, p. 298.
16. *Contra Apionem* II, 17 (18), §175; text cited above, p. 26.
17. Fragment of *Hypothetica*, book I, in Eusebius, *Praeparatio Evangelica*, viii, Loeb ed.
18. Cf. A. Buechler, 'The Reading of the Law and the Prophets in a Triennial Cycle' in *Jewish Quarterly Review* 5 (1893) 420–68; 6 (1894) 1–73; J. Mann, *The Bible as Read and Preached in the Old Synagogue*, vol. I: *The Palestinian Triennial Cycle* (Cincinnati, 1940), on Genesis and Exodus; vol. II by J. Mann and Isaiah Sonne (Cincinnati: Hebrew Union College, 1966), on Leviticus and Numbers; see review by N. M. Sarna indicated above in note 12. Mann's belief that the midrashic homilies were based on the *Hafṭarôth*, and not on the readings from the Pentateuch, is not borne out by an analysis of the texts; further bibliography on the Palestinian cycle in Le Déaut, *op. cit.*, pp. 45f. Aileen Guilding takes a Palestinian triennial cycle as the basis for her work, *The Fourth Gospel and Jewish Worship*, Oxford, 1960. This triennial cycle is also at the basis of R. G. Finch's work, *The Synagogue Lectionary and the New Testament*, London, 1939; likewise C. H. Cave in *New Testament Studies* II (1965) 374–87 (see p. 377); he has promised a larger work on the subject. He believes the triennial cycle originated before the Maccabean age. P. Carrington seeks to prove the relationship of the Gospel of Mark with the Jewish lectionary tradition and with the primitive Christian calendar (*The Primitive Christian Catechism*, Cambridge, 1940; *The Primitive Christian Calendar*, Cambridge, 1952). See critique of his position by W. D. Davies in *Christian Origins and Judaism* (London: Darton, Longman & Todd, 1962), pp. 67–92. P. Levertoff in *A New Commentary on Holy Scripture*, Gore ed. (London, 1928), pp. 128ff, also attempted to trace a connection between the Jewish year and the Gospels; critique of this view in Davies, *op. cit.*, pp. 92–95.

The Aramaic rendering

The need for a rendering into the Aramaic vernacular of the passage read in Hebrew was a necessity in communities with little or no knowledge of Hebrew. Hebrew might be the 'sacred tongue'; yet the very purpose of the Scripture reading was to make the mass of the people acquainted with the Law of Moses.

The Mishnah gives considerable detail on how this rendering into Aramaic was to be done. The interpreter (called the *Meturgeman*) had to be distinct from the reader. Any competent person, even a minor, could act as interpreter, subject, naturally, to the control of the head of the synagogue. As far as the Pentateuch was concerned, each single verse was rendered into Aramaic immediately after being read out in Hebrew. For the Prophets, three verses could be read before being translated (*Meg.* 4,4).

Certain texts, detrimental to the honour of Israel or the ancients, were read out in Hebrew and not rendered into Aramaic. These texts, listed in *Meg.* 4,10, are: the story of Reuben (Gen 35:22); the second story of the golden calf (Ex 32; exact verses uncertain); the blessing of the priests (Num 6:24–26); the story of David and Bethsabee (2 Sam 11:2–17); and the story of Amnon and Tamar (2 Sam 13). It was the oral rendering in the synagogue, not the consigning of a translation of these texts to writing, which was forbidden. Yet, it is interesting that all the Pentateuch passages are left untranslated in Codex Neofiti. In fact, this text even leaves untranslated the words detrimental to Reuben's honour in Gen 49:4.

The Aramaic translation had to be given orally. It was forbidden to use written texts for this purpose. One reason given for this is that the written law should be transmitted in writing and the oral law by word of mouth (Palestinian Talmud, *Meg.* 4,1,74d,l. 16). Another reason given in the Babylonian Talmud (*Meg.* 32a) is that of impressing on the people the difference between the sacred text and its interpretative translation. This law may have been operative already in New Testament times. Jesus's disciples distinguished between the words of Scripture on Elias and the scribes' understanding of these words (Mt 17:10; Mk 9:11).

In the second century A.D., R. Judah ben Ila'i gave as a principle of translation: 'He who translates a verse literally is a liar, and he who adds to it is a blasphemer' (Tos., *Meg.* 4,41; *Kiddushin* 49a). To illustrate this he adduces Ex 24:10; 'They saw the God of Israel.' To translate this literally would be a lie, since no man can be said to have seen God. To insert 'angel' for God would be blasphemous since a creature would then be substituted for the creator. The proper rendering according to R. Judah is: 'They saw the *glory* of the God of Israel.' This, in fact, is substantially how the text is rendered in all targums to the passage, and was a rendering very probably current long before R. Judah's day. The mentality which inspired it can be seen in John 12:41 where Isaiah is said to have seen the *glory* of Christ (cf. Is 6:1,5).

By the time the Mishnah rule came to be codified, and probably long before, the task of the meturgeman was scarcely that of rendering the Hebrew text into Aramaic for the first time. Nor was he likely to have had the liberty to render the Hebrew text at will. The interpretative tradition had already been formed. His was rather the duty of conveying this traditional understanding of the text to the people. That this was so, would seem to follow from the nature of the case. The purpose of the reading of the Law and of the Aramaic rendering was to have the congregation understand the message of Moses. This was a very important function in which the meturgeman would surely be bound by tradition. That the 'interpreter' transmitted a traditional rendering of the text seems implicit, too, in rabbinic texts referring to the translation of the Scriptures in the synagogues. In the Mishnah, *Meg.* 4,9 it is laid down that anyone who translates Lev 18:21 — 'And you shall not give any of your seed to make [them] pass [through fire] to Moloch' — as: 'You shall not give any of your seed to have them become with child in heathendom', be put to silence with a rebuke. We may presume that the translation censured was known to have been used in some synagogues. It was one rendering already in some way 'traditional'. It is, in fact, substantially the rendering of Lev 18:21 still found in Pseudo-Jonathan, the Peshitta and in a gloss to Neofiti.[19] The principle that the targum belonged to the oral law to be transmitted orally seems to indicate that it was looked on as a form of fixed tradition.

19. See further McNamara, *The New Testament and the Palestinian Targum . . .*, pp. 49–51.

On the supposition that the meturgeman repeated a traditional rendering rather than gave a new one of his own, we can readily understand how minors were permitted to act as interpreters. We shall return to this point again when we come to consider the origin and transmission of the Palestinian Targum to the Pentateuch.

The Homily[20]

By New Testament times the homily, in Palestine given in the Aramaic vernacular, was an independent part of the synagogue service. That such was the case in Palestine we know from the Gospels (e.g. Luke 4:16–21). The same was true of the Hellenistic synagogues. Paul, as we know, availed of the synagogue homily to preach the gospel to the Jews of the Dispersion. In Acts 13:14–41 Luke has recorded a homily delivered by the Apostle of the Gentiles in Pisidian Antioch. We have also the evidence of Philo. Referring to the Sabbath observance he says:

> Innumerable schools of practical wisdom and self-control are opened every seventh day in all cities. In these schools the people sit decorously, keeping silence and listening with the utmost attention out of a thirst for refreshing discourse, while one of the best qualified stands up and instructs them in what is best and most conducive to welfare, things by which their whole life may be made better.[21]

The subject matter of this discourse was piety and holiness towards God and humanity and justice towards men.[22] In another passage he tells us that in these assemblies the Law (of Moses) was expounded:

> He [Moses] required them to assemble in the same place on these seventh days, and sitting together in a respectful and

---

20. Cf. G. F. Moore, *Judaism* I, pp. 305–06; P. Billerbeck, *Kommentar zum N. T. aus Talmud und Midrasch* IV, part 1 (Munich: Beck, 1928), pp. 171–188; M. Maher M.S.C., 'Reflections on Jewish and Christian Preaching' in *The Irish Ecclesiastical Record* 108 (1967) 226–42; A. G. Wright, *art. cit.*, *The Catholic Biblical Quarterly* 28 (1966) 127f; 432–36.

21. *De specialibus legibus* II, 15, §§61–62, translation found in Moore, *op. cit.*, p. 306. Another slightly different translation in the Loeb edition of Philo's works, vol. VII, pp. 345, 347.

22. *Ibid.* §63; Loeb edition, p. 347.

orderly manner hear the laws read so that none should be ignorant of them. And indeed they always assemble and sit together, most of them in silence except when it is the practice to add something to signify their approval of what is read. But some priest who is present or one of the elders reads the holy laws to them and expounds them point by point until about the late afternoon, when they depart, having gained both expert knowledge of the holy laws and considerable advance in piety.[23]

It would be interesting to determine the general pattern and content of the homilies delivered in the synagogues of Palestine during the time of Christ and earlier. The task of so doing is by no means an easy one. Unlike the rendering of the Scriptures into Aramaic no rules are laid down in the Mishnah, Tosephta or any other such source regulating the matter or the method of the homily. The greatest liberty would seem to have been allowed to the homilist and the nature of the homily probably varied with time and circumstance. At Pisidian Antioch Paul delivers his homily at the request of the heads of the synagogue and in it he takes his listeners through sacred history from the Exodus to the resurrection of Jesus. On the other hand, Jesus seems to have based his homily at Nazareth on the passage from the Prophets read in the synagogue service (Luke 4:16–21).

The form of the early homilies is probably conserved in the Jewish homiletic midrashim, although these come from a later date and generally follow the Palestinian triennial cycle of Scripture readings. Of the older homilies the homiletic style is clearest in the collection known as the *Pesikta* (*de-Rab Kahana*). A feature of these midrashic homilies, which begin with the liturgical passage from the Pentateuch or the Prophets read in the synagogue, is their liberal use of biblical quotations, not merely from the Law and the Prophets but also from the Hagiographa which were not read in the synagogue service. Peder Borgen has made a study of homilies which he believes he has isolated in the works of Philo (*De mutatione nominum,* 253–63; *Legum allegoriae* III, 65–75a; 162–68; 169–73; *De*

---

23. Fragment of the first book of Philo's *Hypothetica* found in Eusebius, *Praeparatio evangelica* 8,7,12–13; Loeb edition of Philo, vol. IX, pp. 430–33, with English translation given here. Both this and the preceding text of Philo can be taken to refer to the homily; see Billerbeck, *op. cit.,* p. 172, note *c*.

sacrificiis Abelis et Caini 76–87; *De somniis* II, 17–30). All these
he considers similar in structure to the homily in John 6:31–58.
And the homily of John and those of Philo he considers con-
structed on a homiletic pattern found in the later Palestinian
homiletic midrashim.[24] There may then have been a continuity
in Jewish homiletic method from the first century onwards.

We are ill-informed on the origins of the homily and on the
relation it may have borne in earlier times to the Scriptures
rendered into the vernacular. The Jewish homily is a fine
example of haggadic midrash, applying the biblical text as it
does to later situations. In the New Testament homilies the
actualization consists in showing how the biblical texts are
fulfilled in the person of Christ (cf. Luke 4:21; Acts 13:26–41).
It may be that at some early time both the translation of the
Scriptures into the vernacular and the homily were combined
and that the Palestinian Targum of the Pentateuch represents
this earlier period. G. F. Moore writes:

> It is hardly to be questioned that the early interpreters in
> some cases exercised considerable freedom in paraphrase.
> The Palestinian Targums, as we have them, come from a
> much later date, but in the freedom with which paraphrase
> runs into midrash they may be taken to illustrate the fashion
> of the older interpreters . . . It is even possible that in the first
> stage of the institution translation and homily were not yet
> differentiated, and the interpreter was also the expository
> preacher.[25]

Renée Bloch is of the same opinion. Of the Palestinian Targum
she writes:

> This cannot be looked on as a translation. It is sufficient to
> read it to become aware of this. Whereas the Targum of
> Onkelos . . . [is] a kind of peshat, an interpretation of the
> Torah according to the talmudic halakah, the Palestinian
> Targum, for its part, comes nearer to the derash. It is much
> closer to midrash than to translation. It is even quite probable

24. P. Borgen, *Bread from Heaven* (Leiden: Brill, 1965), pp. 28–98.
25. *Judaism* I, p. 304. Moore, writing in 1927, shared the view then common that the
Palestinian Targum was of more recent origin.

that originally it was a sort of homiletic midrash, or simply the outline-sketch of a series of homilies, given in the synagogue after the public reading of the Torah. It already contains the entire structure and all the themes of midrash.[26]

26. Article 'Midrash' in *Dictionnaire de la Bible, Supplément*, vol. 5 (Paris: Letouzey, 1957), cols. 1278f. Wright (*art. cit.*, pp. 422f) justly remarks against Bloch that the Palestinian Targum is both targum and midrash. It is targum when it translates, midrash in its expansions. The point which interests us here is merely Bloch's view on the relation of the Palestinian Targum to the homily.

4

Aramaic as the Language of the Jews

In order to understand the origins of the targums and to grasp the problems involved in a scientific study of extant targumic texts, it is first necessary to consider the evolution of the Aramaic language and its use by the Jews.

The Aramaeans enter historical records in the late twelfth century B.C. as a nomadic people invading the territory of the Assyrian Empire. About the tenth century B.C. one branch of these nomads, known as Chaldaeans, settled in southern Mesopotamia. The Aramaeans penetrated Syria to a much greater extent and founded there a number of city-states, which retained an independent existence until they fell to the advancing Assyrian Empire in the eighth century. After this the Aramaeans survived as traders and merchants, and groups of them are later found in different parts of the Persian Empire, even as far south as Elephantine in Egypt.

Old Aramaic—The earliest recorded Aramaic is found in inscriptions from the Aramaean states of northern Syria. This earliest form of the language lasted from about 950 to 700 B.C. The evidence of the inscriptions reveals that during this period there existed no uniform standard Aramaic. What we have are a number of Aramaic dialects, each influenced by the Semitic but non-Aramaic language of the surrounding district.

Official Aramaic (ca. 700–300 B.C.)—Being a much easier language to learn and write than Accadian (the language of Assyria and Babylon) and due to the somewhat ubiquitous character of the Aramaeans, Aramaic in time came to be accepted as the international language of diplomacy and trade. From 2 Kings 18:26 (= Is 36:11) we learn that in 701 B.C. it was understood and spoken by the diplomats of Assyria and Judah, but not by the ordinary people of Jerusalem. About a century later a Palestinian king (probably that of Ashkelon)

54

writes for help to the king of Egypt in Aramaic. During the Persian period Aramaic is the language used by the Persian chancery, and is widely employed for trade purposes and international correspondence. It is used by the Jews in Egypt. Inscriptions and other texts in Aramaic are found from places as far apart as Egypt, Arabia, Palestine, Asia Minor, Syria, Mesopotamia, Persia, Afghanistan and Pakistan. Because of its use by the chancery of the Persian Empire, the Aramaic of this period is also known as *Imperial Aramaic* (*Reichsaramäisch*). The language of these texts is uniform; there is no evidence of any dialectical differences. From this, however, one would not be justified in concluding that dialects did not exist in the spoken language, as they had in the earlier period. The influence of the Persian chancery is sufficient to explain the uniformity of this literary Aramaic. We can ascribe the Aramaic portions of the biblical book of Ezra to this period.[1]

Middle Aramaic (*ca.* 300 B.C.–A.D. 200?)—With the advent of the Greek Empire, Greek replaced Aramaic as the official language of the chanceries. When new peoples came to write down Aramaic, dialectal differences are noticeable. The earliest attested form of Middle Aramaic is that of the book of Daniel (*ca.* 166 B.C.).[2] To Middle Aramaic also belongs *Nabataean,* the language used for inscriptions and official acts by the Nabatenes, who were Arabs. They probably took this language from Idumaea, after their penetration of the region. Arabic, however, has also influenced Nabataean. Our earliest Nabataean texts are from the early first century B.C.; the latest from the third century A.D.[3] Closely allied to Nabataean in many respects is *Palmyrene*, found in texts from Palmyra and Doura-Europos and elsewhere from the first century B.C. to the third century A.D. Palmyrene, as Nabataean, while belonging to Official Aramaic, already reveals some features of what will

---

1. Its pronominal suffixes are of the form found in the Elephantine papyri, e.g. *-hôm* ('their') and *-kôm* ('your', plural).
2. In the Aramaic of Daniel the form of the pronominal suffixes is the later one, e.g. *-hôn, -kôn* ('their', 'your', plural). Further into the vexed question of biblical Aramaic we need not go here.
3. The Nabataean form of Aramaic preserves some very old features (pronominal suffixes in *-hôm, -kôm*), probably an indication of the archaic character of the Aramaic spoken in Idumaea.

later appear as Eastern Aramaic.[4] This is possibly due to an oriental influence in Palmyra. From the second century A.D. we have the *Aramaic Hatra inscriptions*[5] where two peculiarities of oriental Aramaic are already visible.[6]

Coming now to Jewish Aramaic of this period we have the new texts from Qumrân, Murabba'ât, and the letters of Bar Cochba. Apart from this we have precious little: the *Ta'anith* Scroll (late first century A.D.), short inscriptions on tombstones and ossuaries, a few Aramaic words in the New Testament and in Josephus, and short sentences and texts in Tannaitic literature. To these we shall return in greater detail later.

Later Aramaic (ca. A.D. 200–700). We now have two clearly defined branches of Aramaic. On the one hand *Western Aramaic,* which included Syro-Palestinian Christian Aramaic, Samaritan Aramaic and Palestinian (or Galilaean + Judaean?) Jewish Aramaic; on the other hand *Eastern Aramaic,* i.e. Syriac, Babylonian Jewish talmudic Aramaic and Mandaic. We may add that a highly corrupt form of Aramaic is still spoken in three villages of Syria and in some few areas of Iraq.

The reader will excuse this schematic presentation of Middle and Later Aramaic. The dates given are those of J. Fitzmyer.[7] The question of the evolution of Aramaic and the early presence of dialects is an extremely complicated one. What the evidence for the centuries around the turn of the era reveals is the presence of dialects showing through on various occasions. Our interest here is the language spoken by the people during this period and the material at our disposal is not the most apt to reveal this to us. Much of the evidence comes from inscriptions or formal contracts. Both of these, the former in particular, tend to be archaic. The Qumrân writings, and some at least of the rabbinic texts, are of a literary nature. Neither one nor the

---

4. For example, plural emphatic in *-ê,* not in *-ayya,* as in official and in later western Aramaic.

5. See A. Cacquot in *Syria* 29 (1952) 111; 32 (1955) 56, no. 53; J. Starcky in *Dictionnaire de la Bible, Supplément,* vol. 6 (fasc. 32, 1958), col. 1082.

6. That is, the plural in *-ê;* also the imperfect in *l-,* where official and later western Aramaic will have the imperfect in *y-;* Syriac *n-.* But the earlier Syriac texts, such as in the inscription of A.D. 73, still have the imperfect in *y-,* not in *n-;* see K. Beyer, 'Der reichsaramäische Einschlag in der ältesten syrischen Literatur' in *Zeitschrift der Deutschen Morgenländischen Gesellschaft* 116 (1966) 242–54, esp. p. 243, note 1.

7. In *The Genesis Apocryphon of Qumran Cave 1* (Rome: Biblical Institute Press, 1966), pp. 19f.

other need reproduce the language spoken by the people. But of this anon.

Use of Aramaic among the Jews

At the Exile (as in 701 B.C.) the language spoken by the Jews was Hebrew. In New Testament Palestine the language generally spoken by them was Aramaic, although in some areas Hebrew, in its later mishnaic form, continued to be used. Greek was also known and used to some extent. When the general change-over from Hebrew to Aramaic took place we cannot say. It may be that at the return from the Exile or shortly afterwards the Jews, in the main, spoke Aramaic.

In the latter half of the fifth century B.C. Nehemiah set himself to remedy the problem of mixed marriages in Judah. Many of the Jews had married women of Ashdod, Ammon and Moab. 'And half of their children spoke the language of Ashdod [Hebrew: *ashdodith*], and they could not speak the language of Judah [Hebrew: *yehudith*], but the language of each people' (Neh 13:24). The 'language of Judah' is probably Hebrew which was then being neglected in favour of the surrounding languages or dialects. These were probably, but not certainly, Aramaic dialects spoken by the neighbouring non-Jewish populations of Ashdod,[8] Ammon and Moab. The Jews of Judah themselves were probably bilingual at this same period. Their co-religionists in Egypt were at this very time corresponding with Jerusalem on religious matters through the medium of Aramaic. The strong Aramaic influence on the later Hebrew books of the Old Testament argues towards a growing use of Aramaic among the Jews of Palestine. The fact that almost half the book of Daniel is written in Aramaic is a strong argument that by 166 B.C. this language was commonly spoken among them. This it certainly was by the first century A.D.

Aramaic in first-century Palestine

Determination of the precise form of Aramaic used in Palestine in the time of Christ is of capital importance for a study of the

---

8. J. T. Milik, however, notes that *ashtodith* in Neh 13:24 means Phoenician at that particular period, and thinks that the language in question may have been Phoenician as spoken on the coasts of Palestine; see *Ten Years of Discovery . . .*, p. 131. Phoenician is more closely related to Hebrew than to Aramaic.

Aramaic substratum of the Gospels and other New Testament writings. It is also important to ascertain whether the Aramaic of the Palestinian Targum to the Pentateuch can be taken to represent the spoken language of Palestine, or of some area in Palestine, in Christ's day.[9] This question being of an extremely delicate nature, it is necessary to move cautiously, not allowing preconceived ideas to colour one's judgment. We must first of all consider the evidence, asking the reader to bear with the introduction of some philological details indispensable to any discussion of the problem.

From the first century B.C. to A.D. 70, but mainly from about A.D. 1 to 70, we now have a good number of Aramaic texts from Qumrân, some of them published, others yet to be published.[10] As already noted, from the first century we also have the rabbinic text *Megillat Ta'anit* ('Scroll of Fasting'), some Aramaic words or phrases in the New Testament and in the works of Josephus, as well as a few inscriptions on tombstones and ossuaries.

Dating from a later period (A.D. 70–135), from Wadi Murabba'ât and the neighbouring area we have Aramaic texts containing contracts and some letters written by Bar Cosba (Bar Cochba), leader of the second Jewish revolt (A.D. 132–35). From the third century onwards we have a number of Jewish inscriptions and other texts in Aramaic.

Palestinian Aramaic, as found in the Palestinian targums, the Palestinian Talmud and the Palestinian midrashim, has certain peculiarities which distinguish it sharply from Old Testament Aramaic, from the Aramaic of Qumrân and Murabba'ât and from that of the Targum of Onkelos and of the 'Babylonian' Targum of the Prophets. Thus, for instance, in Palestinian Aramaic 'to see' is expressed by $\d{h}^a ma$, in the Aramaic of the other texts by $\d{h}^a za$; 'for' or 'because' (=Hebrew $k\hat{\imath}$) is expressed by *'arûm*, absent from Qumrân and expressed in the Targum of Onkelos and in the Targum of the Prophets by *'arê*. In certain cases in Palestinian Aramaic the letter

9. On the problem of the language spoken by Christ, see the bibliography in J. Fitzmyer, *Genesis Apocryphon* . . ., pp. 20–21, and H. Ott, 'Um die Muttersprache Jesu Forschungen seit Gustav Dalman' in *Novum Testamentum* 9 (1967) 1–25.
10. For a list of these texts see J. Fitzmyer, *Genesis Apocryphon* . . ., pp. 17f, note 55; *Catholic Biblical Quarterly* 30 (1968) 420.

He (= h) is elided, whereas in the other texts it is written. Thus, for instance, 'his servants' in Palestinian Aramaic is *ʿabdôi*, but in the other texts *ʿabdôhî*; 'his brother' is *ʾaḥui*, in the other texts, *ʾaḥûhi*; 'on him' is *ʿalôi*, in the other texts *ʿalôhi*. Another distinguishing feature of the Aramaic of the Palestinian Targum is that when it distinguishes the accusative by the use of a special particle (called *signum accusativi*), the particle it uses is regularly *yat*, whereas in Qumrân Aramaic the *signum accusativi* is the letter *l* prefixed to the accusative.

The absence of these distinguishing characteristics of the Aramaic of the Palestinian Targum from the Aramaic of the first-century texts from Qumrân necessarily raises the question, whether one can legitimately consider the Aramaic of the Palestinian Targum as a language spoken in Christ's day. From this comes the further question whether we can legitimately take it into account in a consideration of the Aramaic substratum of the Gospels and other parts of the New Testament.

Matthew Black and others have used it. Criticizing Black's third edition of *An Aramaic Approach to the Gospel and Acts,* J. Fitzmyer insists that it is quite illegitimate to do so.[11] In his view the latest form of Aramaic that should be used for *philological* comparisons of the Aramaic substratum of the Gospels and Acts is that of Qumrân and other first-century Aramaic texts such as tomb and ossuary inscriptions. The Aramaic of the Palestinian Targum he considers a later development.

On this we must observe that the Aramaic of Qumrân is a *literary* form of the language. Of itself it fails to let us know what the *spoken* form of Aramaic was. It by no means rules out the possibility that the spoken language in Palestine, or in part of it, was the Aramaic found in the Palestinian Targum to the Pentateuch, i.e. Palestinian Aramaic. The Aramaic of Qumrân is itself a more developed form of Aramaic than that found in the Bible. In the words of J. Fitzmyer the Aramaic of the *Genesis Apocryphon* from Qumrân 'is best described as a transitional type between the biblical Aramaic of Daniel and that of the Palestinian Targums or Christian Palestinian Aramaic'.[12]

11. *Art. cit.*, p. 420.
12. *Genesis Apocryphon . . .*, p. 19.

How far the spoken language had evolved beyond that of Qumrân we cannot say. In the *Genesis Apocryphon* (21,34) we have a single occurrence of a typical feature of Palestinian Aramaic, i.e. *'ḥwy* (*'ᵃḥûi*), 'his brother', instead of the usual *'ḥwhy* (*'ᵃḥûhî*) found elsewhere in the same work (22,3.5.11). This sole occurrence may be due to the influence of the spoken language rather than to a scribal error. We find a similar elision of the *He* in the first of the Bar Cosba letters: *'lwy* (*'ᵃlôi*) instead of the usual *'lwhy* (*'ᵃlôhî*).[12a]

A consideration of the Hebrew language during the Qumrân period may help us to evaluate the Aramaic evidence better. In the Qumrân texts we have two types of Hebrew: Neo-classical Hebrew imitating the Hebrew of the Old Testament, and literary mishnaic Hebrew.[13] The Qumrân texts, we may recall, have shown us that Hebrew, in its later mishnaic form, was spoken in Judaea during the first century A.D. Yet the literary Mishnaic of Qumrân is not quite the same as the Mishnaic spoken at the time; it is a higher and literary form of it.[14] We are very fortunate in having one text, the Copper Scroll (3Q15), written about A.D. 30–70 in this popular Mishnaic Hebrew,[15] differing from the texts in literary Aramaic in all the ways in which a spoken language differs from a literary one.[16] Did we have a similar text in *popular* Aramaic from the same period, we would be able to pass a more definite judgment on the relation of Palestinian Aramaic to the language spoken by Jesus. In default of this, judgment must be suspended.

The Aramaic of the Bar Cosba letters is a more developed

12a. In one instance at least the language of the Qumrân *Genesis Apocryphon* appears to represent an earlier form of Aramaic than that spoken by Jesus. This is in the Aramaic for 'my father', both in the vocative (*pater mi*) and other cases. On the lips of Jesus (Mk 14:36) and elsewhere (Rom 8:15; Gal 4:6) the form is *Abba* (*ho patêr*), *Abba* being in reality the emphatic case ('the father') of *'ab*. *Abba* is used for 'my father', in the vocative and other cases in targumic Aramaic, which in this represents the spoken language of Christ's day. The proper and earlier form is *'abî*, found in Daniel 5:13 (nominative case). It is this earlier and *pre-Christian* usage that we find in *Genesis Apocryphon* 2,19,24; 3,3: 'Then I . . . ran to . . . my father [*'by*] . . . And he said to . . . his father, "O my father [*y' 'by*]". . . for in the days of Jared, my father [*'by*].'
13. See Milik, *Ten Years of Discovery . . .*, pp. 130f.
14. *Ibid.*
15. See J. T. Milik's commentary on the Copper Scroll in *Discoveries in the Judaean Desert of Jordan*, vol. 3 (Oxford University Press, 1966), pp. 221–35.
16. *Ibid.*, pp. 225, 227, 275–76.

form of the language than that of the Qumrân texts. Apart
from the instance of the elision of the *He* mentioned above, it
agrees with Palestinian Aramaic in having *yat* as the *signum
accusativi*. Yet it can in no way be classed as Palestinian Aramaic.

Palestinian Jewish inscriptions and other texts from the
third century onwards are, as far as they provide material for
comparison, in Palestinian Aramaic. How much earlier than
the third century this form of Aramaic became the spoken
language of Palestine we cannot, however, say. Matthew
Black and others argue for a first-century date for the Aramaic
of the Palestinian Targum from the fact that it has many
Greek loan-words. The Greek borrowings would be an indication that the Aramaic comes from a period when Greek,
not Latin, was the dominant language. Fitzmyer, on the
contrary, sees in the presence of these Greek words a good
argument for a date later than the first century, 'since they
relate to a well-known phenomenon of Syriac (and Aramaic
in general) of the third and later centuries'.[17] He further notes
that there are no Greek loan-words in the Aramaic texts from
Qumrân. Neither objection is really valid. Rabbinic and
popular Judaism was more open to Greek borrowings than
was the learned society of Qumrân. Borrowings from Greek,
and occasionally from Latin, are very much a feature of the
Hebrew of the Mishnah, compiled from earlier sources about
A.D. 180. So too was spoken mishnaic Hebrew, as we now
know from the Copper Scroll. This text abounds in Greek
loan-words, and precisely of the kind found in the Mishnah,
Targum and Talmud![18]

Borrowings from Greek are, then, an indication of the early
date of the Aramaic of the Palestinian Targum, rather than
the contrary. It is quite possible that this form of Aramaic
later used for written documents existed as the spoken language
of the people already in New Testament times and even
earlier. That this was so is, however, by no means certain. The
question is still open.

Palestinian and Judaean Aramaic

The Targum of Onkelos (and that to the Prophets) is written
in a form of Aramaic different from that of the Palestinian

17. *Art. cit.*, pp. 420f.
18. See Milik, *Discoveries in the Judaean Desert . . .*, pp. 230, etc.

Targum, the Palestinian Talmud and midrashim. G. Dalman was of the view that the Aramaic of Onkelos represented the language of Judaea, while the other form of Aramaic was the dialect of Galilee. P. Kahle challenged this opinion, maintaining that there was only one form of Aramaic in the whole of Palestine: that found in the Palestinian Targum and midrashim. The language of Onkelos he considered to be an artificial, scholastic Aramaic. Y. Kutscher came to the defence of Dalman's position, finding support for his viewpoint in the Aramaic texts of Qumrân. A. Díez Macho, however, holds that the language of the Bar Cosba letters is more closely related to the Aramaic of the Palestinian Targum than to that of Onkelos or the Targum to the Prophets. In these letters he sees a provisional confirmation of Kahle's position that all over Palestine, apart from minor differences, only one form of Aramaic was spoken.

This discussion must be viewed in the light of what has been said on the use of Palestinian Aramaic in first-century Palestine. If we take it that this language was then spoken there, the problem is further complicated by the Qumrân evidence which seems to indicate that Hebrew rather than Aramaic was the language of Judaea. We must also reckon with the fact that after the second Jewish revolt was quelled in A.D. 135, Judaea was almost totally depopulated.

5

Early Written Targums

I. Targum of Job from Qumrân

The oldest known manuscript of a targum is *11 Q Targ Job,*
found in 1956 by Bedouins in a cave, now known as Cave 11.
The manuscript doubtless once carried an Aramaic rendering
of the entire book of Job. The extant manuscript contains long
sections from the ending of the book, from 37:10 to 42:11,
together with fragments of the rendering of 17:14 to 26:33.
The script, of the type known as Herodian (37 B.C.–A.D. 70),
permits us to date the writing of the present manuscript to
about A.D. 50. The Aramaic of the scroll, however, is of an
older form than that of the Qumrân *Genesis Apocryphon*. Fr. J.
van der Ploeg, to whom (with A. A. van der Woude) the task
of editing the work has been committed, believes it may possibly
have been composed about 150–100 B.C.[1]

This Qumrân targum does not appear to bear any relation
to the one traditionally known as the Targum of Job. Unlike
the latter, the targum from Qumrân is a straightforward
version, without long paraphrases. It does, however, occasionally add extra words to the Hebrew text and is more interested
in giving the sense than rendering slavishly *ad pedem litterae*.
Van der Ploeg thus describes its paraphrase:

> In the poetic parts, the author follows his text faithfully
> enough. But he does not feel himself obliged to do this in a
> slavish fashion; he takes the liberty of making slight modifica-
> tions so that the reader may better understand what the

---

1. Both have given us a preliminary report on the MS.: J. van der Ploeg, *Le targum de*
Job de la grotte 11 de Qumrân (11 Q Tg Job), *Première communication*, Amsterdam, 1962;
A. S. van der Woude, 'Das Hiobtargum aus Qumrân Höhle XI' in *Vetus Testamentum,*
Supplements, vol. 9 (1963, Leiden), pp. 322–31. See also J. van der Ploeg, 'Un targum
du livre de Job' in *Bible et vie chrétienne* 58 (1964) 79–87.

translator has taken to be the sense of a passage. His translation intends to be a guide (a guide which betrays, evidently,
the ideas of the author), but a guide which reads agreeably.
He attains this end by embellishing his text by the addition
of unnecessary words which make no difference to the sense
or the context, and by other means, examples of which will
be given below. He has also a tendency to rationalize when
it appears to him that the expressions of the text should not
be understood according to their literal sense. Job 38:7
presents a striking example of this tendency: the Hebrew
text has the stars 'sing' at the moment of creation, while the
'sons of God' shout for joy; the Targum, however, renders:
'Then when the morning stars shone together and all the
angels of God shouted together for joy.'[2]

Linguistically, as said above, his work belongs to Official
Aramaic, not to that of the Palestinian Targum.[3]

4 Q Targ Job—A few fragments of another copy of the same
targum have been found in cave 4. The fragments are very
worn and contain only a few words of Job 3:4–5 and from
4:16 to 5:4.[4]

The two texts show that a number of copies of this targum
were in circulation. Whether it originated within the Qumrân
Essene community is uncertain. According to van der Ploeg
the targum from cave 11 shows no trace whatever of any
Essene doctrine.

Targum of Job known to early rabbis—In rabbinic literature
(Tos., *Shabbath* 13,2; Bab., *Shabb.* 115a; Pal. *Shabb.* 16,1, 15c,
top; *Sopherim* 5 and 15) mention is made of a targum to Job
having been known to Rabbi Gamaliel I (*ca.* A.D. 25–50) and
having been used by his grandson, R. Gamaliel II (A.D. 90–110).
It occurs in the following account given by R. Jose ben Halaphta
(second century A.D.):

It happened once that R. Halaphta [father of R. Jose] went
to Rabban Gamaliel at Tiberias. He found him seated at the
table of Johanan [son of] the excommunicated, and in his

---

2. *Le targum de Job*, p. 12. The 'traditional' Targum of Job renders this verse: 'when
the morning stars rendered praise together, and all the choirs of angels shouted for joy.'
3. The suffix of the third per. sing. is *-ôhî*, not *-ôi*.
4. 'To see' is expressed as *lᵉza*, not *lᵉma* and the third per. sing. suffix is *-ôhî*.

hands there was a book of Job in targum [i.e. a targum of Job] and he was reading it. R. Halaphta said to him: 'I remember Rabban Gamaliel the Elder, your grandfather, who was seated on a stairway on the Temple Mount and a targum of Job was brought to him and he told the masons to immure it under the course of stones.'

Both van der Ploeg[5] and F. M. Cross[6] believe that the targum in question may have been a copy of that now known from Qumrân. This may well be so, but it is no more than a possibility. Why Rabban Gamaliel ordered that the targum be immured we cannot say. It was hardly because he considered written targums forbidden by Jewish law. His grandson seems to have no scruple in reading it. And he played his part in reorganizing Judaism after the fall of Jerusalem.[7] It is interesting to know that the family of Paul's teacher was acquainted with at least one written targum. We may also note that the text of the Babylonian Talmud speaks of 'Johanan the excommunicated' where the Tosephta has 'Johanan the son of the excommunicated'. Some writers have thought that the Johanan in question is John the Apostle. Both the pauline and johannine writings are closely related to the targums.[8]

The Septuagint ending of Job and the Targum—In some manuscripts of the Septuagint (MSS. Aleph, A, B and C) there is an epilogue which is introduced with the words: *houtos ermeneutai ek tês syriakês bibliou*. Some authors have taken this to mean that the passage is translated from an Aramaic (= Syriac) targum. Others now think that the *Vorlage* of the addition may well be the targum found in Qumrân. P. Winter, however, has pointed out that we cannot render the Greek as 'this is translated from the Syrian (= Aramaic) book'. *Houtos* must refer to Job. Had the translator intended to refer to the addition he would have written *touto* (*hoc, illud*), not *houtos* (*hic, ille*). *Ek* ('from') he takes as a corruption of *en* ('in') and proposes that we understand the passage as: 'This (man) is referred to in the Syriac

5. *Op. cit.*, p. 10. He envisages nothing more than 'une certaine possibilité'.
6. *The Ancient Library of Qumran*, p. 26. For him the Qumrân text 'appears to be the targum condemned by Rabbi Gamaliel I'.
7. See above, p. 40.
8. Cf. M. McNamara, *The New Testament and the Palestinian Targum* . . ., pp. 254–56, for a summary of the evidence.

book as dwelling in Ausis . . .'[9] This, in fact, is how Sir Launcelot Lee Brenton had already rendered it in 1844 in his English translation of the Septuagint: 'This man is described in the Syriac book as living in the land of Ausis . . .'[10] The Syriac book in question may well be some Aramaic apocryphal work.

II. *Qumrân fragments of a targum to Leviticus (4 Q Targ Lev)*

Fr. J. T. Milik is to publish two small fragments of an Aramaic rendering of Lev 16:12–15 and 16:18–21, and has orally described the fragments to A. Díez Macho as belonging to 'a literal Aramaic translation, like that of Onkelos and in Imperial Aramaic . . . They appear to be of the first century B.C.'[11] The literal nature of the rendering reminds one of the Targum of Onkelos; the language of the fragments is similar to that of Onkelos and unlike that of the Palestinian Targum. The Aramaic is in keeping with Qumrân Aramaic in general. These fragments have importance for the history of Onkelos in Palestine. R. Le Déaut, however, has noted that the rendering of these fragments often agrees with Codex Neofiti against Onkelos.[12]

III. *The Syriac translation of the Pentateuch*[13]

That the Syriac (i.e. Eastern Aramaic) translation of the Pentateuch, the *Peshitta*, is in some way connected in its origins with the Targum to the Pentateuch seems undeniable. How to explain this relationship is much less certain. The problem was already posed by J. Perles in his *Meletemata Peschittoniana* (Wrocklaw, 1859). In 1875 J. Prager propounded the view that the Peshitta Pentateuch is ultimately based on a targum from the second to first century B.C.

The question has been taken up once more in our time, particularly by P. Kahle, S. Wohl, C. Peters, A. Baumstark and A. Vööbus, all of whom see a strong influence of the Palestinian Targum to the Pentateuch on the Syriac Pentateuch.

9. *Zeitschrift für die neutest. Wissenschaft* 45 (1954) 59.
10. Reprinted in *The Septuagint Version of the Old Testament with English Translation* (London: Bagster, no date), p. 698. See also L. Ginzberg, *The Legends of the Jews*, vol. V, Notes (Philadelphia, 1925), p. 384, note 14.
11. *Oriens Antiquus* 2 (1963) 107, note 42.
12. *Introduction . . .*, p. 65.
13. For bibliography see *The New Testament and the Palestinian Targum . . .*, p. 51, note 34.

Kahle's view is that the Peshitta Pentateuch is made directly from à Palestinian targum sent from Palestine to the Jewish proselytes of Adiabene shortly before the Christian era. The Syriac Peshitta would then be merely a rendering of a Western Aramaic dialect into the Eastern Aramaic of Adiabene. Kahle himself sees a particularly close relation between the Peshitta Pentateuch and the Palestinian Targum especially as found in the Cairo fragments he published in 1930.[14]

P. Wernberg-Møller has recently challenged this theory of Kahle.[15] For him the relationship lies not with the Palestinian Targum but with that of Onkelos. R. Le Déaut does not find Wernberg-Møller's arguments convincing: the Peshitta agrees too often with the Palestinian Targum against Onkelos.[16]

The Christians of Palestine, too, had their own rendering of the Pentateuch in Christian Palestinian Aramaic. Portions of this rendering survive, and A. Baumstark believes that it, too, was made from an old Jewish targum.[17] M. Black, however, is of the opinion that the influence of the targum may here be only indirect—through the Peshitta.[18]

K. Beyer has recently put forward a different explanation of the facts, and of the origin of targums in general.[19] While maintaining that the *spoken* language of Palestine from the first century B.C. onwards was Western Aramaic (proof: Western Aramaisms of Palestinian literary Imperial Aramaic texts, Aramaisms of Hebrew Qumrân texts, of the Mishnah, of the New Testament and of Greek transcriptions), he holds that until the end of the second century A.D. the *literary* language of Palestine was Imperial Aramaic.[20] The Syriac translation found in the Sinaiticus and Curetonianus manuscripts he takes as a Syriac adaptation of a Palestinian translation made in Imperial Aramaic. The earlier targums would all have been in Imperial Aramaic. Only later did these diverge

14. *The Cairo Geniza*, 2nd ed. (Oxford: Blackwells, 1959), pp. 272f.
15. *Studia Theologica* 15 (1961) 128–80; *Journal of Jewish Studies* 7 (1962) 253–66.
16. *Introduction . . .*, p. 63.
17. *Oriens Christianus* 10 (1935) 201–24.
18. *An Aramaic Approach to the Gospels and Acts*, 2nd ed. (Oxford: Clarendon Press, 1954), pp. 23f; 3rd ed. (1967), pp. 26f; also in *A Christian-Palestinian Horologion* (*Studia Semitica et Orientalia*, vol. 2, Glasgow, 1945), p. 336.
19. 'Der reichsaramäische Einschlag in der ältesten syrischen Literatur' in *Zeitschrift der Deutschen Morgenländischen Gesellschaft* 116 (1966) 242–54.
20. *Ibid.*, p. 251.

to give us the Babylonian (Onkelos and Jonathan to the Prophets) and Palestinian texts. The relation of the Peshitta to the targums is then to be explained through the underlying Imperial Aramaic, not through any influence of Western (i.e. Palestinian) Aramaic. The Peshitta, in turn, served as a basis for the Christian-Palestinian and for an Arabic translation of the Old Testament.[21]

The problem is complicated by a number of factors, not least among them the recensions which the Peshitta has undergone. There was, in Beyer's view, a recension in the fourth century A.D. aimed at normalizing the Syriac. Then again, the text was to a certain extent brought into line with the Greek Septuagint rendering. The Peshitta's relation to the targums, and to the Palestinian Targum in particular, still remains open.[22] That on many points the Syriac Pentateuch is closely related to the Palestinian Targum is clear.[23] But the differences must also be borne in mind. Nor should we restrict ourselves to language alone when speaking of points of contact. Sometimes the Peshitta has the interpretation of the Palestinian Targum and of Onkelos but expressed in slightly different language. We have an example of this in the paraphrase of Ex 19:6.[24] Other times the interpretation is the same while the words used to express it differ. A good example of this latter is Deut 6:5, where *me'od* (generally rendered 'might': 'love the Lord with all your might') of the Hebrew text is rendered in all Aramaic translations (and understood in the Mishnah, *Berakoth* 9,5[7]) as 'riches'. Yet each rendering has a different word to express the same idea. The Palestinian Targum (as the Mishnah) has 'wealth' (*mamônkôn*); Onkelos (and the Targum of 2 Kings 23:25) has 'property' (*niksak*), while the Peshitta has 'possessions' (*qnynk*). Here there is dependence on a general interpretative tradition rather than on any particular targumic text.

21. *Ibid.*, p. 253.
22. *Ibid.*, pp. 242, 253.
23. Cf. e.g. *The New Testament and the Palestinian Targum* . . ., pp. 50f, 109, 229f. Among clear points of contact we may note the rare words found only in the Targums to the Pentateuch and in the Peshitta, e.g. *qarḥuta* in Lev 13:42f; likewise in the names of rare birds (Lev ch. 11); see J. A. Emerton, 'Unclean Birds and the Origin of the Peshitta' in *Journal of Semitic Studies* 7 (1962) 204–11.
24. Cf. *The New Testament and the Palestinian Targum* . . ., pp. 227–30.

6

Characteristics of Targumic Renderings

In an earlier chapter we have seen how certain principles guided the understanding of Scripture in post-exilic Judaism. It was there also remarked that these same principles are operative in the translations found in the extant targums. It now remains for us to say something on the targumic method itself. We have here a field that has been but relatively little explored, yet one deserving of serious study, particularly with regard to the relation of this method to the Jewish canons of interpretation.[1]

All the examples we use here are drawn from the Palestinian Targum to the Pentateuch, as represented by the one or other of the texts of Neofiti, Pseudo-Jonathan, the Fragment Targum and the fragments of the Cairo Geniza. The reader desirous of more information on any of these can turn to the Appendix of the present work. What is said here on targumic rendering with reference to the Palestinian Targum will hold good in the main for other targums also. It is, in any event, prudent, if not altogether necessary, to treat of the targumic method of each group of targums separately in view of the differences in the original intent, the time of composition and the history of composition of the various targums.

I. Paraphrase must adhere to biblical text

The translator of the targum in the synagogue differed from others who handed on Jewish tradition in that he was bound

1. The matter has been treated by J. F. Stenning, *The Targum of Isaiah* (Oxford: Clarendon Press, 1949), pp. xii-xvii, but with special reference to the paraphrase of Isaiah. See also R. Le Déaut, *La nuit pascale* (Rome: Biblical Institute Press, 1965), pp. 56–60; *idem, Liturgie juive et Nouveau Testament* (Rome: Biblical Institute Press, 1965), pp. 18–37. Chapter 4 of the same writer's *Introduction à la littérature targumique* (not yet published) is on 'Nature of the Aramaic Translations. The Targumic Method'. See also A. G. Wright, *The Literary Genre Midrash* (Staten Island: Alba House, 1967) =*Catholic Biblical Quarterly* 28 (1966) 105–38; 417–57.

to translate the Hebrew text of the Bible. It would be wrong
to conceive of the Palestinian Targum as pure midrash. It is
both translation and expansion, *peshat* as well as *derash* or
midrash. The interpretative tradition could not ignore the
biblical text. When a free paraphrase, or a midrash, is given,
it has to be inserted into the rendering of the biblical text,
occasionally to the detriment of syntax. This results in what
we may call 'targumic interpolations' in the text itself. Sometimes in order to give meaning to a passage of the Palestinian
Targum in translation, it is necessary to change the order of
the Aramaic text. Minor interpolations of this nature can be
compared with the glosses already found in the Hebrew text
of the Bible and considered above in an earlier chapter. We
shall illustrate these 'targumic interpolations' by some examples
in which italics denote the interpolated expansion:

> And whatever Adam called *in the language of the sanctuary* a
> living creature, that was its name (Pal. Targ. Gen 2:19).

> And he [Moses] reached the mount *over which the glory of
> the Shekinah of the Lord was revealed* Horeb (Neofiti Ex 3:1).

> And when the Canaanite, the king of Arad, who dwelt in
> the south heard *that Aaron the pious man for whose merit the
> clouds of the Glory had led forth Israel had died* [literally: 'was
> taken up'] *and that Miriam the prophetess, for whose merits the
> well used to come up for them, had died* [literally: 'had been taken
> up'], that Israel had reached the way by which the spies
> used to come up [Hebrew text: 'the way of Atharim'], he
> waged war on Israel and took some of them captive (Neofiti
> Num 21:1).

II.   *Interpretation intended for the unlearned*

In explaining the Scriptures, particularly in interpreting the
Law of Moses, the targumist had 'to give the sense and make
the people understand the reading' (see Neh 8:8). This would
entail giving the literal meaning, the plain sense of the text or
the *peshat*. This he would do in the translation proper. But more
was required of him. We have seen how intimately the
Palestinian Targum is connected with the homily; perhaps

at an earlier period it served as the synagogue homily. The targumist, then, had to bring out the meaning of the text for his audience. This he would do by *derash* exegesis. The faithful had to receive the text of the Law together with the doctrinal and halakic development which had taken place since the days of Moses and the formation of the biblical tradition. The homily and the synagogue rendering thus became the vehicles of tradition. Text and interpretation went naturally together.

Since this exposition of the Scriptures was for the masses, not merely for the learned, the manner in which it was done had to be adapted to the minds of the synagogue congregations and be of a popular nature. Otherwise the people would not understand, or would misunderstand, the biblical message.

The text to be explained was the inspired Word of God, valid for all ages. Reverence for the inspired Scriptures meant the utmost respect for every word of the written text. Being God's Word it could not err; and being the Word of the living God it had a message for each generation. Difficulties in the biblical text had to be explained, or explained away. Some sense had to be made out of, or read into, obscure passages. Earlier and cruder biblical expressions which might sound ill to the ears of later generations had to be paraphrased, not rendered literally. This deep reflection on the inspired Word, and profound reverence for it, is seen in the targumic paraphrases.

III. *Explanation of difficulties and contradictions*

Many of the apparent and real contradictions found in the Pentateuch can now easily be understood in the light of the variety of sources that have gone to compose it and the long period of development in doctrine and law it records. Modern disciplines such as Source Criticism and Form Criticism were unknown to the ancients, who approached the Bible as the inerrant Word of God. Having no idea of a development in revelation, for the ancient Jewish expositors there was no *before* and *after* in Scripture. Difficulties had to be explained in the light of their understanding of Scripture. From this attitude to the Bible comes a whole series of interpretations which to us may seem quite fanciful.

Gen 28:11, for instance, appears to say that Jacob used more

than one stone for a pillow at Bethel. Yet Gen 28:18 says he
used only one stone. How explain this difference? Because,
says the Palestinian Targum (Gen 28:10), God by a miracle
made one stone out of the many.

Then there is the question of the biblical chronology found
in the early chapters of Genesis. Today we say that this chronology is artificial and fictitious, and is in no way to be taken to
represent the real course of events. Things were different for
earlier generations. In Gen 11:10–11, for instance, Shem is
said to have lived for six hundred years, five hundred years
after the birth of his son Arpachshad. When this age is compared
with the life spans of succeeding patriarchs we see that he must
have been alive in the lifetime of Isaac and Jacob, some ten
generations later. And so in fact he was—according to the
Palestinian midrash, found in the Palestinian Targum on
Gen 14:18; 24:62; 38:6.

Some biblical texts require an explanation. Why was Tamar
led forth to be burned (Gen 38:24) rather than put to death
in some other way? Burning, according to the Law of Moses
(Lev 21:9), was the punishment reserved for the daughters of
priests who had given themselves to prostitution. So in Ps.-Jon.
Gen 38:24 Tamar is said to have been the daughter of a priest,
even of the high priest Shem the Great (Ps.-Jon. Gen 38:6)
who in rabbinic and targumic tradition (Pal. Targ. Gen 14:18)
is identified with Melchisedech and who, as we have said, is
considered to have lived on until the days of Isaac and Jacob.

There are many other biblical texts which raise questions in
the mind. Thus for instance in Gen 15:1 we read: 'After these
things the word of the Lord came to Abram in a vision, "Fear
not, Abram . . ."' What does 'after these things' mean? And
why should Abram fear precisely 'after these things'? The
paraphrase in the Palestinian Targum explains (italics denote
biblical text):

After these things, after the kings had gathered together and
fallen before Abram [as recounted in the preceding chapter
of Genesis] . . . Abram thought in his heart and said: 'Woe
now is me! Perhaps I have received the rewards of my
meritorious deeds in this world, and perhaps there shall be
no portion for me in the world to come!' And then *the word*

of the Lord was with Abram in a vision, saying : 'Do not fear; ...
although these fall before you in this world, the reward of
your good deeds exceeding great is kept and prepared before
me for the world to come.'

'The Lord called Moses and said to him from the tent of meeting'
(Lev 1:1) seems a rather abrupt way in which to begin a book
of Scripture. The Palestinian Targum gets over the difficulty
by prefixing a long midrash to the words in question.

If the Jews were miraculously fed with manna and given to
drink during the desert wanderings, why in Deut 2:6 does
God say to them: 'You shall purchase food from them [the
sons of Esau] for money that you may eat; and you shall also
buy water from them for money that you may drink'? The
Palestinian Targum explains away this difficulty by para-
phrasing:

> You have no need to buy food from them for money because
> manna descends for you from heaven; and you have no
> need to buy water from them for money, because the well
> of water comes up with you to the tops of the mountains
> and [goes down] with you to the depths of the valleys.

Here we have one occurrence of the targumic tradition (found
also in other Jewish sources, e.g. Tosephta, *Sukkah* 4,9 referred
to in the first chapter) that a (rock-)well followed Israel during
the desert period. This tradition is used by Paul in 1 Cor 10:4.

After Nehemiah's campaign against the marriage of Jews to
foreign women (Neh 13:23–27) it must have been embarrassing
to read twice in Num 12:1 that Moses was married to a non-
Jewish Cushite (Septuagint: 'Ethiopian') woman. Pseudo-
Jonathan (Num 12:1) explains that Moses was constrained
against his will to marry this Ethiopian woman and that he
later divorced her. Onkelos paraphrases 'Cushite' as 'beautiful'.
Other texts of the Palestinian Targum retain the word 'Cushite'
but go on to explain at length that she was not a Cushite
ethnically speaking, but merely *like* a Cushite in complexion!

IV. *Reverential manner in speaking of God*

This characteristic of the targums is well known. In them an
attempt is made to avoid anthropomorphisms, but is not

carried through systematically. Some anthropomorphic expressions are allowed to remain. The reason for the avoidance of anthropomorphisms is that some of the earlier Jewish ways of referring to God were likely to give a false impression, or even cause scandal, to later generations. Consequently, in the Palestinian Targum, as in the targums in general, God in his relation to the world is said to act through his Word (*Memra*), Glory, Shekinah, Glory of his Shekinah, etc. Rather than say God repents, grows sorrowful, etc., the targums speak of there being repentance, sorrow, etc., before God. The hands, arms, face, etc., of God spoken of in the biblical text become in the targums the might, presence, power, Memra, etc., of God. Many examples of this feature of the Palestinian Targum will be given in the opening chapters of the second part of this work.

V.   *Respect for the elders of Israel*

We have seen that this principle led to the rubric that certain passages of the Bible were to be read out but not translated in the synagogue service.[2] This respect for the elders has influenced the rendering of certain passages in the Palestinian Targum. In the biblical text of Gen 29:17 we read that the eyes of Leah, wife of Jacob and mother of some of the twelve tribes, were weak. The Hebrew text is rendered literally in the Fragment Targum. The rendering found in this representative of the Palestinian Targum was objected to by R. Johanan about A.D. 250, apparently on the principle that it was a statement derogatory to Leah. Onkelos paraphrases: 'Leah's eyes were beautiful'; Neofiti has 'Leah's eyes were raised in prayer'. I earlier thought that Neofiti's rendering was due to a later rabbinic ruling such as that of R. Johanan and that, consequently, we have in Neofiti's rendering an indication that this work has undergone a rabbinic recension.[3] In view of the fact that the principle of respect for the elders of Israel is already operative in the Septuagint translation, and possibly even in the Elohist source of the Pentateuch,[4] no argument for a later rabbinic recension of Neofiti can be drawn from its paraphrase of Gen 29:17.

2. See above, p. 48.
3. *The New Testament and the Palestinian Targum* . . ., pp. 53f, 62.
4. See above, pp. 21, 34.

VI.   Later doctrine read into the interpretation

A certain amount of paraphrase is necessary in any translation intended for the general public. Even in our own day the paraphrastic *Jerusalem Bible* and the *New English Bible* are more easily followed than is the more literal rendering of the *Revised Standard Version*, even though the last-mentioned is more faithful to the original text. By the very nature of the case a greater amount of paraphrase was called for in the Palestinian Targum. Sometimes paraphrase was necessary to bring out the meaning of the original. The Hebrew text speaks of both men and sacrificial animals being 'perfect'. The Targum rightly renders 'perfect' in the former case as 'perfect in good work(s)', in the latter as 'perfect without blemish' (cf. 1 Pet 1:19). For the same reason 'seed' of the biblical text is rendered as 'children' in the targums (cf. Gal 3:16).

In these examples there is question of the plain meaning of the text, i.e. *peshat*. Very often, however, the targumist goes beyond the plain sense to give extensive paraphrase or to include midrash. In many of the passages where the Aramaic translator gives an expanded interpretation, i.e. *derash*, which we see as a later development, he very probably took his understanding of the passage as the obvious and only meaning of the inspired Word of God. For him the text and its interpretation went together. This would clearly be the case in those passages interpreted messianically, e.g. Gen 49:10f; Num 24:17f. This phenomenon of linking text and interpretation is not peculiar to Judaism. It has also been a characteristic of Christianity from its origins until fairly recent times. We may recall how Catholic exegetes and theologians for long took the literal meaning of Gen 3:15 to refer to Mary. This understanding of the verse probably goes back beyond the days of St. Jerome and explains how *hû'* (= 'he', 'it') of the Hebrew text and *autos* ('he') of the Septuagint gave way to *ipsa* ('she') in the Latin Vulgate rendering. The understanding of verse 15 of the Hebrew text has in itself certain difficulties. The *Revised Standard Version* renders: 'he shall bruise [in Hebrew *shûph*] your head and you shall bruise [*shûph*] his heel.' *Shûph* can mean either 'bruise' or 'lie in wait for', and it is by no means certain whether it is to be rendered in the one way in both the occurrences in this verse. The Palestinian Targum is intent on bringing out all the possible meanings and implications of the text. It renders *shûph* both as 'to aim at and bite' and 'to bruise'. The biblical text speaks of an enduring struggle between the seed of the woman and that of the serpent. For the targumist the outcome of the fight will depend on the attitude of the woman's children to the Law. Final victory will come with King Messiah when the children of the woman will effect a crushing (*shephiyyûta,* from the root *shûph*), that is, a crushing victory, over the serpent.[5]

Certain biblical texts must have had a given interpretation attached to them, an understanding that was naturally inserted into the Aramaic paraphrase. Deut 33:6 says: 'Let Reuben live and not die.' This would have meant little to Jews of a later generation unless paraphrased. In the Palestinian Targum it becomes: 'Let Reuben live *in this world* and not die *in the second death, in which death the wicked die in the world to come.*' Thus paraphrased it becomes a reminder of the future life.

'In the end of the days' or its equivalent is a phrase used in certain biblical texts with the meaning of 'in the days to come'. With an evolution in eschatological and messianic teaching these phrases in due time came to be seen as referring to the end of the world or the advent of the Messiah. Thus, for instance, in Gen 49:1 Jacob says to his sons that he will tell them what will befall them in the days to come. This in the Palestinian Targum becomes: 'I will show you the mysteries that are hidden, the appointed times that are concealed; what is the recompense of reward in store for the just, the punishment in store for the wicked, and what the joys of Paradise are.'

In later Judaism almost all sacrifice was considered to have expiatory value. Not so the earlier religion. In Ex 24:8 the biblical text, speaking of the Sinai covenant, simply says: 'Moses took blood . . . and sprinkled it on the altar.' This in the paraphrases of Pseudo-Jonathan and of Onkelos becomes: 'Moses took blood . . . and sprinkled it on the altar *to make atonement for the people.*'

By New Testament times Judaism had developed a rich theology on the Passover. The biblical text itself had said that

5. On the targumic rendering of Gen 3:15 and its relation to the New Testament see *op. cit.* (note 3 above), pp. 217–22.

the Passover night was to be for all Jews a night of vigil through-out all their generations (Ex 12:42). In later times the Messiah was expected to come at the Passover. All this leads to the insertion in the Palestinian Targum at Ex 12:42 of a hymn of four nights, all probably Passover nights, the last of which is that of the Messiah's coming.[6]

The exodus from Egypt was the first great liberation or redemption of Israel. It inspired in her the hopes of a future redemption. Hence where the biblical text speaks of Israel's coming out of Egypt, the Palestinian Targum paraphrases *coming* as *redeemed* out of Egypt. In the Targum Israel's God is he who has redeemed and will again redeem Israel.

In Ex 3:14f God reveals his divine name Yahweh to Israel. For his people Yahweh was the God who acts, who is ever at his people's aid. The Aramaic paraphrases of Ex 3:14f are at pains to bring out the attributes of God and consequently interpret the divine name so that it would connote God's eternal existence and active providence towards his people. We find such paraphrases of it as: 'I am he who is and who was and who will be'; 'I am he who spoke and the world was, and who is yet to speak and the world will be; I am he who was with you in the bondage of Egypt and who will be with you in every bondage.'[7]

What was the tree of life mentioned in the Paradise account of Genesis?, the ordinary Jew could ask. The Targum explains: 'The Law is the tree of life for all who labour in it; and anyone who observes its precepts lives and endures like the tree of life in the world to come' (Pal. Targ. Gen 3:24).

All these examples show that the Aramaic renderings were made the vehicle of instruction. They brought out the lessons thought to be included in the inspired Word of God. This is very much a feature of midrashic interpretation, particularly of the homiletic midrashim.'The primary aim [of the targums] was to make the Bible relevant, to make the Bible come alive and serve as a source of spiritual nourishment.'[8] In order to attain this end symbolical interpretation was occasionally

6. This hymn is the subject of Le Déaut's doctoral dissertation: *La nuit pascale*, Rome, 1963.

7. See *op. cit.* (note 3 above), pp. 106–12.

8. A. G. Wright, *Catholic Biblical Quarterly* 28 (1966) 132.

employed. Ex 13:18 speaks of the people of Israel coming up from Egypt *armed for battle*. In the Palestinian Targum the italicized words become 'armed with good work(s)'. This was the moral lesson of the passage, valid for all times.

VI.   *Homiletic nature of certain passages*

In these and in many other ways the popular nature of the Palestinian Targum is revealed. The homiletic nature of certain passages is shown by the opening words: 'My people, children of Israel . . .'[9] This is an expression used in the synagogue.[10] It is found in the Palestinian Targum of the Pentateuch to introduce exhortations to fidelity to God's Law, and opens the paraphrase of each of the commandments, e.g.:

> My people, children of Israel, you shall not be adulterers, nor companions or partners with adulterers, and adulterous people shall not be seen in the congregation of Israel; lest your children rise up after you and they also learn to be an adulterous people; for by the sins of the adulterer pestilence comes upon the land.

These few examples will give us some idea of what the targums are. They are free paraphrases, yet governed by certain laws. These laws have yet to be studied in greater detail, but were in the main operative in pre-Christian Judaism as is evidenced by the later history of the Old Testament canon and by the Septuagint version.

---

9. For examples see Pal. Targ. on Ex 20:7, 12–17; 23:2; 34:20,26; 35:5; Lev 19:16; 22:28; Num 28:2; Deut 25:4,18,19; 28:6,12, etc.

10. Cf. I. Elbogen, *Der jüdische Gottesdienst in seiner geschichtlichen Entwicklung*, 2nd·ed. (Frankfurt a.M., 1924; 4th ed. Hildesheim, 1962), pp. 88, 192.

7

Origin and Transmission of the Palestinian Targum

Jewish tradition from a very early date believed that targums were already used in the days of Ezra; Neh 8:8 was interpreted in this light. We have already cited Neh 8:1–8 when speaking of the reorganization of Judaism in the mid-fifth or possibly the early fourth century B.C.[1] Ezra had brought the Book of the Law of Moses with him from the East and was now to set about teaching it to Israel. The community was gathered together before the Water Gate of Jerusalem in solemn assembly to hear the Law of Moses from Ezra and the Levites: 'And they read from the book, from the law of God, *mephôrash*, and they gave the sense, so that the people understood the reading.'

In the Babylonian Talmud (*Meg.* 3a) this text is understood as referring to the targum:

> What is meant by the text: 'And they read in the book, in the law of God, *mephôrash*, and gave the sense and caused them to understand the meaning'? 'And they read in the book, in the Law of God': this indicates the Hebrew text; *mephôrash*: this indicates the targum; 'and they gave the sense': this indicates the verse stops; 'and they caused them to understand the reading': this indicates the accentuation or, according to another version, the Masoretic notes. These had been forgotten and had now been established again.

Mephôrash is the Pual particle of *parash*, meaning 'to separate', 'to cut', 'to decide' (the sense). Some think that here it means 'in sections'. The *Confraternity Version* has 'distinctly', the RSV has 'clearly'. By giving the marginal variant 'with interpretation', the RSV recognizes the possibility of another rendering. And in point of fact *mepharash* (the Aramaic

---

1. Above, pp. 22f.

equivalent of *mephôrash*) found in Ezra 4:18 is probably to be understood as 'translated'. It was customary for the Persian chancery to have documents translated into the language of the different countries of the empire.[2] Some modern writers take it that Neh 8:8 speaks of the law being translated from Hebrew into Aramaic. A. Gelin in the *Jerusalem Bible* renders the passage simply as 'translating and giving the sense'. (See also his note on Neh 13:24.) F. L. Moriarty comments on verse 8: 'The task of the Levites was to translate the Hebrew read by Ezra into Aramaic, the language of the people in post-exilic Palestine, and, finally, to explain its meaning and application to the community.'[3] R. Le Déaut, too, believes that the sense of the *mephôrash* in Neh 8:8 seems to be that given by the rabbinic tradition.[4]

That there is question of an Aramaic translation in Neh 8:8 would by no means be conceded by all. It would depend to a certain extent on whether or not the mass of the Jews then spoke Aramaic rather than Hebrew. And this, as we have seen,[5] is again uncertain, although Neh 13:24 seems to be an indication that they spoke Aramaic.

In any case, it is generally granted that by the first century B.C. Aramaic translations of the Torah, and probably of other books of the Bible as well, were being made among the Jews.

Our main concern here is with the Targum to the Pentateuch. This was certainly the first targum to be formed. How it came into being, whether all at once or gradually over a long period, is difficult to determine. It is only natural to see its origin in the synagogue service, as a rendering of those sections of the Torah read in public. As we have seen, the earlier manner in which the Torah reading was carried out is uncertain. Apart from the fixed readings for certain feasts, the choice of passage read may have been left at first to the head of the synagogue or to the reader. If this was the case, the origins of the targum would have been somewhat haphazard, and the rendering of the passages read assured of a greater antiquity than other parts. By New Testament times there very probably was a

---

2. See R. Le Déaut, *Introduction* . . ., pp. 29f.
3. *Ezra and Nehemiah* (*Old Testament Reading Guide*, Collegeville, 1966), p. 53.
4. *Loc. cit.*
5. Above, p. 57.

lectio continua of the Pentateuch and an Aramaic rendering of the entire work. Josephus can boast:

> For our people, if anyone do but ask any of them about our laws, he will more readily tell them all than he will tell them his own name, and this in consequence of our having learned them immediately as soon as we became sensible of anything, and of our having them as it were engraven on our souls (*Contra Apionem* ii, 17[18] §178).

This knowledge of the Law of Moses the majority of the Israelites would have got from the synagogue rendering of the targums. It was already Ezra's mandate and intention to bring them this knowledge of the Law of Moses, and the principle must have led the religious leaders of Judaism long before the Christian era to provide an Aramaic rendering of the entire Law.

The question now arises as to the characteristics of these earlier targumic renderings. The Qumrân texts present rather literal translations. This leads R. Le Déaut to ask whether the older written targums were not rather guides which followed the text quite closely, leaving to each the task of adding haggadic embellishments drawn from oral tradition. The more paraphrastic targums to arise later correspond to a time when midrashim were also written down, and would then represent a fusion of two literary genres.[6] Here we should probably distinguish between literary targums and liturgical paraphrases. The targums from Qumrân may well have been intended for a different public than were those in use in the synagogue, the targums in which we are principally interested. Its purpose would have been 'to give the sense of the biblical text and make the people understand the Scripture passage read' (see Neh 8:8). Our extant Palestinian Targum to the Pentateuch, and in a lesser degree the Targum to the Prophets, express sentiments found also in the synagogue liturgy. It is then natural to see the origin of this targum in the synagogue liturgy itself. Further, the Targum of Onkelos also contains midrash, and some of its paraphrases seem to presuppose the Palestinian targumic tradition. This would appear to indicate

6. *Introduction* . . ., p. 65.

that the Palestinian paraphrastic targumic tradition was formed at a very early date. The midrash and paraphrase is hence better considered something intrinsic to the targumic tradition itself. The indications, then, are that the synagogue targumic tradition originated at an early date in pre-Christian times and was formed in accord with the manifold laws of considering the text of Scripture which we have treated in chapter two.

A further question which needs consideration is the *language* of these early paraphrases. Was it official, literary Aramaic or the Aramaic of the people, when it so happened that one differed from the other? When the difference between the literary language and the spoken dialect was noticeable, it is legitimate to presume that the synagogue paraphrase was in the language of the people. The purpose of the paraphrase, after all, was to bring the message of the Scriptures to the people. There would be little sense in translating from an unknown language to a literary one but little known to the people. It might then well have been that in Palestine the language of the paraphrase was Palestinian Aramaic, while written records were in the literary language then in use. Another natural consequence of this principle is that the language of the synagogue paraphrase would evolve without necessitating any change in the paraphrase itself. In other words, from the nature of the language one cannot determine the date of origin of the paraphrase.

There remains the question of *written targums*. In 1832 Leopold Zunz wrote that 'written translations of most of the books of the Bible certainly existed under the Hasmonaeans' (i.e. 134–36 B.C.).[7] The texts from Qumrân appear to bear him out. These are literal renderings. Could it be that the older parts of Pseudo-Jonathan were at that time consigned to writing? Some of its midrash is very old. One passage (Deut 33:11) is taken by some authors to be a prayer for John Hyrcanus (135–105 B.C.) and to have originated during his reign.[8] In some respects the language of certain passages is

---

7. *Die gottesdienstlichen Vorträge der Juden*, 1st ed. (Berlin), p. 61; cf. 2nd ed. (Frankfurt a.M., 1892; reprinted 1966), p. 65.
8. See below, pp. 179f.

archaic (personal suffixes *-hôm, -kôm*) as in Middle Aramaic
and Nabataean.

Written targums must have existed in Jewish circles in the
early Christian centuries; they are legislated for in Mishnah,
Yadaim 4,5. We have already spoken of the written targums of
Job known to Rabban Gamaliel ɪ and used by his grandson
Rabban Gamaliel ɪɪ. In *Genesis Rabba* 79,7 (to Gen 33:19)
we read of R. Hiyya the Elder, R. Simeon ben Rabbi
and R. Simeon ben Halaphta (all from about A.D. 200) having
forgotten (i.e. not knowing) some words from the targum and
of their having gone to Arab territory, probably Nabataea, to
find out their meaning.[9] This is a good indication that the
Jews were interested in the targums, and moreover that the
targum in question was something already formed—not merely
in the process of formation—something whose language could
present difficulties to the learned.

We cannot say whether this particular targum was oral or
written. A written work would suit the context well. Some
fifty years later we find R. Joshua ben Levi (*ca.* A.D. 250)
giving advice to his children on how to prepare the weekly
parashah, i.e. the weekly section of the Pentateuch read in the
synagogue:

> Even so did Joshua ben Levi say to his children: 'Complete
> your *parashah* together with the congregation, twice the
> Hebrew and once the Targum' (Bab., *Berakoth* 8b).

Half a century later R. Ammi gives the same advice to all Jews:

> R. Huna ben Judah says in the name of R. Ammi: 'A man
> should always complete his *parashah* together with the con-
> gregation, twice the Hebrew text and once the targum,
> even such verses as Ataroth and Dibon [Num 32:3], for if
> one completes his *parashoth* together with the congregation
> his days will be prolonged' (Bab., *Berakoth* 8ab).

'Completing the *parashah* together with the congregation'

9. The original form of this text is, unfortunately, uncertain. Some mss. have it in
Hebrew, others (including *Vat. Ebr. 30*) in Aramaic. It was probably a text of the
Babylonian Talmud (*Meg.* 18a, *Rosh ha-Shanah* 26b), which has led P. Billerbeck
(*Kommentar . . .*, vol. III, p. 30) to render 'targum' of the passage as '(aus einem)
arabischen Targum'. Surely an Arabic targum or translation of the Old Testament is
out of the question for A.D. 200.

means studying at home the Scripture passage to be read and rendered in the synagogue. It is hard to see how this could be done from any but a written targum. Because of this W. Bacher,[10] I. Epstein[11] and G. F. Moore[12] see a reference to a written targum in the above passage, and rightly so, it would appear. Moore remarks: 'The latter prescription [i.e. that of R. Ammi] supposes that copies of an Aramaic version were in the hands of the educated.'[13] He also notes that written targums may also have been used as aids by students in the study of the targum in the schools and by the meturgeman in preparation for his oral rendering in the synagogue.[14] About A.D. 300 mention is also made of a written targum in an episode narrated of R. Samuel ben Isaac (Pal. *Meg.* 4,1,74d top).

Rabbi Joshua, R. Ammi and R. Isaac were all Palestinian rabbis. One naturally asks what kind of written targum would have been known to them. Moore believes it would have been Onkelos. This is highly improbable. Palestinian sources show little or no acquaintance with Onkelos before A.D. 800 or so. When we do find targumic citations in rabbinic sources from Palestine they are drawn mainly from the Palestinian Targum. Elsewhere I have studied in some detail fifteen such citations from the first(second) century to the fourth and found that thirteen of them agree with the Palestinian targum text as found in Neofiti.[15] This may well have been a semi-official text in Palestinian Judaism.

The inference from all this evidence seems to be that the tradition enshrined in the Palestinian Targum was formed at an early date, and even in pre-Christian times; that this targum was known in early times among Palestinian rabbis; and that certain written targumic texts existed, texts which probably carried the Palestinian Targum to the Pentateuch more or less as we now know it. Owing to the fact that no written text

10. *The Jewish Encyclopedia*, vol. 12 (New York, 1907), p. 58.
11. In his English interpretative rendering of the text in the Soncino translation of the Babylonian Talmud: '[*reading*] twice the Hebrew text and once the [*Aramaic*] Targum'. Italics mine.
12. *Judaism* I, pp. 174f. He still considers reference to a written targum no more than probable.
13. *Ibid.*, p. 175.
14. *Ibid.*, p. 174.
15. *The New Testament and the Palestinian Targum* . . ., pp. 45–56; *Rivista degli studi Orientali* 41 (1966) 1–15.

of such a work is mentioned by Origen or Jerome,[16] it is probable that such written texts were few.

The Cairo Geniza shows that texts of the Palestinian Targum to the Pentateuch were being written in the seventh to eighth centuries. With the aid of these texts we can trace the history of the work from the seventh or eighth to the eleventh century. From the opening years of the eleventh century we have numerous citations from this work in the lexicon (known as the *Arûk*) of R. Nathan ben Yehiel. We shall see further below how the main targum used by him seems to have been practically identical with Codex Neofiti.[17] Citations between the eleventh and the sixteenth century help somewhat to bridge the gap between R. Nathan's *Arûk* and the date of most extant copies of the Palestinian Targum.[18]

In conclusion we can say that there is a good likelihood that the present texts of the Palestinian Targum to the Pentateuch transmit substantially the paraphrase of the Pentateuch formed in pre-Christian times and known to Palestinian Judaism of the early Christian period. Used in accord with strict scientific principles, this paraphrase is of immense importance in reconstructing the beliefs of those to whom Christ and his apostles preached.

16. Jerome, however, knew of a rendering of Gen 25:3 which coincides with that of the Palestinian Targum; cf. McNamara, *op. cit.*, p. 55.

17. Below, pp. 187f.

18. See *op. cit.*, pp. 56–60, for references.

8

Date of the Palestinian Targum

In the preceding chapters we have considered evidence which appears to indicate that the Palestinian Targum to the Pentateuch is, in substance, very old. Further arguments for an early date of this rendering will be seen in the more detailed consideration of the extant texts of this targum which is given as an Appendix to the present work.

In this chapter arguments are brought together which to me seem to indicate that the Aramaic paraphrase found in the representatives of the Palestinian Targum known to us is very old indeed, and even basically pre-Christian.

1) *Principles underlying the paraphrase*—These were to a good extent already in use in pre-Christian Judaism. This seems established by a comparison of the characteristics of targumic paraphrase (chapter 6) with what we know of the development of Judaism in the post-exilic period (chapter 2).

2) *Relation of paraphrase to early Jewish liturgy*—We have seen how the spirit of the prayers used in the early synagogue liturgy is also found in the Palestinian Targum. Both speak of the resurrection of the dead, look forward longingly to the coming of the Messiah. We have also seen how Neofiti Gen ch. 1 gives indications of having been used in the synagogue before the destruction of the Temple.[1]

3) *Antiquity of the paraphrase*—G. F. Moore, who believed that our present texts of the Palestinian Targum to the Pentateuch date from some centuries after Christ, had to admit, by the strength of the evidence, that the nature of the paraphrase (particularly in the freedom with which translation runs into midrash) was characteristic of a very early period. It could be from the earliest days of the synagogue homily, when

---

1. Above, p. 37.

the Scripture translation may well have served as version and expositional homily at once.

4) *Geography*—There appears to be nothing in the geographical terms of Neofiti, to be studied below in the Appendix, which would necessitate a date after the time of Christ for the formulation of the tradition found in this text.

5) *Early form of midrash*—G. Vermes has made a deep study of certain midrashic themes in Judaism, going back from recent forms of a tradition to its earliest attested form (i.e. by the retrogressive method). This has convinced him of the early form of the midrash as found in the Palestinian Targum and has borne out Renée Bloch's contention that the Palestinian Targum stands midway between the Scripture text and later Jewish midrashic haggadah:

> On studying the Targum of Jerusalem [i.e. Palestinian Targum to the Pentateuch] it has appeared to us as quite evident that it lies at the base of the later haggadic tradition; that, placed in the immediate prolongation of the scriptural data, it constitutes a sort of joint, a gateway between the Bible and the later rabbinic literature; that it represents the starting-point, not indeed of the midrashic genre as such (which is already present in the biblical literature), but of *midrash* properly so called, of which it already contains the entire structure and all the themes.[2]

Rabbi M. Kasher, a specialist in rabbinic literature, writes of Codex Neofiti:

> It is my firm conviction that the contents are largely 200 years older than the earliest date given by some scholars for Targum Jonathan. It certainly contains much material of a later date, but its origins go back to the early days of the Second Temple, when at the direction of Ezra, scribes and scholars (the two were then just about synonymous) interpreted the Bible to the people in Aramaic (their spoken language), and began to record their translations cum interpretations.[3]

2. *Recherches de science religieuse* 43 (1955), 202f.
3. In a letter to A. Díez Macho, reproduced in A. Díez Macho, 'Magister-Minister. Prof. P. E. Kahle through Twelve Years of Correspondence' in *Recent Progress in Biblical Scholarship* (Boars Hill, Oxford: Lincombe Research Library, 1965), p. 43.

6) *Form of the halakah*—A. Marmorstein considers the halakah (i.e. Jewish Law) of Ps.-Jon. similar to that of Philo (first century A.D.). Rabbi M. Kasher believes that the halakah of Codex Neofiti is older than that found in Tannaitic sources: 'I consider it certain that in the Targum MS. we have material which served as a source for the Mishnah and the halakhic midrashim of the Tannaim, such as Mekhilta, Sifra and Sifre.'[4] These are weighty words, coming from a specialist in his field. Much more detailed study by scholars of Jewish law is, however, required before any definitive judgment can be given on the nature and age of the Palestinian Targum halakah.

7) *Relation to the New Testament*[5]—In recent years special attention has been devoted to the bearing of targumic evidence on the understanding of the New Testament writings. The parallels between them seem to favour an early date for the tradition found in the Palestinian Targum.

The convergence of all these arguments provides a very strong indication that the bulk of the material which we have in the Palestinian Targum to the Pentateuch comes from pre-Christian times. It likewise permits us to assume that by the days of Christ the tradition enshrined in this paraphrase was already formed and has, in the main, been faithfully transmitted.

The dating of Jewish traditions

It does not follow that the form of Aramaic in which the tradition was transmitted did not evolve with the ages. Such linguistic evolution is a feature of a living tradition. We have a clear example of it in Irish literature. And the evolution of Aramaic can be seen by a comparison of extant texts among themselves. Nor does the assumption of an early age for the targumic tradition as a whole preclude the intrusion of some later material and the change of certain earlier texts to 'update' them. The task still remains of proving, where possible, the age of any given targumic tradition.

This we must do by seeking evidence for its existence in dated texts.[6] Such dated evidence we have in the following:

4. *Ibid.*
5. See M. McNamara, *The New Testament and the Palestinian Targum* . . .; summary of the evidence for an early date, p. 257.
6. The basic study in this question is that of Renée Bloch, 'Note méthodologique pour l'étude de la littérature rabbinique' in *Recherches de science religieuse* 43 (1955) 194–227.

a) *Patristic writings,* some of which show acquaintance with Jewish tradition. Outstanding among the Fathers in this field is Jerome (fourth century A.D.) who makes several explicit references to the Jewish understanding of Scripture in his own day. At other times Jewish influence is present in his writings even when his source is not mentioned. The Jewish (and targumic) understanding of Scripture has even influenced his Vulgate rendering. Jerome's *Hebraicae quaestiones in Genesim* is replete with the understanding of Genesis found in the Palestinian Targum. Origen, and others, have also their contribution to make. Through the new interest in Judaeo-Christianity today, we shall probably be made aware how much targumic tradition influenced the early Jewish Christians. This latter is a point which is particularly worthy of study.

b) *Early Jewish art.* To take but one example: the frescoes of Doura-Europos (from about A.D. 250) depict scenes from extra-biblical Jewish tradition. In one of these frescoes some scholars see depicted the sacrifice of Isaac on the Temple Mount—a tradition found in the Palestinian Targum (Gen 22) as well as in other Jewish sources.

c) *Ancient Jewish writings* to which a definite date can be ascribed; e.g. the Dead Sea Scrolls, Pseudo-Philo's *Biblical Antiquities,* the *Book of Jubilees.*

d) *Ancient translations of the Old Testament,* such as the Septuagint and the Peshitta, which are occasionally witnesses to Jewish exegesis.

e) *Jewish liturgy.*

f) *The New Testament.* To give but two examples: in 1 Cor 10:4 Paul speaks of a rock which followed the Israelites during the desert wanderings. The Old Testament has no mention of this, although it does mention that the Israelites were miraculously given to drink from a rock. There is, on the contrary, a well-attested Jewish tradition on the well, in rock form, which followed the Israelites in the desert. The text from Paul is testimony to the early age of this tradition. Again, in 2 Tim 3:8 we read of Jannes and Jambres opposing Moses. No mention of these names is found in the Old Testament. They are found, however, in varying forms, in Jewish tradition and exactly in the form given in 2 Tim in the Targum of Pseudo-Jonathan Ex 7:11; 1:15.

PART TWO:

The Palestinian Targum and New Testament Studies

After this introductory consideration we come now to see what light the Palestinian Targum has to shed on the New Testament. In this second part we shall consider the Palestinian Targum in its setting within Jewish life. It is after all but part of the vast literature of Judaism and is intimately connected with liturgical texts and rabbinic writings.

The better to situate targumic evidence, we draw on the writings of the rabbis and on the Jewish liturgy as occasion requires. The evidence of the former tends to show, I believe, how embedded targumic tradition is in Jewish tradition. The testimony of the latter reveals how close is the relationship between the liturgy and the Palestinian Targum to the Pentateuch, which we look on here as a liturgical rendering, one which took its origin from within the liturgical services of the synagogue.

We shall occasionally treat of targumic texts other than ones from the Palestinian Targum to the Pentateuch. But this will be very much the exception, and only because they present material related to that of the Palestinian Targum. In the concluding chapter we go beyond the New Testament into a brief consideration of the bearing of the Palestinian Targum on Judaeo-Christian studies.

9

Reverential Manner in Speaking of God

I. Actions done 'before God'

The reverential attitude in speaking about God, already noticeable in the later writings of the Old Testament, is very much in evidence in the Aramaic paraphrases. When speaking of God's relations with the external world, the targumists shy away from making deity the direct subject or object of an action. To effect this, active verbs of the biblical text become passive in the Aramaic renderings, sometimes with a certain amount of violence being done to the Aramaic language. According to the biblical text of Gen 1:4, 'God saw the light (*ra'ah 'et ha'ôr*) that it was good.' This in the Targum (Neofiti) becomes: 'And it was manifest *before the Lord* that the light was good' (literally: 'and it was manifest before the Lord the light [*yt! nhwr'*] that it was good'). Likewise, throughout the entire chapter 'God saw' becomes 'it was manifest before God'. 'And God saw the earth, and behold it was corrupt' of Gen 6:12 becomes 'and the earth was manifest [*wgly qdm YY yt 'r'*] *before the Lord,* and behold had become corrupt' (cf. further Gen 31:12,42). 'God heard their groaning' of Ex 2:24 is rendered in the Targum 'and their plaint was heard *before the Lord*'. Likewise 'God saw the people of Israel and God saw their condition' of Ex 2:25 is translated as 'the servitude (*yt š'bwd*) of the sons of Israel was manifest *before the Lord . . .*'[1] 'God will provide himself a lamb' of Gen 22:8 is rendered '*Before the Lord* is a lamb prepared'. Instead of the Bible's 'I know you fear God' (Gen 22:12), the targumist writes 'I know that you *fear before the Lord*'; God cannot be the direct object of

---

1. Cf. further J. Levy, *Chaldäisches Wörterbuch über die Targumim* (Cologne: Melzer, 1959), pp. 114f.

an action. Instead of 'tempt the Lord' (Ex 17:2), the Targum has *'tempt before the Lord'.*

This religious mentality which spoke of things being done before the Lord is not peculiar to the targums nor indeed to Israel. We find it for instance in the Palmyrene inscriptions of Doura-Europos: 'May Malikû . . . . be remembered *before* [the god] *Yarhibol'* (Inscr. no. 15, A.D. 103).[2] In a Jewish inscription from Doura we read: 'that Ahiah . . . may be remembered for good *before* [*qdm*] *the God of the heavens'.*[3]

This way of speaking about God is abundantly illustrated by gospel texts. No more than in the targums are human emotions predicated of God. The Palestinian Targum renders Gen 6:6 ('And the Lord was sorry that he had made man . . .') as 'and there was regret before [*qdm*] the Lord that he had created man'. In Lk 15:10 Jesus says that 'there is joy *before* [*enôpion*] angels of God [or 'in heaven', v.7] over one sinner who repents', i.e. God rejoices over the conversion of a sinner. Sparrows are not forgotten *before* (*enôpion*) God (Lk 12:6), i.e. God remembers them.[4]

The prodigal son confesses (Lk 15:18,21): 'Father, I have sinned against heaven (*eis ton ouranon*) and *before you* (*enôpion sou*)'. 'To sin before' someone is a phrase not found in the Hebrew texts, nor in the Septuagint. The expression used there is 'to sin against' (*hata' le-; hamartanein eis*). 'To sin before' is a good targumic phrase. The targums, in fact, use both the phrase 'to sin against' and 'to sin before'. The latter is generally used when referring to a sin against God; the former when there is question of a sin against man. Thus for instance in Neofiti Gen 20:6: 'And the Word of the Lord said to him [i.e. Abimelech] in a dream: "It is also manifest before me that you did this in the integrity of your heart, and I have also restrained you from sinning *before me*".' Three verses later Abimelech says to Abraham: 'What have I sinned *against you*?' Joseph says to his master's wife: 'How can I do this great evil and sin *before* my God?' (Neofiti Gen 39:9). And the Lord said

2. Cf. Compte du Mesnil du Buisson, *Inventaire des inscriptions palmyréniennes du Doura-Europos* (32 avant J.-C. à 256 après J.-C.), new ed. (Paris: Paul Geuthner, 1939), pp. 7, 15f, 45f; another example in inscription no. 45. See also J. B. Frey, *Corpus inscriptionum Iudaicarum*, vol. II (Vatican City, 1952), no. 825, p. 74.

3. Frey, *op. cit.*, no. 845, p. 87.

4. Cf. Palestinian Talmud, *Shebiith* 38c: 'Not a bird perishes apart from heaven.'

to Moses: 'Whoever has sinned *before me,* I will strike out from the book of my Law' (Neofiti Ex 32:33). Ps 51:6 says: 'against you (*leka*) alone have I sinned'. This in the Targum becomes 'before you alone have I sinned' (literally: 'incurred debt', *habêt*).

According to Lk 12:8f, Christ says that those who confess him or disown him before men will be confessed or disowned before (*emprosthen*) the angels of God. The parallel passage in Mt 10:32f has 'before my Father who is in heaven'. Dalman believes it probable that Luke has inserted 'the angels of God' merely to avoid the use of the divine name.[5] Which, if either, is the original form of the logion is hard to say. The Jews of Christ's day may have mentioned both the angels of God and the Father in heaven in contexts such as this. In the Palestinian Targum to Gen 38:25 we find mention of 'the just fathers'. In the text in question Judah says: 'It is better for me to blush in this world, which is a passing world, than to blush *before my just fathers* in the world to come' (Neofiti).

II. *Good pleasure before God*

In Mt 18:14 Christ says: 'There is not will before (*ouk estin thelema emprosthen*) my [*v.l.* your] Father who is in heaven that one of these little ones should perish', i.e. 'it is not the will of my Father . . .' Again in Mt 11:26 (= Lk 10:21) Christ says: 'Yea, Father, for thus was there good pleasure before you' (*houtos eudokia egeneto emprosthen sou*), i.e. 'for such was thy gracious will' (RSV).

Here we are very much in targumic terminology, the corresponding Aramaic phrase—*ra'awā min qodam Adonai*—being of extremely common occurrence in the Aramaic paraphrases. *Ra'awā* is a word none too easy to translate precisely. It is used to render such Hebrew words as *rasôn* ('goodwill', 'favour', 'will'), *hešeq* ('desire') and *hepes* ('pleasure'). It can be rendered by 'will', 'goodwill', etc. The Greek translators of the early Christian tradition were faced with the same difficulty as any modern translator. In Mt 18:14 it is rendered as 'will' (*thelema*); in Mt 11:26 (Lk 10:21) as 'good pleasure' (*eudokia*). As just said, the expression 'good pleasure before the Lord' is

---

5. *The Words of Jesus,* Eng. trans. (Edinburgh: T. & T. Clarke, 1902), p. 210.

very frequent in the targums and is by no means restricted to passages where the Hebrew text has one or other of the three words it is used to translate. Balaam says to the noblemen of Balac: 'Go to your country because there is not good pleasure before the Lord [*lêt ra'ᵃwah min qᵒdam YY*] to allow me to go with you' (Num 22:13, Neofiti, etc.). Later Balac says to Balaam: 'Come, now, I will take you to another place; perchance there will be good pleasure before the Lord [*yihwê ra'ᵃwah min qᵒdam YY*] and you will curse them for me' (Num 23:27; Neofiti, Onkelos, Pseudo-Jonathan). Many more examples could be given. The expression, which does not occur in the Hebrew Bible or in the Septuagint, is also found in Hebrew, in the prayer formula: *yᵉhî raṣôn millᵉpanêka*: ('may it be well-pleasing in thy sight', literally: 'may there be [good] will before you'). Its antiquity is attested by 1 Mac 3:60: 'as there is the will in heaven . . .' It may underlie Lk 12:32: *eudokêsen ho patêr hymôn*, 'it has pleased your Father'. We should also compare Lk 2:14, for which a Hebrew equivalent has been found in a Qumrân text.[6]

Another word of extremely common use in the targums is *'itre'ê*, the Ithpe of *re'ê*, *re'ā*, meaning 'to be pleasing', 'acceptable', 'to delight in', 'to be well pleased in', etc. It is used, among other things, to render the Hebrew word *baḥar*, 'to choose', especially when the subject of the action is God. The targums also use the word *bᵉḥar*, 'choose', when the subject of the action is man (Gen 13:11; Ex 17:9; 18:25—Neofiti). Divine election, then, is seen as the effect of God's goodwill and good pleasure. To be a chosen one is to be one in whom God is well pleased. Bearing this in mind we find it easier to see a reference to the Servant of Yahweh in the divine voice at the baptism of Jesus: 'This is my beloved Son, *in whom* (Mk, Lk: 'in you') *I am well pleased*'—*en hô (soi) eudokêsa* (Mt 3:17; Mk 1:11; Lk 3:22; cf. Mt 17:5; 2 Pet 1:17). In the final phrase there seems to be a reference to the first Servant Song of Is 42:1: 'Behold my servant, whom I uphold; my chosen one in whom my soul delights' (*baḥîrî raṣᵉtah napšî*). This in the targum becomes: 'Behold my Servant, I will bring him near; my chosen *in whom* my Word (*Memra*, i.e. I) is *well pleased*.' The

6. Cf. J. Fitzmyer, '"Peace upon Earth among Men of His Good Will" (Lk 2:14)' in *Theological Studies* 19 (1958) 225–27.

Septuagint has: 'my soul has accepted him'. (*prosedexato auton hê psychê mou*). The same targumic religious terminology is found again in Mt 12:18: 'my beloved with whom my soul is well pleased' (*hon eudokêsen psychê mou*).

The way in which the citation from Ps 39 (40) found in Heb 10:6 deviates from the Septuagint text may be due to the same mentality. The citation in Hebrews runs: 'in burnt offerings and sin offerings thou hast taken no pleasure' (*ouk eudokêsas*); the Septuagint reads: 'burnt offerings and sin offerings thou didst not require' (*ouk êtêsas*). The Masoretic Text has: 'sacrifice and offering thou didst not desire' (*lô ḥapaṣta*); the verb would naturally be rendered as 'you have taken (no) pleasure in'. Although rendered by *ṣebîta* in our present targum to Ps 40:6 (7), *ḥpṣ* in the targums is very often translated by the verb *reʻê*, 'to be well pleased in', 'take pleasure in', as e.g. in the targum to verse 9 of Ps 39 (40).

God and Creation

The expression of divine truths in human language will always present a problem to mortals. The Yahwist has given us both a deep psychology and a profound theology in anthropomorphic and mythical dress. Yahweh fashions man from clay, converses with him, walks in the garden of Eden, descends from heaven to see the tower of Babel. This manner of speaking about God must have appeared to many as not entirely becoming. In the Elohist, God appears to man rather in dreams, or sends his angel as messenger. For the Priestly writer God is the Almighty One who created the world by a word. And yet, despite his earlier anthropomorphisms, in Ex 33:20 the Yahwist has Yahweh say to Moses: 'You cannot see my face, for man shall not see me and live.'

The task confronting later Jewish interpreters of the Old Testament was that of removing or explaining any expression which might be offensive to their audiences, or might be misunderstood by them. This led the targumists to remove anthropomorphisms, substituting references to the 'Word' (*Memra*), 'Glory' (*Yeqara*, *'Îqar*) or 'Presence' (*Shekinah*; Aramaic: *Shekinta*) of the Lord when speaking of his relations with the world. In communicating his will to man we read of 'the Holy Spirit' or the *Dibbera* (Word) rather than the Lord himself. For a Jew, of course, these were merely other ways of saying 'the Lord'. They were reverential ways of speaking about the God of Israel.

I. Word, Glory and Shekinah of the Lord

In the targums such phrases as 'he went down', 'went forth', 'came', etc., when referring to God, are naturally omitted. In their stead we read that God *'tgly*, *'itgᵉlî* (Ithpeel), 'revealed himself', or preferably, 'was revealed'. We read repeatedly in

the targums that God, the Word (*Memra*) of God, the Glory
of the Lord, the Glory of the Shekinah of the Lord (this last
mainly in Neofiti), is revealed. 'The Glory of the Shekinah of
the Lord was revealed to see the city and the tower that the
sons of man had built' (Gen 11:5, Neofiti). With such language
we should compare Stephen's words in Acts 7:2: 'The God of
glory was seen [*ôphthê*, was revealed] to our father Abraham.'

In the second century A.D. a dictum ascribed to Rabbi
Judah ben Ilai gives as a principle for rendering the Hebrew
text: 'He who translates a verse quite literally is a liar, while
he who adds anything thereto is a blasphemer.'[1] He illustrates
through Ex 24:10, which in the biblical text runs: 'and they
saw the God of Israel'. To translate this literally would give a
false sense, since no man can see God and live. To insert the
word 'angel' for God would be blasphemous: an angel would
be substituted for God. The only possible rendering of the
verse according to him is: 'and they saw the Glory [*yeqara*]
of the God of Israel', which is substantially the rendering of
all extant targums. This shows that this form of targumic
rendering must have been current in the second century A.D.
and even earlier. We are not surprised to see that according
to Targum Isaiah 6:2,5, Isaiah saw 'the Glory of the Lord',
'the Glory of the Shekinah of the King of Ages'.

In some texts in Neofiti 'Glory of the Lord' is a metonym for
God and one which could equally well be replaced by 'the
Word (*Memra*) of the Lord'. Thus, for example, in Genesis:

> *The Word of the Lord* created the two large luminaries . . .
> (1:16) . . . and the *Glory of the Lord* set them in the firmament
> (1:17) . . . *The Word of the Lord* created the son of man [i.e.
> man] . . . (1:27) . . . And the *Glory of the Lord* blessed them and
> the *Word of the Lord* said to them: 'Be strong and multiply'
> (1:27) . . . And on the seventh day the *Word of the Lord*
> completed the work which he had created . . . (2:2) . . .
> and the *Glory of the Lord* blessed the seventh day (2:3).

Apart from these texts, however, the Glory of the Lord in the
targums is employed in connection with God's relations to the

---

1. Tosefta, *Meg.*, end; Babylonian Talmud, *Kiddushin* 49a.

world. It is revealed to see the work of the men of Babel (Gen 11:5, Neofiti), and it is revealed to the patriarchs. Aaron, Nadab and Abihu saw the Glory of the Lord, or the Glory of the Shekinah of the Lord (Ex 24:10).

This is the religious terminology we find in the New Testament. Whereas according to the biblical text of Is 6:2,5 Isaiah saw the Lord, Yahweh, Jn 12:42 speaks of him as having seen the *Glory* of Christ. This is good targumic language. We may also recall how John generally speaks of the glory of Christ in conjunction with 'seeing' and 'revealing', as the targums do of the glory of the Lord.

II. The glory of the Lord dwells with Israel

In the Palestinian Targum the usual expression is not 'the Glory of God' but 'the Glory of the Shekinah of God', or 'the Glory of the Shekinah of the Lord'. The insertion of 'Shekinah' may be a further attempt to remove any trace of anthropomorphism. 'In the evening you will know that the Lord has led you out redeemed from Egypt, and in the morning you will see the Glory of the Shekinah of the Lord' (Ex 16:6f, Neofiti). 'Shekinah',[2] i.e. presence, dwelling, calls to mind 'the Glory of the Lord', or his dwelling presence with Israel. 'Moses led out the people from the camp to meet the Glory of the Shekinah of the Lord . . . And the Glory of the Shekinah of the Lord was revealed upon Mount Sinai' (Ex 19:17,20, Neofiti). 'And Moses drew near to the cloud on Mount Sinai, where the Glory of the Shekinah of the Lord dwelt' (Ex 20:21, Neofiti). It also dwelt in the wilderness (Ex 18:5, Neofiti). It leads Israel in the desert wanderings (Deut 1:30; 31:3,6,8, Neofiti). God promised to make the Glory of his Shekinah dwell among his people in the sanctuary (Ex 25:8). He also promised to sanctify the tent of meeting and said to Moses: 'And I will place my Shekinah in the midst of the children of Israel, and my Word (*Memra*) will be for them a Redeemer God. And they will know that I am the Lord their God who brought them out of the land of Egypt so that the Glory of my Shekinah might dwell among them' (Ex 29:45f).

These are but a few of the many texts which speak of God's

---

2. On the Shekinah see, among others, P. Billerbeck, *Kommentar zum Neuen Testament aus Talmud und Midrasch* II, pp. 314f.

Glory dwelling with Israel (see e.g. Pal. Targ. Gen 49:17; Lev 16:16; Deut 14:23f; 16:2,6,11; 25:20; 26:15; 31:17; cf. Gen 28:16). We shall see the bearing of this on the New Testament after we have devoted some study to the *Memra* of the Lord.

III. Memra of targums and Logos of John[3]

At the end of a very long excursus on 'The Memra of Yahweh' (Jn 1:1), P. Billerbeck concludes:

> The inference that follows from the foregoing statement with regard to the Logos of John can be in no doubt: the expression 'Memra of Adonai' was an empty, purely formal substitution for the Tetragrammaton and is consequently unsuitable to serve as a starting-point for the Logos of John.[4]

That the *Memra* of the Lord is merely a reverent circumlocution for 'the Lord', another way of expressing the same thing and in no way a hypostasis, is now generally held by students of Judaism. As H. A. Wolfson says: 'No scholar nowadays will entertain the view that it is either a real being or an intermediary.'[5] An examination of its usage in the targums appears to substantiate this view. The word is confined to the targums, occurring nowhere else in Jewish literature. In the targums it is inserted in passages speaking of God's being at Israel's aid, of man's believing in him, in passages of an anthropomorphic nature, etc. On occasion it seems indifferent to the paraphraser whether it was omitted or inserted:

> And *the Word of the Lord* said: 'Let the waters swarm forth a swarm of living creatures . . .' And *the Lord* created . . . every living creature which the waters swarmed forth (Gen 1:20f, Neofiti). And *the Lord* said: 'Let us create man . . .' And *the Word of the Lord* created the son of man [= man] . . . and the *Glory of the Lord* blessed them . . . (Gen 1:26f, Neofiti).

3. Cf. P. Billerbeck, *op. cit.*, pp. 302–33; M. McNamara, 'Jewish Liturgy and the New Testament' in *The Bible Today* 33 (December 1967) 2324–32, esp. 2328f; '*Logos* of the Fourth Gospel and *Memra* of the Palestinian Targum (Ex 12:42)' in *The Expository Times* 79 (1968) 115–17.

4. *Op. cit.*, p. 333.

5. *Philo*, vol. I (Harvard, 1948), p. 287. See also G. F. Moore, *Judaism* I, pp. 417–19.

'The Word of the Lord' is extremely frequent in the marginal glosses of the Neofiti MS. (glosses drawn apparently from complete MSS. of the Palestinian Targum which are now lost) where the text has merely 'the Lord'. One might conclude from this that the expression could, in very many cases, be inserted or omitted almost at will. This, however, would probably be a false approach. There may very well have been development in the use of the periphrasis in the course of history. When Moore writes[6] that the creative word of God is not his *Memra*, he is apparently going on the texts of Onkelos and Pseudo-Jonathan to Gen 1–2 where *Memra* never occurs.[7] Apparently there was a rabbinic ruling against its use there.[8] It is different in Neofiti (and in all texts of the Palestinian Targum to Ex 12:42, as we shall see), which mentions 'the *Memra*' repeatedly in these chapters. A new study of the *Memra* in the targums is called for, and is in fact being prepared by a Spanish student.[9]

Present-day scholars tend to reject the targumic Memra as a background to, or contributing factor towards, John's doctrine of the *Logos*. This they prefer to see prepared in the prophetic word (*dabar*) and in the Wisdom literature. This neglect of targumic evidence is unfortunate. Granted that the *Memra* of God and the Lord is but another way of saying 'God' or 'the Lord', it by no means follows that John was not influenced by targumic

---

6. *Op. cit.*, p. 418.

7. Cf. Billerbeck, *op. cit.*, pp. 316, 307. Billerbeck notes (p. 316) the presence of the expression in the Fragment Targum (Targum Yerushalmi 2) Gen 1:3 with the remark: 'For this, however, nothing follows for the praxis in the liturgy. Targum Yerushalmi 2 is a collection of supplements and additions to the official targum which some Jewish scholar had put together for his own personal purposes, and in the writing down of which he followed his own peculiar viewpoints and expressions'! On the Fragment Targum, its relation to the Palestinian Targum, and on the various views on its origin, see below, pp. 181f. In the course of his extensive treatment of the Memra in the targums (which runs to thirty-two pages) P. Billerbeck does not even once cite or refer to the text of Ex 12:42. Nowhere, in fact, in the entire four volumes of the *Kommentar* is the relevant part of the verse cited.

8. Cf. A. Díez Macho, 'El Logos y el Espiritu Santo' in *Atlantida* 1 (1963) 392f; Billerbeck, *op. cit.*, pp. 316, 307.

9. The generally accepted view on the meaning of Memra in the targums is that put forward in the monograph of V. Hamp: *Der Begriff 'Wort' in den aramäischen Bibelübersetzungen*, Munich, 1938. 'A thesis by Domingo Muñoz has taken up once again this problem of the value of the formula *Memra of Yahweh* and reaches conclusions quite different from those of the classical work of V. Hamp' (R. Le Déaut, *Ephemerides theologicae lovanienses* 44 [1968] 25, note 90).

usage in his choice of Logos as a designation for Christ. For John, too, 'the Word was God' (Jn 1:1). John got his doctrine on the nature of the Logos from the New Testament revelation. The question at issue for us is the sources from which he drew the concepts and terms in which he expressed it.

If targumic background there be to chapter 1 of John, we would expect to find it in the Aramaic paraphrase of the opening chapter of Genesis. In the textant targums to this chapter, however, there is little help to be found. But the targums to Genesis ch. 1 are not the only place in the Aramaic renderings where the creation of the world is spoken of. It is mentioned again in the Palestinian Targum to Ex 12:42 (Ex 15:18 in the Paris MS. of TJ 2) in a song in honour of four nights. This liturgical composition is a kind of Jewish *Exultet*, summing up the course of sacred history in four nights, possibly four Passover nights. The first night is that of creation; the second, that in which the promise of posterity was made to Abraham; the third was that of the first Passover in Egypt; the fourth will be that in which King Messiah comes.

The paraphrase is extant in Neofiti and TJ 1 and 2. All these texts have essentially the same poem, but occasionally with minor differences. The first night is thus described in Neofiti:

> The first night when the Lord was revealed above the earth to create it. The earth was void and empty and darkness was spread over the face of the abyss. *And the Word [Memra] of the Lord was the light and it shone [wmmryh dYY whwh nhwr' wnhr]*; and he called it the first night.

The relevant part of this text, given above in Aramaic, should be rendered literally: 'And the word of the Lord *and it* was [whwh] the light and it shone.' The *waw* ('and') before *hwh* is evidently a scribal error, due to numerous *waws* of the context. That this is so seems clear from the texts of the Fragment Targum in Walton's London Polyglot and in the Paris MS. The former text runs: 'And the Word of the Lord was shining [hwh nhyr] and illuminating.' Paris 110 reads: 'and in his Word he was shining [hwh nhyr] and illuminating.'

These two texts are in substance the same as Neofiti. If the Word of the Lord shone at creation, this can only be because it was the light. It is identified with the primordial light.

Neofiti states explicitly what the other texts imply: at creation the Word of God was the light and it shone.

This is precisely what John in his Prologue says of the Logos. 'In the beginning was the Word . . . and the Word was God. In him was light and the light shines in darkness' (Jn 1:1–3). And like the targumist, John is speaking of the activity of the Logos at creation. He was then light, and this light still shines in Christ.

In view of the close connection of the Prologue with Pal. Targ. Ex 12:42, and considering the manifold relations of Johannine literature to Jewish liturgy,[10] it is legitimate to assume that John is very much under the influence of the targums in the formulation of his doctrine of the Logos. A. Díez Macho thinks that the entire Prologue is equally so.[11] In his view, John draws on the then current Jewish concepts of Memra, Glory and Shekinah (presence, dwelling) to express the incarnation and the mystery of Christ. He renders Jn 1:14 into Palestinian Aramaic as follows:

U-MEMRA bisra 'it‘abed,
we-'ašrê ŠEKINTEH bênan,
wa-ḥamînan yat-YEQAREH,
Yeqara hêkema yeḥîda min 'abba,
melê ḥesad u-qešut.[12]

And the *Word* was made flesh,
and placed his *Dwelling* among us;
and we saw his *Glory*,
the glory as of the only Son from the Father,
full of grace and truth.

It is possible, in view of this, that when speaking of light and darkness the johannine literature is more under the influence of Jewish liturgy and less under that of Qumrân than is now generally conceded. While admitting the rather evident influence of Qumrân on certain texts, we should not be too prone to see it in every New Testament passage in which we

10. On this point cf. M. McNamara, *The New Testament and the Palestinian Targum . . .*, pp. 255f, 145–49.
11. *Art. cit.*, pp. 389f.
12. *Ibid.*, p. 389.

find the contrast of light and darkness. That 2 Cor 6:14–16 ('What fellowship has light with darkness? What accord has Christ with Belial?') shows typical Qumrân terminology is clear.[13] Matters are different in 1 Pet 2:9:

> But you are a chosen race, a royal priesthood, a holy nation, God's own people, *that you may declare the wondrous deeds of him who called you out of darkness into his marvellous light.*

The background here is the Jewish Paschal liturgy, not Qumrân. A well-known text of the Jewish Passover liturgy, already found in Mishnah, *Pesaḥim* 10,5, says:

> In every generation a man must so regard himself as if he came forth himself out of Egypt . . . Therefore are we bound to give thanks, to praise, to glorify, to honour, to exalt, to extol, and to bless him who wrought all these wonders for our fathers and for us. He brought us out from bondage to freedom, from sorrow to gladness, and from mourning to a festival day, and *from darkness to a great light* . . . so let us sing before him the Hallelujah.[14]

It is quite possible that in many, if not all, texts speaking of light and darkness, the johannine literature, too, is dependent on Jewish liturgy rather than on that of Qumrân. Christ, the Word, was the light which shone at the first creation, on the first night. The second creation for John would be the fourth night of the poem of the Palestinian Targum to Ex 12:42. While no mention is made in this poem of the Messiah's dissipating the darkness, this does not mean that the johannine literature is not dependent on it when speaking of the work of the Messiah. The very fact that it was the fourth *night* implies the presence of darkness. For John, at Christ's coming the world was in darkness. He, the Word, is the light which shines in this darkness (Jn 1:5). All who are not attached to him by faith and good works walk in the night; they are still in the darkness (Jn 8:12; 1 Jn 1:6; 2:9,11). They who refuse to come to him do not benefit from the new age; they love darkness more than the light (Jn 3:12). They, on the contrary, who

---

13. See J. A. Fitzmyer, 'Qumran and the Interpolated Paragraph in 2 Cor 6,14–7,1' in *Catholic Biblical Quarterly* 23 (1961) 273–80.

14. In Danby's English translation, p. 151.

come to him walk no more in darkness (Jn 8:12), having submitted to the hypostatized Light of the new creation.

This creation, given in John ch. 1 as the counterpart of the first creation, began when the Word was made flesh. The true light then began to shine in the darkness. The progress of the Gospel is, consequently, the dissipation of this darkness and 1 Jn 2:8 can say: 'the darkness is passing away and the true light is already shining'. Those who believe in the Messiah, the Word of God, the light, are the sons of the light (see Jn 12:36). Those who do not believe can be called sons of darkness, even though the expression does not occur in John, where we read rather of the contrast 'children [*tekna*] of God' (Jn 1:12; 1 Jn 3:1,2,10), 'children [*tekna*] of the devil' (1 Jn 3:10; cf. Jn 8:44).

The Holy Spirit

References in the targums to the holy spirit are few but significant, and in order that their import for New Testament exegesis be properly understood they must be read in the light of Judaism as known from Tannaitic and Amoraic sources.[1]

I. The holy spirit in Judaism

For Judaism the holy spirit (*rûaḥ haqqodeš*) is God conceived of as communicating his mind and will to man. The term is used in Tannaitic literature chiefly in passages saying that in a given biblical text the speaker in question is God.[2] Expressions commonly used in such contexts are: 'the holy spirit says',[3] 'has said', 'the holy spirit cries (*ṣowaḥat*) and says'.[4] Prophets and other persons communicate God's will etc., because the holy spirit rests on them (*šarat ʿal[êhem*, etc.] *rûaḥ haqqodeš*). Possession of the holy spirit leads to the resurrection of the body.[5]

The holy spirit, then, was God's gift to Israel. But before the Torah was given God spoke to the Gentiles also. They had the holy spirit. 'After the Torah had been given to Israel the holy spirit was withheld [literally: 'ceased'] from the nations' (*Seder Olam*, ch. 15, end).

---

1. Cf. W. Bacher, *Die exegetische Terminologie der jüdischen Traditionsliteratur* (reprinted, Darmstadt, 1965): vol. I, *Die bibelexegetische Terminologie der Tannaiten*, pp. 180–82; vol. II, *Die bibel- und traditionsexegetische Terminologie der Amoräer*, pp. 202–07.
2. Cf. *op. cit.*, I, pp. 180f.
3. Cf. Mt 10:20.
4. Cf. Rom 8:15f.
5. Mishnah, *Sotah* 9,15 (end), 306f., in Danby's translation: 'R. Phineas b. Jair (*ca.* A.D. 200) says: Heedfulness leads to cleanliness, and cleanliness leads to purity, and purity leads to abstinence, and abstinence leads to holiness, and holiness leads to humility, and humility leads to the shunning of sin, and the shunning of sin leads to saintliness, and *saintliness leads to the gift of the Holy Spirit, and the Holy Spirit leads to the resurrection of the dead*;' cf. Rom 8:11.

The holy spirit was God himself conceived of as speaking with Israel. Rabbinic texts can express the same idea in other ways. In some contexts 'the holy spirit' can be replaced by such terms as 'the Shekinah', 'the Dibbêra' (Word) and 'Bath Qôl' (Voice). In point of fact, where in one text we find 'holy spirit', in parallel texts we read one of the others, these being more or less synonymous in certain contexts.

To understand the targumic evidence we need pay special attention to the *Dibbêra* (in Hebrew it means 'divine discourse' or 'revelation'). It is the *nomen actionis* of the verb *dibber*, when this is referred to God.[6] In the plural (*Dibberôth*) it is used in Hebrew for the Decalogue, the ten words (*Debārîm*). In Jewish sources of the Amoraic period (third century and later) the form used is not *Dibber* but *Dibbûr*, a form not attested in Tannaitic times.

In the targums to the Pentateuch (except in Neofiti), whereas *Dibbêra* (the Aramaic form of the Hebrew *Dibber*) is used in the singular for one of the ten words, and in the plural (*Dibberayya*) for the Decalogue, the word used for God's address to Israel (when it does occur) is not *Dibbêra* but almost invariably *Dibbûra*. From this P. Billerbeck[7] and others have concluded that these texts of the targum are dependent on the Amoraim and not earlier than the third century A.D. We can grant that the targumic form *Dibbûra* may be influenced by later sources. But the earlier form of the word could have been different: *Dibbêra* and not *Dibbûra*. And, in point of fact, the form in Neofiti throughout is *Dibbêra*, never *Dibbûra*—a further indication of the venerable age and faithful transmission of this text of the Palestinian Targum.

We now turn to the bearing of the targumic evidence on the New Testament. According to the biblical text, in Ex 33:16 Moses says to God:

> For how shall it be known that I have found favour in thy sight, I and thy people? Is it not in thy going with us, so that we are distinct, I and thy people, from all the people that are on the face of the earth?

6. Cf. W. Bacher, *op. cit.*, I, p. 19.
7. *Kommentar* II, pp. 316–19.

Apart from an inserted reference to the Shekinah, Neofiti renders this passage without significant additional paraphrases. Pseudo-Jonathan, however, translates it as:

> And now, how is it that I have found mercy before you, I and your people, except in the *converse of your Shekinah* with us? *And distinguishing signs will be wrought for us when you withhold the spirit of prophecy from the nations and speak in the holy spirit* [*b*^e*ruaḥ qudša*] *to me and to your people*, by which we shall be made different from all the nations that are upon the face of the earth.

The holy spirit was God's gift to Israel. By it she knew herself as God's people, distinct from all the other nations of the earth. One is reminded immediately of Acts 19:44–48; 11:15–18 in which Peter recognizes that the Lord has chosen the Gentiles by giving them the holy spirit, just as he had done to the earlier Jewish Christians. Possession of the holy spirit indicates membership of the people of God.

Dibbûra (Neofiti: *Dibbéra*), i.e. the Word, is, as we said, the term generally used in the Palestinian Targum when reference is made to God's communicating his will to man. Pal. Targ. Gen 29:10 says that the Word (*Dibbêra*) desired to speak with Jacob. The Word (*Dibbêra*) of the Lord spoke to Moses from Sinai (Ex 19:3, Neofiti). The place where God spoke with Moses was in the tent of meeting, from between the two cherubim. 'When Moses had completed the tent of meeting, the Word [*Dibbêra*] called him, and the Lord [*v.l.*: 'Memra of the Lord'] spoke to him' (Lev 1:1, Pal. Targ.). Ex 33:11 tells us that in the tent of meeting, the Lord used to speak to Moses face to face, as a man speaks to his friend. This in Pseudo-Jonathan (unlike Neofiti) becomes:

> He [Moses] used to hear the voice of the *Dibbûra* but the features he used not see, as a man speaks with his friend. And after the voice of the *Dibbûra* had ascended, he returned to the camp and related the words to the congregation of Israel.

Num 7:89 is a parallel passage to that of Ex 33:11 just cited. This long chapter narrates how the tent of meeting was erected.

The final verse (7:89) is a generalizing account of Moses's relation with God within it. The biblical text reads:

> And when Moses went into the tent of meeting to speak with the Lord, he heard *the voice* speaking with him from above the mercy-seat that was on the ark of the testimony, from between the two cherubim; and it spoke with him.

This in Neofiti becomes:

> And when Moses used to go into the tent of meeting to speak with him, he used to hear the voice of the *Dibbêra* speaking with him . . . from between the two cherubim; from there the *Dibbêra* used to speak with him.

Dibbêra or *Dibbûra* of all these texts could equally well be expressed by 'the holy spirit', 'the spirit'. And, in fact, this is what we find in Pseudo-Jonathan to Num 7:89:

> And when Moses went into the tent of meeting to speak with him, he heard *the voice of the spirit* [*qal rûḥa*] that conversed with him when it descended from the highest heavens above the mercy-seat, above the ark of the testimony, from between the two cherubim; and from there the Word [*Dibbêra*] conversed with him.

Returning now to Paul's midrash on the veil of Moses (2 Cor 3:7;4:6) we may recall that throughout the greater part of it Paul appears to be presenting a midrashic development of Ex 32;33, a midrash as found especially in Pseudo-Jonathan, e.g. for the glory of Moses's face (3:7,10f) and the removal of the veil from the heart by conversion. We may then legitimately ask whether the Palestinian Targum to these chapters, and Pseudo-Jonathan in particular, has any light to throw on the enigmatic *ho de kyrios to pneuma estin* of 2 Cor 3:17.

II. *'The Lord is the Spirit'*[8]

Paul's midrash on the veil of Moses (2 Cor 3:7;4:6), culminating in his identification of the Lord with the Spirit in 3:17, has presented difficulties to commentators right down to our own time. In this passage the Apostle is contrasting the Old Covenant

---

8. For greater detail see *The New Testament and the Palestinian Targum* . . ., pp. 168–88.

with the New, showing how much the second surpasses the first. The chief, if not sole, Old Testament background of his thought is Ex 32:15;34:35, on the second and definitive giving of the Law to Moses. Some of the difficulties of the passage are occasioned by the fact that the Apostle has passed from the biblical text itself to a midrashic development of it. If we could come to identify the midrash he is following, we would probably find it much easier to follow his train of thought and his meaning.

Of recent years a certain amount of light has been thrown on the passage by Jewish sources. When Paul speaks of Moses's face having been in glory (2 Cor 3:7) as he came down from the mountain, he is clearly under the inspiration of the Jewish traditional understanding of Ex 34:29f,35. In these verses the biblical text merely says that the skin of Moses's face shone because he had been talking with God. In Jewish tradition (the Septuagint included) this passage is interpreted to mean that (the skin of) Moses's face was rendered glorious.

In a midrashic development of the veil of Moses (cf. Ex 34:29–35) Paul notes that a veil lies over the hearts of unconverted Jews whenever they read Moses, i.e. the Old Testament (2 Cor 3:15). Only in Christ is this veil taken away (3:14). 'But when a man turns to the Lord the veil is removed' (2 Cor 3:16). Here we have an evident reference to Ex 34:34: 'But whenever Moses went in before the Lord . . . he took off the veil.' The difficulty is that while for Paul the expression 'turn to the Lord' means 'repentance', 'conversion', in the Exodus passage (34:34)—whether in the biblical text or versions (Septuagint and all targums)—it is used in a purely local sense. R. Le Déaut has shown how the pauline passage in question is paralleled in Ps.-Jon. Ex 33:7f. The biblical text speaks of the individual Israelite seeking the Lord in the tent of meeting which was outside the camp. This in the Targum becomes: 'And anyone who used to turn in repentance, in a perfect heart, before the Lord, used to go out to the tent . . . which was outside the camp, confessing his sin [literally: 'debt' or 'guilt'] and praying on account of his sin ['debt'] and praying he was forgiven.'

The Lord is the Spirit. Having noted that 'when a man turns to the Lord the veil is removed', Paul goes on to state: 'Now the Lord is the Spirit [*ho de kyrios to pneuma estin*] and where the Spirit of the Lord is, there is freedom.' In the tent of meeting, to which the repentant Israelite withdrew, God was enthroned. From between the cherubim he spoke with Moses and Israel. God so speaking with Israel is often referred to as *Dibbêra*, 'the Word'. We have seen how he could equally well be referred to as 'the holy spirit'. This is, in fact, the case in two examples from Pseudo-Jonathan just cited: 'And distinguishing signs will be wrought for us when you . . . *speak in the holy spirit to me and your people* . . .' This is from Ex 33:16, just a few verses after the targumic parallel to 2 Cor 3:16. Again, according to Ps.-Jon. Num 7:89, in the tent of meeting Moses heard '*the voice of the spirit* (*qal rûḥa*) that conversed with him'.

For the paraphrase of Pseudo-Jonathan, in the tent of meeting the spirit conversed with Moses and the individual Israelite. And the Lord, i.e. Adonai, the God of Israel, was the spirit. But for the spirit to speak it was necessary to turn to the Lord in repentance, in order to hear his voice. So too in Paul's midrash. The Israelite must turn (i.e. in repentance) to the Lord to have the veil removed. And the Lord of which the passage speaks is the Spirit.

In view of this it seems better to take 'the Lord' (*Kyrios*) of 2 Cor 3:16f as 'the God of Israel', and not as Jesus Christ. When Paul says that 'the Lord is the Spirit' he then seems to identify the Lord of which the passage of Exodus speaks with the Spirit, God; but now in that richer sense which the New Testament revelation has given. As L. Cerfaux has put it: 'The whole context [of 2 Cor 3:17] is that of a midrash and Paul means that *Kyrios* in Ex 34:34, upon which he is commenting, should be understood as the Spirit, "the Spirit of the Lord", who has revealed himself in the Christian community.'[9]

Texts such as this, and there are others, show the special importance of Pseudo-Jonathan as a repository of ancient material of importance for New Testament studies. Apparently Paul is merely christianizing a midrash already formed within Judaism. We should note how Pseudo-Jonathan (like Paul in 2 Cor 3:17) uses the term *spirit* not 'holy spirit' which was the usual Jewish expression. We should also compare John 4:24:

9. *The Christian in the Theology of St Paul* (London: G. Chapman, 1967), p. 351; cf. also pp. 266f and note 7 to p. 266.

'God is spirit' (*pneuma ho theos*), bearing in mind the manifold ways in which Paul's teaching parallels that of the Fourth Gospel. Could their resemblances be explained as a christianization of basically identical Jewish concepts? It may seem strange that Paul should use such Jewish traditions in a letter directed to mainly Gentile Christians. The explanation probably lies in the fact that the Apostle of the Gentiles never succeeded in being anything in his mental make-up but a Hebrew of the Hebrews. The more stirred his soul was, the more did he reveal his true religious upbringing.

III. Other Palestinian Targum texts on the holy spirit

Apart from the texts given above, the Palestinian Targum speaks on a number of occasions of the 'holy spirit' or 'the spirit of prophecy', both meaning the same thing. 'And Jacob fled with all that was his. And he arose and crossed the river, setting his face to the mountain of Gilead' (Gen 31:21); the marginal gloss of Neofiti continues: 'because *he had seen in the holy spirit* that redemption would be wrought there for Israel in the days of Jephthah of Gilead'. 'And Pharaoh said to his officers: "Where will we find a man like this [i.e. Joseph] on whom there is a *holy spirit* from before the Lord"?' (Gen 41:38, Neofiti) 'And Jacob *saw in the holy spirit* that corn was being sold in Egypt' (Gen 42:1, Neofiti). From marginal notes of Neofiti we may mention Ex 2:12: '[And Moses looked] in *a spirit of prophecy* in this world and in the world to come and saw, and behold, there was no innocent man to come forth from that Egyptian.' Another gloss on the same passage reads: 'Moses saw the two worlds *in the holy spirit* and behold there was no proselyte destined to arise from that Egyptian.'[10]

In the New Testament, too, 'the holy spirit' must at times be taken in this general sense of a divine power moving man to prophesy, praise God, etc. (e.g. Lk 1:41,67;2:25–27).[11]

IV. The voice from heaven (Bath Qôl)

We have seen how a synonym for 'the holy spirit' and *Dibbûra, Dibbêra* in Judaism is 'the voice' (*Bath Qôl*). Thus, for instance, whereas Sifra to Leviticus 10:4 (46 a 1) says: 'The *holy spirit*

---

10. Cf. also Neofiti Ex 31:3; 35:31; Ps.-Jon. Gen 27:5; 37:33; 43:14.
11. Cf. A. Díez Macho, *art. cit.* in *Atlantida* 1 (1963) 394–96.

answered them', the parallel passage in Bar., *Kerithoth* 5b has:
'A voice [*Bath Qôl*] went forth and said'.[12] In point of fact, in
many of the passages cited above in relation to 'the Word'
(*Dibbûra, Dibbêra*) or 'the spirit', the underlying Hebrew text
speaks of the voice (*Qôl*) of God (see Ex 33:11; Num 7:89). The
'holy spirit', as *Dibbêra*, meant the voice of God from heaven.
Bath Qôl (literally: 'the daughter of a voice') means 'echo',
but is used extensively in Jewish literature and also in the
targums in the sense of a mysterious divine voice from heaven.
It is also mentioned by Josephus who designates it simply as
'a voice' (*phônê; Jewish Antiquities*, 13,10,3, §282). The word
of God came to Israel through the prophets. After the cessation
of prophecy heaven communicated with earth only occasionally,
and then by a heavenly voice (*Bath Qôl*). As the Tosephta puts
it: 'When the last prophets, Haggai, Zechariah and Malachi,
died, the holy spirit ceased out of Israel; but nevertheless it was
granted them to hear communications from God by means of
a *Bath Qôl*' (*Sotah* 13,2).

Frequent references to the *Bath Qôl* from all periods of
Israel's history are to be found both in rabbinic literature and
in the targums. As Isaac was about to be sacrificed, 'in that
hour, a voice came forth [*npqt bt qwl*] from the heavens and said:
Come and see two singular persons who are in my world'
(Gen 22:10, Neofiti). When Judah confessed his sin with
Tamar, 'a voice came forth (*qlh . . . npqt*) from the heavens and
said: They are both just' (Gen 38:25, Neofiti).

On three different occasions a voice came from heaven
confirming Jesus's ministry: at the baptism (Mt 3:17 and
parallels: *phônê ek tôn ouranôn*), the transfiguration (Mt 17:5
and parallels) and before his passion (Jn 12:28,39: *êlthen . . .
phônê ek tou ouranou*).

12. Cf. W. Bacher, *op. cit.*, I, p. 181; II, pp. 206f.

12

The Father in Heaven

'Father in heaven' (*ho patêr ho en* [*tois*] *ouranois; ho patêr ho ouranios*) occurs among the words of Jesus twenty times in Matthew, once in Mark (11:25), but never in Luke, although Lk 11:13 (*ho patêr ho ex ouranou*) shows a certain similarity with the designation and seems to indicate that the source of Luke contained the form as found in the other two Gospels. The question immediately arises, whether Jesus himself ever, or often, used this designation; whether, that is, it is introduced into his text by the first evangelist or generally omitted by the others from the sources they used.

The expression 'Father in heaven' never occurs in the Gospels without some qualifying pronoun such as 'my', 'your', etc. This designation of God as 'your' ('my') 'Father in heaven' is attested in rabbinic Judaism from about the end of the first century A.D. It is found neither in the Old Testament nor in the Apocrypha. In the Old Testament Israel is called God's son (Ex 4:22f), God's sons (Deut 30:9; 32:5; Is 1:4; Hos 2:1; 1 Chr 29:10, etc.). In Jer 3:4,19 Israel calls God her father; so also in Is 63:16; 64:7. In Jer 31:8(9) and Mal 1:6 God professes himself Father of Israel.

In later Judaism mention is made but rarely of God as Father of Israel. There seems to have been a tendency to avoid the designation. This tendency is noticeable in the Targum to the Prophets, where the word 'father' is replaced by some other word, or the text is made to say that God is *as* a father. Thus 'Thou art our Father' of Is 63:16 becomes in the targum: 'Thou art he whose compassions towards us are more than those of a father towards his children.' Likewise in Targ. Proph. 64:7. In Targ. Proph. Jer 3:4,19 it is replaced by 'master'; in Targ. Proph. Jer 31:8(9) and Mal 1:6 it is preceded by 'as', 'like' (a father).

Things are different in the Palestinian Targum to the Pentateuch. In one text (Deut 4:30, Neofiti) 'the Lord your God' is replaced by 'your Father' (*'abukôn*). In the Palestinian Targum to the Pentateuch alone among the targums do we find the designation of God as 'Father in heaven'. As in the New Testament, it is never found alone, but is always accompanied by a qualifying pronoun, 'your', 'their', 'our' (Father who is in heaven). Like most of the New Testament occurrences of the expression, in the targums too it is found chiefly in certain definite contexts, i.e. in reference to prayer, merit or divine will.

A final way in which the targumic evidence must be compared with that of the New Testament is in terms of the literary and synoptic problem posed in both bodies of literature.

I have found a total of thirteen occurrences of the expression 'Father in heaven' in the Palestinian targums: three in Pseudo-Jonathan, seven in the Fragment Targum and three in Neofiti. The texts are as follows: Gen 21:33 (TJ 1); Ex 1:19 (TJ 1 and 2, Neofiti); Ex 17:11 (TJ 2); Lev 27:28 (TJ 1); Num 20:21 (TJ 2, Neofiti); Num 21:9 (TJ 2; Neofiti missing); Num 23:23 (TJ 2); Deut 28:32 (TJ 1); Deut 32:6 (TJ 2); Deut 33:24 (Neofiti). In only one instance (Ex 1:19) do all three representatives of the Palestinian Targum carry this particular designation of God. As in the Gospel evidence, we may ask, in which is it original and in which added? Is its absence or presence due to the date of composition or to later editorial work? Perhaps like 'holy spirit', *Shekinah*, *Dibbêra* and *Bath Qôl*, 'Father in heaven' was another of the expressions which could easily be replaced by a synonym. The question will be clearer when we have considered the individual texts.

I. Prayer to the Father in heaven

Ex 1:19, Ps.-Jon.:

> Before the [Egyptian] midwife comes to them [i.e. the Israelite women], they lift up their eyes in prayer, *supplicating mercy before their Father who is in heaven* who hears the voice of their prayers [Frag. Targ. and Neofiti: 'who answers them'] and at once they are heard and delivered in peace.

Num 21:9, Frag. Targ.:

When anyone was bitten by a serpent, and *his face was lifted up in prayer to his Father who is in heaven* and he looked upon the brazen serpent, he lived. [Unfortunately this verse is missing from Neofiti; Ps.-Jon. reads: 'he gazed upon the brazen serpent, with his heart intent on the name of the Word of the Lord'.]

Gen 21:33, Frag. Targ.:

And our father Abraham discoursed to them of him who said [= spoke] and the world came to be by his word: *'Pray before your Father who is in heaven,* from whose bounty you have eaten and drunk.' [Ps.-Jon. reads: 'And he proclaimed to them there: Confess and believe in the name of the Word of the Lord, the God of the world.' Neofiti reads: 'You have eaten from him who said and the world was', without any reference to the 'Father in heaven'.][1]

Deut 28:32, Ps.-Jon.:

In your hand there will be no good work by which you prevail *in prayer before the Lord, your Father who is in heaven,* that he may save you. [Neither TJ 2 nor Neofiti has any reference to the 'Father in heaven' in their paraphrase of this verse.]

Ex 17:11, Frag. Targ. (Paris MS. only):

And when Moses had lifted up his hands *in prayer to his Father who is in heaven,* those of the house of Israel prevailed. ['To his Father who is in heaven' is not found in Ps.-Jon., Neofiti or in the polyglot text of Frag. Targ. Hence it is a suspect reading, possibly an addition to the Paris MS. alone.]

II. Reward before the Father in Heaven

Num 23:23, Frag. Targ.:

At that time it will be said to Jacob and to Israel: 'What favour and consolation is the Word of the Lord to bring upon you of the house of Jacob.' He [Balaam] said, too, in his parable of prophecy: 'Blessed are you, the just ones! How good a *reward is prepared* for you in the world to come, *before*

---

1. The foregoing texts should be compared with Mt 6:6,8.

your Father who is in heaven' (*ma' 'agar tab mittaqqen lekôn gabbê 'abûkôn dibšamayya*).

Neofiti speaks of reward 'before the Lord in the world to come'. The paraphrase of Pseudo-Jonathan is quite different: 'How praiseworthy are the signs and wonders which God has done for them.'

III.   *'Be you merciful as your Father in heaven'*[2]

In Mt 5:48 Christ concludes his exhortation to the better righteousness with the words: 'You shall therefore be *perfect* [*teleios*] as your heavenly Father is perfect.' The form of this logion in Luke (6:36) is: 'Be you merciful as your Father is merciful.'

The words of Christ are found in the Targum of Pseudo-Jonathan to Lev 22:28: 'My people, children of 'Israel, *as our Father is merciful in heaven* [*hêkemah di'abûnan raḥaman bišmayya*] so shall you be merciful on earth.' Thus the *editio princeps* (1593) of Pseudo-Jonathan, which text would be a very strong indication that Luke is nearest the original words of Christ. Matthew probably changed 'merciful' to 'perfect', the better to bring out his teaching on the new righteousness.

Unfortunately, we are not sure of the original form of the words in Pseudo-Jonathan either! 'Our Father' in the mouth of God seems strange. And two other variants of this translation of Lev 22:28 are known. That of the London ms. of Pseudo-Jonathan reads: 'as I (*'anā*) am merciful in heaven'. This too is the form found in the text of this rendering as found in the Jerusalem Talmud, *Berakoth* (5,3) 9c. The parallel passage of the Jerusalem Talmud, *Megillah* (4,9) 75c, however, has: 'as *we* are merciful in heaven', the reading preferred by G. Dalman.[3]

Notwithstanding the uncertainty of the reading 'our Father', the text still retains its value for the Gospel, and is a strong argument that Luke, and not Matthew, is nearer the original words of the Christian logion in question. The paraphrase is now found in Pseudo-Jonathan alone. I have elsewhere[4] given arguments indicating that it was once part of the other texts

---

2. *The New Testament and the Palestinian Targum* . . ., pp. 133–38.
3. *The Words of Jesus*, p. 191.
4. *Op. cit.*, pp. 137f. On the place of the Shema' in the Jewish liturgy, see above, ch. 3.

of the Palestinian Targum from which it was later omitted owing to a rabbinical censure.

IV. Other texts

In Deut 32:6 Moses says to Israel: 'Is he not your father who created you?' Whereas Pseudo-Jonathan and Neofiti are content to reproduce the biblical text without addition, the Fragment Targum paraphrases: 'Is he not *your Father in heaven*, who established you?'

In his blessing of Asher, Moses says (Deut 33:24): 'Blessed above sons may he be; welcomed in the tribes between his brothers and *their Father who is in heaven*.' The reference to 'the Father in heaven' is proper to Neofiti.

According to the Fragment Targum and Neofiti Num 20:21, Israel turned away from Edom 'because they were *commanded by their Father who is in heaven* not to wage war on them'. Instead of 'by their Father who is in heaven', Pseudo-Jonathan has: 'from before the Word [*Memra*] of the heavens'. This text of the Fragment Targum and Neofiti is to be compared with that of Matthew (7:21; 12:50) which speaks of the will of the Father in heaven.

13

Sin and Virtue

In Mt 6:12 'sin' and 'sinner' are called 'debt' (*opheilêma*) and 'debtor' (*opheiletês*): 'forgive us our debts as we forgive our debtors.' So also in Lk 13:4. The designation of sin as 'debt' and of sinners as 'debtors' is very frequent in the Palestinian Targum to the Pentateuch. In Neofiti Ex 32:31 Moses says: 'This people have sinned great sins'; literally: 'have sinned great debts' (*ḥattûn . . . ḥôbîn rabrabîn*). In Neofiti Gen 18:20–26 sin is called *ḥôba*, and a sinner *ḥayyeb*. It is, in fact, very often difficult to get a proper English term for the Aramaic words *ḥôba* and *ḥayyeb*. The fundamental meaning is 'debt', 'debtor', but they must often be rendered as 'sin', 'sinner', 'guilt', 'guilty person'.

I. The sin of Adam

According to the Palestinian Targum, God placed Adam in the garden of Eden to 'observe the commandments of the Law and fulfil its precepts' (Pal. Targ. Gen 3:22). It may be that the targumist is reading back into Genesis ch. 3 a situation obtaining only after the giving of the Law to Moses. Yet we may recall that even for Paul, commandment and a law were laid on Adam (compare Rom 5:14 with Rom 4:15). It appears that according to Pseudo-Jonathan at least, Adam and Eve were considered to be in the state of glory in Eden, a glory they lost by their sin. This seems to follow from Ps.-Jon.'s rendering of Gen 2:25 ('and they were not ashamed'): 'they did not long remain in their glory'. The same idea makes Ps.-Jon. render Gen 3:21 as 'And the Lord God made garments of glory for Adam and for his wife upon the skin of their flesh, from the skin of the serpent, instead of their beauty which had been shed; and he clothed them.' Neofiti (Gen 3:21) too speaks of God's making garments of glory for Adam and Eve, but has no reference to any glory being lost.

This new garment of glory made for Adam and Eve, its transmission to Jacob, and by him to his children, is the subject of a midrash in Pal. Targ. Gen 48:22. What theological idea it enshrines, I cannot say. The belief that through the sin of Adam humanity lost its glory probably lies behind Rom 3:23: 'All have sinned and fall short [*hysterountai*] of the glory of God.'

Ps.-Jon. Gen 3:6 identifies the serpent as Sammael, the angel of death. Late Judaism (Wisd 2:23f) and the New Testament identify him with Satan, the devil, 'who was a murderer from the beginning' (Jn 8:44).

The tradition of the Palestinian Targum identifies the tree of life with the Law:

> For the Law is the tree of life for all who study it, and everyone who observes its precepts lives and endures as the tree of life in the world to come. The Law is good for those who serve it in this world, like the fruits of the tree of life (Gen 3:24, Neofiti).

The outcome of the struggle between the seed of the woman and that of the serpent will be determined by their attitude to the Law:

> And I will put enmity between you and the woman, between the descendants of your sons and the descendants of her sons. And it shall come to pass that when the sons of the woman keep the precepts of the Law, they shall aim at you and smite you on the head. But when they forsake the precepts of the Law you shall aim at them and bite them on their heels. For them, however, there will be a remedy. And they are to effect a crushing in the end, in the days of King Messiah (Gen 3:15, Ps.-Jon.).

II. *The undivided heart*

We have shown elsewhere the relevance of the above text for the New Testament.[1] The tree of life in the Paradise of God figures in the Apocalypse (2:7; 22:2; 14:19). For Paul the source of life is not the Jewish law, but Jesus Christ the true

1. *The New Testament and the Palestinian Targum . . .*, pp. 217–22.

New Law. The inefficacy of the Old Law lay in the weakness of men's hearts. The New Law is written in the hearts of believers. Even though not explicitly stating so, Christ preaches this new law in his teaching on the better righteousness and the intensification or interiorization of religion. Man should set his heart on God alone; blessed are the pure in heart (Mt 5:8). Where man's treasure is, there is his heart (Mt 6:21). No man can serve God and mammon (Mt 6:24), the mammon of iniquity (Lk 16:9). Man should be single-minded; his eye sound (perfect; literally: 'simple'—Mt 6:22f; Lk 11:34–36). We find the same teaching in James 7:8. The double-minded (literally: 'double-souled') man is unstable in all his ways. Sinners, those of a double mind, are told to purify their hearts (James 4:8), i.e. the hearts of believers should be simple and perfect. There should be undivided attention to the Lord and his affairs (1 Cor 7:32–35).

We should compare this with what the Palestinian Targum to the Pentateuch has to say on 'the perfect heart'. Israel was commanded to love God 'with *all her heart*' (Deut 6:5). In the targum full devotion to God is described as a 'perfect heart', i.e. one that is completely set on God, not divided between him and created things. Pal. Targ. Gen 22:6,8 says that Abraham and Isaac 'walked together [to Mount Moriah] with a perfect heart [*b^eleb šalem*]'. After the sacrifice of the animal in Isaac's stead Abraham reminds God: '*There was no division in my heart* the first time that you said to me to sacrifice my son' (Pal. Targ. Gen 22:14), i.e. it was whole, perfect, not divided between God and creatures. At Sinai all Israel '*answered with a perfect heart*' that they would obey God's words (Pal. Targ. Ex 19:8). Finally, in the verse preceding the command to love God with all one's heart, the twelve tribes of Jacob answered together 'with a perfect heart and said: Listen to us, Israel our father, the Lord our God is one' (Pal. Targ. Deut 6:4).

III.   The Shema‛ and true worship of God[2]

The Shema‛, Israel's profession of faith, composed of Deut 6:4–9; 11:13–21 and Num 15:37–41, was recited at the opening of the morning service in the Temple and in the synagogue.

2. See also B. Gerhardsson, *New Testament Studies* 14 (1968) 167–72.

In New Testament times the Shema' was preceded by the recitation of the Ten Commandments. The Shema' contains the very essence of the belief of Israel, faith in One God and the acceptance of the commandments he had given his people. Hence it could truly be said that in reciting the first sentence of the Shema' (Deut 6:4) a man took upon himself the yoke of the kingdom of heaven and then in the other texts proceeded to take upon himself the yoke of the commandments (R. Joshua, *ca.* A.D. 140–165, Mishnah, *Berakoth* 2,2). Faith in God entailed acceptance of his will.

Mark 12:28–34—Debates of Jesus with Pharisees, Herodians and Sadducees are narrated in Mark12:13–27. The Sadducees denied the resurrection of the body because they could find no basis for it in the Law of Moses. Jesus told them that it was implicit in 'the passage about the bush' (Ex 3:6) where God said to Moses: 'I am the God of Abraham, the God of Isaac, and the God of Jacob.' The God of Israel, Jesus explains, 'is not the God of the dead, but of the living'. The principle here is that the words of Scripture have a fuller sense, revealed by the development of revelation. To believe in Yahweh as a living God will ultimately be seen to imply that he is the God of the living, and that the dead will live again before him. Christ came to bring the Law to completion by revealing the riches latent in the revelation made to Moses. It was probably by exegesis such as that employed by Christ that the doctrine of the resurrection had come to be explicitly taught in Israel by the beginning of the second century B.C. (Dan 12:1–3).

The rabbis, and the targums, find the resurrection of the dead in Deut 33:6 by a similar exegetical method.[3] The biblical text (in the RSV) says simply: 'Let Reuben live and not die and let his warriors be few.' This in the Palestinian Targum becomes: 'Let Reuben live *in this world* and not die *in the second death in which death the wicked die in the world to come.*' Onkelos has the same interpretation of the text: 'Let Reuben live *in eternal life,* and not die *the second death.*' The 'second death' in the targums, as in the Apocalypse (20:6), means exclusion from the resurrection. 'Not to die the second death', then, means to arise again to eternal life. Deut 33:6 was, in fact, the *locus*

---

3. Cf. *op. cit.* (note 1 above), pp. 120f.

theologicus in rabbinic Judaism for proving the resurrection of the dead, as we see from the Babylonian Talmud (*Sanhedrin* 92a):

> Rabba [*ca.* A.D. 35] said: How do we prove the vivification [i.e. resurrection] of the dead from the Torah? He said: *Let Reuben live and die not* (Deut 33:6). *Let Reuben live*—in this world; *and die not*—in the world to come.

To return to our text from Mark. Having recounted the debate with the Sadducees, the Evangelist continues (12:28–34; parallels in Mt 22:34–40; Lk 20:39f; 10:25–28):

> And one of the scribes came up and heard them disputing with one another, and seeing that he answered them well, asked him: 'Which commandment is the first of all?' Jesus answered: 'The first is, "Hear, O Israel: The Lord our God, the Lord is one; and you shall love the Lord your God with all your heart, and with all your soul, and with all your mind and with all your strength" [*ex holês tês ischyos sou*]. The second is this, "You shall love your neighbour as yourself." There is no other commandment greater than these.' And the scribe said to him: 'You are right, Teacher; you have truly said that he is one, and that there is no other but he; and to love him with all the heart, and with all the understanding, and with all the strength [*tês ischyos*], and to love one's neighbour as oneself, is much more than all whole burnt offerings and sacrifices.' And when Jesus saw that he answered wisely, he said to him: 'You are not far from the kingdom of God.'

Jesus here gives the opening words of the Shema' as the greatest of the commandments, ordaining as it does to love God with all one's being. 'To love one's neighbour as oneself' is a summary of the second part of the decalogue. By reciting the Shema' the Jew took on himself the yoke of the kingdom of heaven. This the scribe had done. Yet Jesus said that he was not far from the kingdom of heaven (or as Mark says, 'the kingdom of God'). The scribe had not yet reached this kingdom. The expression 'kingdom of God' or 'kingdom of heaven' (both mean the same thing) is one of those expressions so rich in meaning that no one definition can fully express its wealth. It means God's rule, God's sovereignty, God's will, the divine activity in the affairs of men, God's people accepting his divine will. A Jew accepted the yoke of the kingdom by his profession of faith. Before it he blessed the Lord who in his goodness, day by day, renewed the work of creation. Now in Jesus the greatest renewal of all was taking place. The kingdom was being preached in a sense as yet undreamt of. The deep meaning inherent in the Shema' was being revealed.

Mark 10:17–31 (Mt 19:16–30; Lk 18:18–30)—We may presume Jesus cited Deut 6:5 to the scribe in Aramaic. It would be interesting to know what word he used as a rendering of $m^{e'}od$ of the Hebrew text. The Septuagint renders this by *dynamis*, 'might', 'power', etc.; the synoptics use *ischys*, 'strength'. $M^{e'}od$, in the sense found in the Shema', is used only in Deut 6:5 and 2 Kgs 23:25. Elsewhere the word occurs only in adverbial phrases, with the meaning of 'greatly'. The lexicon of Brown–Driver–Briggs gives the fundamental meaning of $m^{e'}od$ as 'muchness', 'force', 'abundance', referring to the Assyrian word *mu'du*, 'abundance'. Palestinian tradition, as found in the Palestinian Targum, Onkelos and the Peshitta, rendered the word in the sense of 'riches', 'abundance', each choosing a different word to express this idea. The Palestinian Targum as found in Neofiti, Pseudo-Jonathan and the Fragment Targum has: '[thou shalt love the Lord] with all your wealth' (*mamônkôn*);[4] Onkelos (and Targ. 2 Kgs 23:25) has 'with all thy property' (*niksak*), while the Peshitta renders 'with all thy possessions' (*qnynk*). We may safely assume, then, that in Christ's day this injunction of the Shema' was taken to mean a command to love God with all one's external possessions.

When the rich man came to Jesus asking what he should do to attain eternal life, Jesus replied that for him this meant putting this injunction of his profession of faith into practice in a particular way. Loving God with all one's riches was now interpreted for the rich man as meaning to sell what he had, give to the poor, and follow Christ. Jesus had here again brought the Law to fulfilment. Yet, the rich man went away sorrowful, 'for he had great possessions'.

The Shema' and the true worship of God—For the pious scribe the Shema' recalled what true religion was: the love of the One

---

4. The Targum also knows of the 'mammon of iniquity' (Lk 16:9,11). Cf. Billerbeck, *Kommentar* II, p. 22.

True God. 'You are right, Teacher; you have truly said that he is one, and that there is no other but he; and to love him . . . is much better than all burnt offerings and sacrifices' (Mark 12:33). In the Palestinian Targum the Shema' is given not as the words of Moses, but as the profession of faith of the twelve tribes gathered together around the bed of the dying Jacob. We find this in essentially the same midrash inserted at Deut 6:4 (all texts) and Gen 49:2 (in Neofiti and the Fragment Targum only):

> When the appointed time came for our father Jacob to be gathered in peace from the world, he summoned the twelve tribes and set them round about his bed of gold. Our father Jacob answered and said to them: 'From Abraham my father's father there arose the worthless [*or:* blemished] Ishmael and all the sons of Keturah; and from Isaac my father there arose the worthless [*or:* blemished] Esau, my brother. Perchance [*dilma'*] you worship the false god which Abraham's father worshipped? Or perchance you worship the false god of Laban, my mother's brother? Or perchance you worship the God of Jacob your father?' The twelve tribes of Jacob answered together with a perfect heart and said: 'Hear, O Israel, our father, the Lord our God, the Lord is one [*YYY 'lhn YYY ḥd hw'*]. May his name be blessed forever' (Deut 6:4, Neofiti).

Here we have the Shema' as a rejection of false worship and as a profession of faith in the true God of Israel, a profession of faith addressed by the twelve tribes to Israel, the father of the nation.

In Neofiti, Deut 6:5 goes on to give the command to love God with all one's being. The transition is somewhat abrupt by reason of the midrash inserted in verse 4. The text of Pseudo-Jonathan is smoother, in that it notes that in verse 4 the twelve tribes profess their faith, whereas in verse 5 Moses exhorts Israel to practise the true worship of their fathers. Its text of the two verses runs:

> And when the time came for Jacob our father to be gathered from the world, he feared lest [*dilma'*] there should be a blemish in his sons. He called them and asked of them:

'Perchance there is guile in your heart.' They all replied together and said to him: 'Hear, O Israel, our father. The Lord our God, the Lord is one [*YY 'elahana' YY ḥad*].' Jacob answered and said: 'May his glorious name be blessed for ever and ever.'

Moses the Prophet said to the people, the house of Israel: 'Follow the true worship [*pûlḥana qashîṭa*] of your fathers, and love the Lord your God with the two inclinations of your heart . . . and with all your wealth.'

For Israel the true worship of God is that professed by the tribes of old, Israelites in whom there was no guile (see John 1:47). The scribe who came to Jesus saw that the worship expressed by the Shema' was better than the Temple sacrifices. Christ will tell the Samaritan woman that God seeks a religion centred neither in Jerusalem nor Garizim, but one in spirit and in truth (John 4:23f).

IV. 'This is my blood of the covenant'

'This is my blood of the covenant', *touto estin to haima mou tês diathêkês* (Mt 26:28, = Mk 14:24) is not good Greek. Against a Semitic (Hebrew or Aramaic) original for these Greek words it has been objected that an exact Semitic equivalent construction with the possessive suffix between the *nomen regens* and the *nomen rectum* is impossible according to the accepted rules of Hebrew and Aramaic grammar. Hence, some take the form of Luke (22:20) and Paul (1 Cor 11:25) to be earlier than that of Mt-Mk. Even if the formula of Mt-Mk were ungrammatical, it could still of course be early and from the lips of Christ. As J. Dupont puts it: Christ could have taken the same liberties with the laws of grammar that he occasionally took with the laws of Moses.[5]

In 1964 J. A. Emerton gave examples from the targums to show that the construction of Mt-Mk is not ungrammatical in Aramaic.[6] As examples of such construction, with possessive adjective between the *nomen regens* and *nomen rectum*, he instances Targ. Pss 110:3 and 68:36: *ᵃmûk dᵉbêt yisrael*: 'Your people

---

5. *Nouvelle revue théologique* 80 (1958) 1032.
6. 'Mark xiv.24 and the Targum to the Psalter' in *Journal of Theological Studies* NS 15 (1964) 58f.

of the house of Israel'; and *bêt maqdᵉšak taqqîpa dᵉyisrael*: 'Your strong sanctuary of Israel'. The latter example is of no value. *Yisrael* is not governed by *bêt maqdᵉšak*, but by *taqqîpa*. The text should be read, in conformity with the Masoretic text: 'Terrible is God, from your sanctuary; the strong one of Israel gives power and strength to his people.' The first example is valid, and all the stronger in that it is not mere translation Aramaic.

More recently the Cistercian J. E. David[7] has shown that the construction with a possessive adjective between the *nomen regens* and its determinative is found in Hebrew, Phoenician and Ugaritic. Consequently he sees no reason why it should not also have been current in Aramaic. In fact in four of the seven biblical examples he gives, this construction is retained in the targum. In the targums, then, the construction must not have sounded too harsh to Aramaic-speaking Jews.

The formula of Mt-Mk is modelled on that of the covenant at Sinai (Ex 24:8): 'Behold the blood of the covenant which the Lord had made with you' (MT: *hinnêh dam hab-berît 'ašer karat Yahweh 'immakem*; Septuagint: *Idou to haima tês diathêkes, hês dietheto kyrios pros hymas*). Neofiti renders the Hebrew literally as *ha 'ᵃdam qᵉyama dᵉqayyem Adonai 'imkôn*. Pseudo-Jonathan's rendering is slightly different: *ha dên 'ᵃdam qᵉyama*, etc.; 'Behold, this is the blood of the covenant . . .' The Aramaic equivalent of Mt-Mk's formula would then be: *ha dên admi* (or: *'idmî*) *(di)qᵉyama*.

Christ's blood is shed for the remission of sins. It has atoning efficacy. Heb 9:18–22, comparing the blood by which the first covenant was ratified with that of Christ, clearly implies that the blood sprinkled by Moses had expiatory value. This has caused difficulty to those who hold that the blood of the peace-offering (such as was that at Sinai) did not atone for sins. Recently Antonio Charbel has attempted to get over this difficulty by suggesting that the text is speaking of more sacrifices than that of Sinai.[8] But in fact there is no difficulty if we keep later Jewish teaching on sacrifice in mind. For Jewish thought, even in the New Testament period, all sacrifice

---

7. '*To haima mou tês diathêkês*. Mt 26;28: un faux problème' in *Biblica* 48 (1967) 291f.
8. *Ẓebaḥ shelamim. Il sacrificio pacifico* (Jerusalem: Commercial Press, 1967), p. 84.

was considered expiatory. Both in Onkelos and Pseudo-Jonathan (Ex 24:8—not however in Neofiti) it is explicitly stated that the blood had expiatory value. Their rendering is: 'And Moses took blood . . . and sprinkled it on the altar *to make atonement for the people* and he said: Behold the blood of the covenant which the Lord has made with you in all these words' (Ps.-Jon.).

V. *The remission of sins*

When Christ spoke of his blood, the blood of the new covenant, being shed for the remission of sins, he was, then, using concepts and language that could be readily understood by the Apostles. The expression 'for the remission of sins' is found in Neofiti Num ch. 7, which renders '[he offered] one male goat for a sin-offering' (see verses 7,16,22,28,34,40,46,52,58,64,70, 76 and 82) as 'he offered one male goat as a sin offering, for the remission of debts [i.e. sins: *lšbqwt ḥwbyn*], and for sins unwittingly committed [*wlšlwwn*], to make atonement by the blood of the goat for his debts [i.e. sins] and for the debts of his tribe unwittingly committed.' Onkelos and Pseudo-Jonathan give merely a literal rendering of the Hebrew text.

In Pseudo-Jonathan the word for 'to forgive (sin)' is *šbq* (*šᵉbaq*). Sins which are not forgiven are reserved, retained—*nᵉtîrîn*. Thus in Gen 4:7 (Ps.-Jon.) God says to Cain: 'If you make good your work, your debt [i.e. sin] will be forgiven you [*yištᵉbeq lak*]; but if you do not make good your work in this world, your sin will be reserved [retained: *nᵉtîr*] for the day of great judgment.' A. Díez Macho,[9] following G. Vermes,[10] has shown how this terminology illustrates *aphête—apheôntai—kratête—kekratêntai* ('whose sins you shall forgive, they are forgiven; whose sins you shall retain, they are retained') of Jn 20:23.

The fundamental meaning of *šᵉbaq* is 'to leave', to 'let go'. To forgive sins, then, is to release them, to loose them. Another word used very much in Palestinian Aramaic for remitting sins is *šᵉrî*, the basic meaning of which is 'to loose', 'to untie'. 'To

9. 'Targum y nuevo Testamento' in *Mélanges E. Tisserant* (*Studi e testi* 231; Vatican City, 1964), pp. 163, 178.
10. In *The Annual of Leeds University Oriental Society*, vol. 3 (1961–62; Leiden: Brill, 1963), pp. 107–11.

forgive sins' is in fact nearly always expressed in Neofiti, and occasionally elsewhere in rabbinic sources, by a combination of both verbs: *šᵉrî ušbaq*. Thus in Neofiti Gen 4:7 we have: 'Certainly, if you make good your work in this world, you will be remitted and forgiven [*yštry wyštbq*] in the world to come.' In *Lev. rab* 5 end, we read: 'Behold it is remitted [*šᵉrê*] to you and behold it is forgiven [*šᵉbîq*] you.'

A translator of the targums is here once again faced with the problem of choosing the most appropriate terms by which to render the Aramaic. The early Aramaic-speaking Church may have expressed the original logion of Christ in different ways, or the Greek translation may have given two variant renderings of the original Aramaic logion. I have elsewhere indicated how this probably happened as regards the word *'istalleq*—'to be raised up', 'to die'.[11] That Jn 22:23 bears some relation to the logia of Mt 16:18 and 18:18 ('Whatsoever you shall bind— *dêsês, dêsête*—on earth shall be bound also in heaven; and whatsoever you shall loose—*lysês, lysête*—on earth . . .') seems obvious. How to explain this relationship is less clear. It is usual to take the relevant terms of these logia of Matthew as representing the rabbinic *'ᵃsar* and *šᵉrî (šerā)*—Hebrew *'asar* and *hiṭṭîr*—'to bind and loose', i.e. 'to forbid and permit'. The sense would then be a legal one, not very much in keeping with the nature of the Church and the kingdom of God. Díez Macho surmises that the original logion underlying both John and Matthew used a double form for each: *'ᵃsar û-nᵉtar* ('to bind and retain') and *šᵉrî û-šᵉbeq* ('to remit and forgive'). The Greek renderings would, then, present two different translations of one original logion. To fully understand either, it is necessary to place it in its setting within the nascent Aramaic stage of the Church.

11. Cf. *The New Testament and the Palestinian Targum* . . ., pp. 145–49; more fully in *Scripture* 19 (1967) 65–73. On page 70, note 16, I suggested that the expression 'he was taken up', used by the apocryphal Gospel of Peter (Fragment 1,1,19) referring to Christ's death on the Cross, might possibly reflect this Aramaic word, and should then be understood as 'he died'. I now find that this is also Chr. Maurer's understanding of the text (in *The New Testament Apocrypha*, E. Hennecke and W. Schneemelcher eds. Eng. trans. by R. McL. Wilson, London: Lutterworth Press, vol. 1, 1963, p. 181): 'The statement "He was taken up" (v. 19) may be simply a turn of expression, of which there are other instances for "to die", in which case we need not think of an ascension from the cross.'

VI. *Good works and reward*

In the Gospels we find the good news presented in the simple language 'understanded of the people'. There is absent from them that polemical theology we find in Paul. This we see, for example, in the reference to good works and reward before God. Good works seen as mere externals, and considered in themselves as a means of salvation, are for Paul a source of boasting before God and the chief danger to salvation which comes from Christ alone. His censures on the works of the Law must be viewed in the light of his polemic against Pharisaic Judaism.

In the Gospels we find repeated references to good works and bad works. These terms, occurring neither in the Hebrew nor Greek Old Testament, are extremely common right through the Palestinian Targum to the Pentateuch. We have already cited Pal. Targ. Gen 4:7. The works of the generation of the flood were evil (Pal. Targ. Gen 6:3). So were the works of the people of Sodom (Pal. Targ. Gen 18:21). Abram is told by God to serve before him in truth and be perfect in good works (Gen 17:7, Neofiti). God reassured him that the reward of his good works was exceeding great, and kept and prepared before God in his favour for the world to come (Pal. Targ. Gen 15:1).

From good works, then, comes merit, *'agar*. This word is used in its original sense of 'wages' in a number of places in the Palestinian Targum (Gen 31:41, etc.). We find it very often, however, in the sense of the reward of good works. Christ says that the just should be glad and rejoice, for their reward is great in heaven (Mt 5:12). They have it 'before [*para tô*] their Father who is in heaven' (Mt 6:4). This is the language we find in the Palestinian Targum: 'Blessed are you, the just ones. What a good reward is prepared [*mittaqqen*] for you before your father who is in heaven [Neofiti: 'before the Lord'] in the world to come' (Num 23:23, TJ 2). The reward of Abraham's good works is kept and prepared (*mittaqqen*) before the Lord in (for) the world to come (Pal. Targ. Gen 15:1).

Christ reminded those who came to hear him that those who perform their good deeds to be seen by men have no reward before God (Mt 6:1). They have already received their reward while on earth (6:2,5,16). Abram, too, feared he would lose his reward in heaven because of favours received while on earth. 'After these things, after the kings had gathered together and fallen before Abram . . . Abram thought in his heart and said: "Woe now is me! Perhaps I have received the *reward* of my meritorious deeds in this world, and perhaps there shall be no portion for me in the world to come . . ." And then the Word of the Lord was with Abram in a vision saying: "Do not fear . . . although these fall before you in this world, the reward of your good works exceeding great is kept and prepared before me for the world to come"' (Gen 15:1, Ps.-Jon.). Likewise in Pal. Targ. Deut 7:10 (Neofiti): 'He repays in this world the rewards of their good works to those who hate him, in order to be avenged of them in the world to come, and he does not delay in giving the good reward to those who hate him. While still in this world he repays them the reward of their small meritorious deeds that are in their hand' (HT: 'He requites to their face those who hate him by destroying them; he will not be slack with him who hates him, he will requite him to his face').

14

Eschatology

Such familiar Gospel expressions as 'this world—the world to come', 'the resurrection', 'the judgment', 'the great day of judgment', 'Gehenna', 'Paradise', etc. are all found in the Palestinian Targum.

I. This world—the world to come

As G. F. Moore observes, in the sphere of eschatology 'there is . . . not merely an indefiniteness of terminology but an indistinctness of conception'.[1] This is particularly true in relation to the meaning to be attached to the expression 'the world (or 'age') to come'. This is due to the historical development of Hebrew thought on the subject. At all periods Israel was conscious of the actual order of things, later described as 'this world'. What 'the world to come' meant is not so clearly defined. It could mean the final order of things after the general resurrection, excluding the days of the Messiah. But it could also mean, or at least include, the days of the Messiah. This is something not without importance for New Testament eschatology.

The clearest distinction of the ages is found in Ps.-Jon. Ex 17:16 (and in *Sifre*, Deut §47): 'The Lord swore that he would fight against those of the house of Amalek and would destroy them for three generations: from the generation of *this world*, from the generation of *the Messiah*, and from the generation of *the world to come*'.

The 'world to come' is called the 'other world' in Pal. Targ. Gen 4:8, where it means what we now call 'the next life': 'There is a judgment and there is a judge and there is anòther world; there is a giving of good reward to the just and retribution is

---

1. *Judaism* II, p. 378.

[exacted] from the wicked in the world to come' (Neofiti). The existence of this other world is given as one of the matters on which Cain and Abel argued. We have seen how Abram thought he may have already received in *this world* the reward which should await one in *the world to come*. God is avenged of the wicked in the world to come (Deut 32:35, Neofiti).

There are other texts where the same meaning of 'the world to come' is less precise. The Lord is 'King of kings in this world; his too is the kingship in the world to come' (Ex 15:18, Pal. Targ.; Ex 12:42, Paris MS. 110).

Sometimes, apparently, by 'the world to come' messianic times are meant. This seems to be the case in Pal. Targ. Deut 33:21: 'As Moses led the people of Israel in this world, so will he lead them in the world to come.' On Pal. Targ. Ex 12:42 we read of Moses's leading the flock (*v.l.* 'in a cloud') in messianic times. Likewise in a marginal gloss to Neofiti (and in Ps.-Jon.) to Ex 2:12 we read: 'Moses saw the *two worlds* [another variant: '*this world* and *the world to come*'] and behold there was no proselyte destined to arise from that Egyptian; and he smote the Egyptian and buried him in the sand.'[2]

Whereas in most of the New Testament passages 'the world to come' clearly designates eternal life, we should not be surprised to find the exact meaning of the words occasionally ambiguous (e.g. Mk 10:30).

The contrast 'this world—the world to come' (*praesens saeculum, futurum saeculum*) is found also in the apocryphal works 4 Esdras (4:2,27; 6:9; 7:12,50,113; 8:1f,52), of the first century A.D., and 2 Baruch (44:11–13). The words are nowhere found in Onkelos and are infrequent in the Targum to the Prophets. On this basis, G. Dalman considered them to be characteristic of the language of the learned in Christ's day, rather than of the language of the people.[3] Since the phrases, while found in all three synoptics, are never found for any given logion or passage in more than one of the synoptics, he concludes that the expressions 'this age' and 'the future age', *if Jesus used them at all*, were not of importance for his vocab-

2. Further occurrences of the expression 'this world—the world to come' in Ex 3:14; Num 15:31 (Ps.-Jon.); Deut 31:16; 32:39.
3. *The Words of Jesus*, p. 151.

ulary.[4] It is Dalman's neglect of the Palestinian Targum evidence and his undue respect for Onkelos which have led him to this conclusion. The synoptic problem involved with regard to their use is no different from that which we have seen in the targumic use of 'the Father in heaven'.

II. *The day of great judgment*

On a number of occasions the New Testament speaks of the dreaded judgment awaiting men at a future date. It is the day when God avenges himself on those who deny him on earth (Mt 10:15; 11:22,44 and parallels). On the day of judgment man shall give an account of every idle word (Mt 12:36). The angels who have sinned and the unjust are being kept in prison until the day of judgment (2 Pet 3:7). It is a day of fear (1 Jn 4:17). Jude 6 calls it 'the judgment of the great day'. The men of Nineveh and the Queen of Sheba will rise at the judgment and condemn the generation to whom Christ preached (Mt 12:36,41f and parallels).

The 'day of great judgment' (*yôm dîna rabba*) is often mentioned in the targums as well as in rabbinic literature. The thought of the judgment to come, and of 'the account and reckoning of all one had done' (Pal. Targ. Gen 3:19) which must be given at it, was a potent deterrent from sin. Joseph refused to sin with Pharaoh's wife 'lest he should be condemned with her in the day of great judgment of the world to come' (Gen 39:10, Ps.-Jon.). Likewise the Israelites were deterred on the plains of Moab (Pal. Targ. Num 31:50).

On that day God will punish the wicked: 'Is not this the cup of retribution, mixed and prepared for the wicked, sealed up in my treasury for the great day of judgment' (Deut 32:34, Neofiti, TJ 2).

In Lk 9:26 Christ says: 'For whoever is ashamed of me and my words, of him will the Son of Man be ashamed when he comes in his glory and the glory of his Father and of his holy angels.' Here we have a reference to the judgment which should be compared with Pal. Targ. Gen 38:26. There Judah confesses his relations with Tamar and says: 'Blessed is every man who confesses his own deeds. . . . Better is it for me to blush in this

4. *Ibid.*, p. 148.

world than to blush [i.e. to be ashamed] in the world to come; better is it for me to burn in a fire that goes out than to burn in inextinguishable fire.' The entire paraphrase of Pal. Targ. Gen 38:25–26, we may add, reads somewhat like a page from the New Testament and has been employed by R. Bloch as a reason for Tamar's inclusion in the genealogy of Christ in Matthew.[5]

III. *The resurrection*

Belief in the resurrection of the dead (called 'vivification of the dead' in the targums and in rabbinism) is implicit in the final judgment. 'Because you are dust and to dust you are to return; and from the dust you are to return and arise and shall give an account and a reckoning of all you have done', were God's words to Adam according to Pal. Targ. Gen 3:19. The resurrection is also mentioned in many other texts of the Palestinian Targum to the Pentateuch.

IV. *Gehenna and paradise*

At the judgment Christ will say to the just: 'Come ye blessed of my Father, possess the kingdom prepared for you from the beginning of the world' (Mt 25:34); but to the wicked: 'Depart from me you cursed into everlasting fire which was prepared for the devil and his angels' (Mt 25:41). Heaven is won or lost by one's attitude to Christ and his law. We read of 'the Gehenna of fire' (Mt 5:22; 18:9); it is unquenchable fire (Mk 4:43); the damned are thrown into Gehenna (Mt 5:29; 18:9). God can destroy both soul and body there (Mt 10:28). Mt 23:33 speaks of the judgment of Gehenna.

With these texts we should compare those of the Palestinian Targum. The paraphrase to Gen 3:24 says:

Two thousand years before the world was created, he [God] created the Law. He prepared the garden of Eden for the just who will eat and nourish themselves from the fruits of the tree of life, because they observed the commandments of the Law and fulfilled its precepts. For the wicked he

5. '"Juda engendra Pharès et Zara, de Thamar": Matth., 1,3' in *Mélanges bibliques rédigés en l'honneur d'André Robert* († 1955) (Paris: Bloud & Gay, no date), pp. 380–97.

prepared Gehenna, which is like a sharp sword, devouring with both sides.

Within it he prepared darts of fire and burning coals, enkindled for the wicked, to be avenged of them in the world to come because they did not observe the precepts of the Law in this world. For the Law is the tree of life for all who labour in it [or 'study it'] and anyone who observes its precepts lives and endures as the tree of life in the world to come. The Law is good for those who serve it in this world, like the fruits of the tree of life.[6]

Abram was given a vision of Gehenna which Pal. Targ. Gen 15:17 describes as follows:

And behold the sun set and there was darkness, and behold Abram looked while seats were being arranged and thrones erected. And behold, Gehenna, which is like a furnace, like an oven surrounded by sparks of fire, into which the wicked fell because the wicked rebelled against the Law in their lives in this world. But the just, because they observed it, will be delivered from the affliction. All this was shown to Abram when he passed between these pieces.[6a]

For Judaism, one's eternal destiny was determined by one's attitude to the Law. For the Christian, it is determined by one's attitude to the Son of Man, Christ the New Law. In this, as in other respects, Christianity predicates of Christ what Judaism predicated of the Law.

V. Redemption

In the Infancy Gospel of Luke (ch. 1–2) we see the pious in Israel intently awaiting the redemption of their people, the salvation to come, according to the promises made to the fathers of old. At the birth of John, his father Zechariah blessed God, 'for he has visited and *redeemed* his people, and he has raised up a horn of *salvation* for us in the house of his servant David, as he spoke by the mouths of his holy prophets of old, that we should be *saved* from our enemies . . . that we might serve him without fear' (Lk 1:68–73). The pious Simeon was 'looking forward for the consolation [i.e. messianic redemption] of Israel . . . and it had been revealed to him that he should not

6. The text given is that of Neofiti.
6a. The text given is that of Neofiti.

see death before he had seen the Lord's Christ' (Lk 2:25f). In
the *Nunc Dimittis* he expresses his gratitude for having seen
God's salvation, i.e. the redemption brought to Israel by God
(Lk 2:30). The prophetess Anna spoke of the infant Jesus to all
who were looking for the redemption of Jerusalem (Lk 2:38).
There must at that time have been many of these in the Holy
City and scattered throughout Palestine. One of them was
Joseph of Arimathea who looked for the kingdom of God
(Mk 15:43; Lk 23:51). The kingdom of God and the redemption
of Israel would have meant more or less the same thing.

There were doubtless various forms of messianic expectations
among the Jews at the coming of Christ. Those pious Jews of
whom the above texts have spoken would have nourished their
piety from the liturgy, and very probably the liturgical texts
themselves were influenced by the beliefs of the pious. The
oldest Jewish prayers we possess make mention of Israel's
redemption. 'Rock of Israel, arise to Israel's aid and, according
to your word, deliver Judah and Israel. Our *Redeemer,* the Lord
of hosts is his name, the holy one of Israel. Blessed are you,
O Lord, who *redeems* Israel' (blessing recited at the recitation
of the Shema', basically pre-Christian). The ninth petition of
the Eighteen Benedictions (*Shemoneh Esreh*) prays God to
promptly bring near the appointed time of redemption. The
Kaddish prays: 'May he cause his kingdom to reign, cause his
redemption to bud forth, lead in his Messiah and redeem his
people in our lifetime and in your days.'

The idea of redemption runs all through the Palestinian
Targum to the Pentateuch. Where the biblical text says that
Yahweh will be Israel's God, the Palestinian Targum as found
in Neofiti paraphrases: 'I will be for you a Redeemer God'
(see Gen 17:8; Lev 11:45; 22:33, etc.). The great redemption,
of course, was that from Egypt and, according to the paraphrase
of TJ 1 and 2, Israel proclaimed its Redeemer King at the
Reed Sea:

When the people of the house of Israel saw the signs and
wonders which the Holy One—may his name be praised—
performed at the Reed Sea, and the might of his hands
between the waves, they answered and said one to the other:
'Come, let us place the crown of majesty on the head of our

Redeemer . . . For his is the crown of kingship; and he is the King of kings in this world, and his is the kingship in the world to come. And his it is and shall be for ever and ever' (Ex 15:18).

Biblical passages speaking of God as having led Israel out of Egypt are so paraphrased as to render the idea of redemption explicit, e.g. 'I am the God who led you *redeemed* out of Egypt'; 'Israel came out *redeemed* from Egypt'. But God is ever for Israel a *Redeemer* God. 'I am the God who has redeemed and will again redeem.'

At the Exodus Israel was told by God she would soon *see* the *redemption* of the Lord (Ex 14:14, Pal. Targ.; Ex 15:3, Paris 110). Later she must have often looked forward to this same redemption, just as the pious encountered in Luke's Infancy Gospel did. These had as their model their father Jacob. The targum on Gen 49:18 has him say:

Jacob our father said when he saw Gideon bar Joash and Samson bar Manoah who were to arise as redeemers: 'Not for the redemption of Gideon do I look nor for the redemption of Samson do I yearn, for their redemption is but the redemption of an hour [i.e. short-lived]; but for your redemption do I look and yearn, O Lord, because your redemption is an eternal redemption.'

Thus Pseudo-Jonathan. For 'your redemption' Neofiti writes: 'To the *redemption of him*, does my soul look which you have said [i.e. promised] to bring to your people, the house of Israel. To you, to your redemption, do I look, O Lord.' The redemption of him who has been promised is the redemption of the Messiah. In Pal. Targ. Gen 49:1 the age in which this was to come is called 'the appointed time of consolation' (cf. Lk 2:25f).

We see from texts such as these how the opening chapters of Luke represent the atmosphere of first-century Judaism, particularly of that form of Judaism we find in the liturgy of the chosen people.

VI. *Day of the Messiah not revealed to the prophets*

'Truly, I say to you', Christ told his disciples, 'many prophets and righteous men [Luke: 'prophets and kings'] longed to see what you see and did not see it, and to hear what you hear and did not hear it' (Mt 13:17; Lk 10:24). We have seen how the pious Jacob looked forward to the redemption of the Lord, or, according to Neofiti, to that of the Christ. Yet he was not given to see it, even in vision. This is made clear in Ps.-Jon. Gen 49:1:

> And Jacob called his sons and said to them: 'Purify yourself from uncleanness and I will show you the *mysteries* which are hidden, the appointed times [*qṣyy'*] which are concealed, what the recompense of reward for the just, the retribution in store for the wicked and the joys of Eden are.'
>
> The twelve tribes gathered together around the bed of gold on which he lay. And after the glory of the Shekinah of the Lord was revealed, *the determined time* [*qyṣ'*] *in which King Messiah is to come was hidden from him.*

The same idea is found in the renderings of this text in Neofiti and the Fragment Targum, albeit in a less explicit manner.[7] We find the same belief again in a reference to Balaam, who in Num 24:17 says he sees a certain individual arising from Jacob, a personage considered in later Judaism and in the targums to be the Messiah. Num 24:3,15 is consequently paraphrased as: '[Balaam] to whom the mysteries hidden from the prophets were revealed'. The other Palestinian Targum texts render: 'What has been hidden from all the prophets was revealed to him.'

The targumic rendering of Gen 49:1 speaks of the Messiah's coming. In general the targums speak of the Messiah as 'being revealed', and the same is true of 4 Esdras and 2 Baruch. We find this language in the New Testament in Jn 1:31 (cf. Jn 7:4) where the Baptist says he came baptizing in water that Christ might be made manifest, be revealed (RSV: *hina phanerôthê*) to Israel.

In the targums the kingdom of God is also referred to as being revealed, as in Luke 19:11, and the *Sibylline Oracles* 3:46–50. It is arguable that when speaking of the *epiphaneia* of Christ and of the grace of God, Paul in 2 Thess 2:13 and the author of the Pastoral Epistles are dependent on Jewish rather than Hellenistic terminology.[8]

7. Cf. *The New Testament and the Palestinian Targum . . .*, pp. 244f.
8. Cf. *ibid.*, pp. 246–52.

The Palestinian Targum paraphrase of Gen 49:10f presents the figure of a warring Messiah, one whose garments have been rolled in blood—a clear reference to Is 63:2. The figure of the Christ we meet in Apoc 19:11ff is the same as the one of the Palestinian Targum. The Apocalypse, here as in many other places, seems to be dependent on targumic tradition in its presentation of the Christian mystery.[9]

9. Cf. *ibid.*, pp. 230–33; 255f.

15

The Targums and Johannine Literature

We have already considered the bearing of the targumic evidence on the Logos doctrine of John and its relevance for the understanding of the Prologue to the Fourth Gospel. In fact, after a consideration of the evidence for the relation of the targums—and of the Palestinian Targum on the Pentateuch in particular—to the New Testament, the present writer has been led to see that the Apocalypse is 'the New Testament book which shows the greatest number of contacts with the Palestinian Targum'.[1] A study of the overall relation of the johannine literature with the targums would be very rewarding. Here we can only note some special points.

I. *Some theological concepts and linguistic expressions*

The use of 'glory' and 'Logos' (*Memra*) in the Fourth Gospel has already been dwelt on.[2] Christ wishes that those whom the Father has given him be with him 'that they might see his glory' (17:24). We are reminded of Neofiti Gen 45:13, where Joseph tells his brothers to relate to his father all his glory in Egypt. Jesus did not seek his own glory, but the glory of his father (Jn 7:18). In the Palestinian Targum the dutiful son is one 'who has consideration for the glory (*'iqar* or 'honour') of his father' (Gen 32:7(8),11(12), TJ 1; Lev 19:3, Neofiti).

We have already considered the manner in which Exodus ch. 32–33 and their midrashic development have influenced St. Paul in his treatment of the nature of the new dispensation.[3] In Ex 33:14 God promises Moses: 'My presence will go with you and I will give you rest.' This in Neofiti becomes: 'The glory of my Shekinah will accompany amongst you [*mdbr*'

1. *The New Testament and the Palestinian Targum . . .*, p. 255.
2. Above, pp. 101ff.
3. Above, pp. 110–13.

bynykwn] and will prepare a resting place for you' (cf. Gen 46:28). This brings to mind Christ's words in Jn 14:2f: 'I go to prepare a place for you.'

An expression typical of the johannine writings is 'from the beginning' (*ap' archês*: Jn 8:44; 15:27; 1 Jn 1:1; 2:7,13f,24; 3:11; 2 Jn 2:5f; 3:8; *ex archês*: Jn 6:64; 16:4). The Aramaic equivalent *min šerûi*—literally: 'from the beginning'—is equally typical of the Palestinian Targum to the Pentateuch and found only there. *Šerûi* itself is found only in Palestinian Aramaic. The Aramaic 'from the beginning' can refer to an absolute beginning, e.g. 'the language [i.e. Hebrew] in which the world was created *from the beginning*' (Gen 11:1,2; 13:4; 21:7). It is, however, also used in other contexts: Naphthali announced to Jacob 'from the beginning' that Joseph was still alive. Issachar saw 'from the beginning' that the land of Israel was good (Gen 49:15), etc.

'Come and see' (plural, Jn 4:27) is also an expression of the Palestinian Targum (Gen 22:8; 28:12). The Semitic equivalent given in Strack-Billerbeck[4] is used only in the singular and in the context of scholastic debates.

Like John and the other New Testament writings, the Palestinian Targum uses the word 'sign' (*nês, sîman*—a Greek loan-word) in the sense of miracle; e.g. 'five signs [= miracles] were worked for Jacob the time he went from Beersheba to Haran' (Gen 28:10).

The exaltation of Christ is a concept about which the Fourth Gospel has developed a rich theology. I have elsewhere[5] indicated how an Aramaic term occurring in the targums may well stand behind the johannine use of *hypsôthênai*, 'to be lifted up', 'exalted', 'crucified'. The Aramaic word in question is *selaq*, 'to ascend', used in the Ithpael with the meaning of 'to go away', 'depart', '*die*', although literally it would mean 'to be raised up', 'exalted'.

The 'hour' of Christ is another term round which John has built up a theology of Christ's redemptive work. There are some targumic texts which come to mind in connection with certain of John's expressions in this context. In Jn 12:27 Jesus prays: 'Now is my soul troubled. And what shall I say?

4. *Kommentar* II, p. 371.
5. See note 11 to chapter 13 above.

"Father save me from this hour"?' The words of Tamar as she was being led out to be burned come to mind: 'She raised her eyes to the heavens on high and said: "I beg by the mercies which are before you, O Lord, answer me in this hour of my affliction"' (Gen 38:25, Ps.-Jon.). We may add that the Palestinian Targum has a number of long texts on the hour of affliction and distress (Gen 22:14; 38:24; Lev 22:27). And in Pal. Targ. Gen 38:26, as in Jn 12:28, a voice came from heaven.

In Apoc 18:10,17,19 'one hour' (*mia hôra*) means a short space of time. So also in Pal. Targ. Gen 49:18; 49:21 ('in a short hour').

Nowhere in the Jewish tradition do we read that Abraham had a vision of the days of the Messiah. It could, however, have been part of a Jewish tradition. In Wisdom 10:10 we read that wisdom showed the righteous man (Jacob) the kingdom of God. C. F. Burney[6] believes the tradition is to be found in Pal. Targ. Gen 15, in which Abraham is assured of divine protection in this world and in the world to come (15:1), and is given a vision of four kingdoms to arise against his people (15:17). 'All this was shown to Abram when he passed between these pieces' (15:17, Pal. Targ.).

The text which principally interests us here is Gen 15:12, which is a midrashic development of the Hebrew *'emah ḥašekah gedôlah nopelet 'ālaw*—literally: 'dread darkness great falling upon him' (i.e. a dread and great darkness fell upon him). In the Palestinian Targum the paraphrase of 15:12 becomes:

And when the sun was about to set, a deep sleep [Neofiti: 'sweet sleep'] was cast upon Abram, and behold four kingdoms were rising to enslave his children: *Dread*—that is, Babylon; *Darkness*—that is, Media; *Great*—that is, Greece; *Fell*—that is, Persia [other texts: 'Edom'], which is to fall and shall never rise again, and whence the people of Israel is to come forth (text of Ps.-Jon.).

This midrash is based on the four kingdoms which according to Daniel precede the eternal kingdom of the Son of Man (Dan 7:1–14). The midrash on Gen 15:17 also reproduces the

6. *The Aramaic Origin of the Fourth Gospel* (Oxford: Clarendon Press, 1922), pp. 111f.

language of Dan 7:9 ('I looked as thrones were being set'). The final kingdom of the Palestinian Targum is Rome, called Edom in most texts, but changed to Persia in Pseudo-Jonathan in order to escape ecclesiastical censors, Edom in medieval Judaism meaning the Christian Empire. (In the MS. of Neofiti the final words are actually erased by the censor.)[7] The final empire will fall and never rise again. This destruction for Judaism would usher in the messianic age, and would most probably be the work of the Messiah. It would mean the ingathering of the exiles, referred to explicitly in the text of Pseudo-Jonathan and implicit in the others. It would be the fourth night of Pal. Targ. Ex 12:42, in which Moses and the Messiah would lead God's people.

II.   The well of Jacob[8]

John's account of Christ's conversation with the Samaritan woman at the well of Jacob (Jn 4:5–23) brings other biblical texts on wells to mind. 'Give me to drink' (4:7) recalls the words of Abraham's servant to Rebekah at the well in Paddan-aram (Gen 24:14). This well, if not the same as that later mentioned in the story of Jacob (29:2,3,8), would very naturally have been identified with it in Jewish tradition. All the biblical text tells us of this well is that although covered by a stone so great that all the shepherds' strength was required to roll it back, Jacob did so unaided. Tradition as found in the Palestinian Targum sees two signs (i.e. miracles) worked for Jacob as regards this well. These are but two of the five signs God worked for him when he went from Beersheba to Haran. The first was that the daytime was made shorter because the Word of God (*Dibbêra*) wished to speak to him (at night). The second was that the stones he used as a pillow in Bethel became one stone: that set up as a sacred pillar at Bethel. The third was that the space between Bethel and Haran was shortened 'and he was found dwelling at Haran'. All five miracles are found in the midrash to Gen 28:10. The last two are:

And the fourth sign: a stone which all the shepherds had come together to roll away from the mouth of the well and

7. See below, p. 184.
8. Cf. J. Ramon Díaz, *Estudios biblicos* 21 (1962). A. Jaubert, 'La symbolique du puits de Jacob' in *L'homme devant Dieu. Mélanges P. de Lubac*, vol. 1 (Paris, 1963), pp. 63–73.

could not, when our father Jacob came he raised it with one hand, and gave to drink to the flock of Laban, his mother's brother. And the fifth sign: when our father Jacob raised the stone from above the mouth of the well, *the well flowed up* and came to its mouth and was flowing up and coming to its mouth for twenty years—all the days that he dwelt at Haran (text of Neofiti).

The midrash occurs again in Pal. Targ. Gen 39:22. It must, then, have been embedded in the tradition.

This tradition may well lie behind Christ's words to the Samaritan woman. The well of Jacob at Sychar was deep and Christ had nothing with which to draw water, yet he told the woman he could give living water (4:10), water that would become like a spring of water welling up to eternal life (4:14). He spoke of himself somewhat as Jewish tradition had spoken of the well of Jacob.

Christ's words are the fulfilment of a number of Old Testament prophecies (Ezek 47:1f, etc.). He may well have spoken of this fulfilment in concepts borrowed from the tradition of his people. The water of life was spoken of again by Christ at the feast of Tabernacles (Jn 7:37–39), on the last day of the feast. His imagery on this occasion is generally explained by the special water rite of this feast.[9] But there may also be a reference to the well of Jacob, inasmuch as in Ps.-Jon. Gen 35:14 the pillar of stone (subject of one of the five miracles in Pal. Targ. Gen 28:10!) erected by Jacob at Bethel was connected with the feast of Tabernacles:

> And the Shekinah of the Lord went up from him in the place where it had spoken with him. And Jacob erected there a pillar of stone in the place where it had spoken with him, and he poured upon it a libation of wine and a libation of water, *because thus was it to be done at the feast of Tabernacles*; and he poured olive oil on it.

III.   Jacob's ladder

Another text of Genesis developed midrashically in the Palestinian Targum (as in rabbinic midrash) is that of Gen 28:12:

9. See also Tos., *Sukkah* 3,3–16; above, pp. 7f.

And he [Jacob] dreamed, and behold, a ladder was fixed
on the earth and its head reached to the height of the heavens,
and behold, the angels who had accompanied him from the
house of his father ascended to bear the good tidings to the
angels on high, saying: 'Come and see a just man whose
image is engraved in the throne of the Glory, whom you
desired ['*ithamedtun*] to see.' And behold, the angels from
before the Lord were ascending and descending and they
observed him.

The biblical text does not tell us why the angels ascended and
descended. The targumic paraphrase supplies a reason. They
ascended and descended to see Jacob. They had desired to see
him until then, knowing only his heavenly image. 1 Pet 1 :12
tells us how the angels long to bend down in order to examine
closely (*parakypsai*) the salvation brought by Christ. Nathaniel
was a just man, a true son of Jacob, an Israelite in whom there
was no guile (Jn 1 :47). But the true Jacob was the Son of Man,
on whom and in whose work, faith would see the angels of God
ascending and descending (Jn 1 :51). Here again, Christ
apparently availed himself of Jewish tradition to explain the
mystery of his own person.

IV.   *The brazen serpent*

In Jn 3 :14 Jesus tells the Jews that 'as Moses lifted up the
serpent in the wilderness, so must the Son of Man be lifted up,
that whoever believes in him may have eternal life'. The brazen
serpent is then a symbol of Christ, belief in whom brings
eternal life.

Jewish tradition had, once more, prepared the way for this
teaching. The brazen serpent raised up by Moses as a cure for
the lethal bite of the fiery serpents (Num 21 :4–9) was considered
to be that later honoured in the temple. Because of the danger
of superstitious practices attached to its veneration, King
Hezekiah had it destroyed (2 Kgs 18:4). To avoid danger
from superstitious and magical beliefs, it was necessary to
remind Israel that it was God alone, not the material serpent,
who healed. This explanation we find in Wisd 16:7: 'For he
who turned toward it was healed, *not by what he saw*, but by
thee [the Lord], Saviour of all.' The paraphrase found in the

Palestinian Targum attributes the healing to God invoked by prayer:

> When anyone bitten by a serpent lifted up his face in prayer to his Father who is in heaven [Ps.-Jon.: 'turned his heart to the name of the Word of the Lord'], and looked upon the brazen serpent, he lived (Fragment Targum).

V.　*The second death*

In the paraphrase of Deut 33:6 found in the Fragment Targum (Paris MS. 110) Moses prays: 'Let Reuben live in this world, and not die in the *second death*, in which death the wicked die in the world to come.'[10] This 'second death' is spoken of also in the Apocalypse (2:11; 20:6), but is found nowhere in Jewish literature outside the targums. Furthermore, there are positive indications that in at least one passage where he uses the term (20:14), John has passed from the biblical text to the targumic rendering of Is 65:15ff.[11]

VI.　*A kingdom of priests and a holy people*

According to Ex 19:4–6, on the third new moon after the Exodus of Israel from Egypt, after they had come to Mount Sinai, Moses at God's call went up to Mount Sinai and God addressed him from the mountain:

> You have seen what I did to the Egyptians, how I bore you on eagles' wings and brought you to myself. Now therefore, if you obey my voice and keep my covenant, you shall be my own possession among all peoples; for all the earth is mine, and you shall be to me a kingdom of priests [*mamleket koh^anim*] and a holy nation. These are the words which you shall speak to the children of Israel.

These verses do not belong to any of the classical sources of the Pentateuch. They are generally taken as redactional, intended to connect the narrative of Israel's arrival at Sinai with the covenant about to be made between Yahweh and his people. They are a summary of Israel's privileges. When the redactor did his work we cannot say; most likely in the sixth to fifth

10. See above, pp. 123f.
11. Cf. *The New Testament and the Palestinian Targum* . . ., pp. 123f.

century B.C., i.e. in the later stages of the formation of the Pentateuch.

The summary is dependent on earlier literature. The influence of Deuteronomy is particularly in evidence. Compare Ex 19:4 with Deut 4:34: 'Or has any god ever attempted to go and take a nation for himself from the midst of another nation, by trials, by signs, by wonders and by war, by a mighty hand and an outstretched arm . . .'; see also Deut 29:2. In the same verse we appear to have an echo of Deut 32:11: 'Like the eagle that stirs up its nest, that flutters over its young; spreading out its wings, catching them, bearing them on its pinions, the Lord alone did lead him . . .' The influence of Deuteronomy may be seen again in the reference to Israel's being a nation apart; cf. Deut 10:14–15. For Israel as a consecrated (or 'holy') nation, see Deut 7:6; 26:19.

The redactor is in the mainstream of biblical tradition for the greater part of his teaching. What, however, does he mean when he refers to Israel as a kingdom of priests (*mamleket koh^anîm*)? Does he merely mean that Israel is God's possession, God's kingdom, provided with a ministering priesthood? This of course Israel was. The emphasis in this case would be on the kingdom, rather than on the priesthood. Possession of a priesthood was not peculiar to Israel among ancient peoples.

The context seems to require a different sense. The priesthood referred to here can scarcely be that of the descendants of Aaron. As it is the entire people who are holy and a nation set apart, so too is it the entire people who are priests. 'Priests' of verse 6, then, bears a different meaning from what it does in verse 22.

In what this priesthood consists is a different matter. Clearly, the redactor does not deny the reality of the priesthood of the descendants of Aaron, nor are we to assume that he confuses the priesthood of the other Israelites with it. The priesthood of the Israelites arises from their consecration to God, from their being his own possession, chosen from among the nations, as the priests of the line of Aaron were chosen from among men (cf. Heb 5:1). More, perhaps, is intended. As the priests of Aaron were chosen from among men to make intercession for them, so is Israel a priesthood among the nations to bring to them God's message. As A. H. McNeile puts it:

They are not only a 'holy', separated people, and a people
that is a possession more valuable to God than all other
nations, but *they are a 'kingdom of priests'—an organized
community under the government of a King, every member of which
has a mediatorial office, to intercede for all other men, and to minister
to them in the things pertaining to God.* It is the only statement
in the book of the true mission of Israel.[12]

Such an understanding of the text is rendered more probable
when we recall that Trito-Isaiah (537–515 B.C.) says much the
same thing in Is 61:6. In the context the prophet speaks of his
mission to Israel and consoles her by reminding her of her role
to humanity. It is the continuation of the passage (61:1–4) in
which he declares that the Spirit of the Lord is upon him to
bring good tidings to the afflicted and to Zion. She shall be
supreme among the nations:

> Aliens shall stand and feed your flocks,
> foreigners shall be your ploughmen and vinedressers;
> but you shall be called priests of the Lord,
> men shall speak of you as the ministers of our God.

The nations shall be Zion's servants in material things, while
she devotes herself to the priestly function of mediating the
divine to them:

> Zion's unique status will be recognized; among the peoples
> of the world she will serve as *priests* just as the Aaronids did
> in Israel (cf. Ex 19:6; 1 Pet 2:9); she will perform the
> priestly functions of instruction and intercession (cf. 45:14–
> 15; 60:14; also 66:21).[13]

The idea of Is 61:6 is that the nations shall see Zion's glory and
acknowledge that her God is the only God (Is 45:14f). They
shall look on the Israelites as priests of the Lord and ministers
of God, and this Israel shall be to them in bringing them a
knowledge of God. Again, this priesthood cannot be confused
with that of the sons of Aaron. We are scarcely to presume that
the author of Trito-Isaiah believed all Israel would be priests

---

12. A. H. McNeile, *The Book of Exodus* (Westminster Commentaries, London, 1908),
p. cxxiii. Italics are mine.
13. James Muilenburg, 'Isaiah', in *Interpreter's Bible*, vol. 5, 1956, p. 712; on Is 61:6.

in the sense that all would function and offer sacrifice as the Levites and the sons of Aaron did. Is 66:21 appears to acknowledge this distinction between the universal priesthood of Israel and that of the official priesthood when it has God say of the converted nations: 'And some of them also I will take for priests and for Levites, says the Lord.'

Carroll Stuhmueller puts the idea well in his concise commentary on Is 61:4–6:

> In two strophes the prophet summarizes this message of glad tidings. The first (vv. 4–6) stresses the victory of humble faith; the second (vv. 7–9), the end of robbery. Both conclude with Israel's sharing her blessings with all nations. Every Israelite becomes a priestly minister of grace. Whoever observes the renewal of Israel will spontaneously confess: 'Here is God!' for God alone could have done that. Israel's priestly role widens as she wins others to the worship of God. Just as the prophetic role of all Israel never dispensed with individual prophets, likewise the priesthood of all men does not remove the separate order of priests. There must always be men totally dedicated to worship and to the apostolate, to keep the priestly, prophetic spirit alive in all hearts.[14]

Later Judaism

Israel in Trito-Isaiah could be described as a kingdom, priests and a holy nation. In fact, she is implicitly so described by the stress placed on the reign of God in Deutero-Isaiah. While it appears that the only possible rendering of *mamleket kohᵃnîm* of Ex 19:6 is 'a kingdom of priests', by the second century B.C. the expression was being understood as 'a kingdom and priests'. The privileges conferred on Israel at the Exodus, then, were three. By the covenant they were made 'a kingdom and priests and a holy nation'. The earliest witness of this tradition is found in the Ethiopic version of the Apocryphal *Book of Jubilees* 16:18, the original of which dates from 153–105 B.C.

In the context of Jubilees 16:18 angels explain how Abraham was blessed through Isaac, and how from the sons of Isaac one (i.e. Jacob) should become a holy seed:

---

14. *The Book of Isaiah. Chapters 40–66* (*Old Testament Reading Guide* No. 20; Collegeville: Liturgical Press, 1965), pp. 135–36.

For he should become the portion of the Most High, and all his seed had fallen into the possession of God, that it should be unto the Lord a people for [His] possession above all nations and that it should become *a kingdom, and priests and a holy nation* (16:18).

Thus the Ethiopic Version which R. H. Charles takes to represent the original Hebrew.[15] The Latin version of Jubilees has *regnum sacerdotale*—the text followed by Enno Littmann in Kautzsch's *Apokryphen und Pseudepigraphen*.[16] This, being the Vulgate rendering of *mamleket koh^{a}nîm* of Ex 19:6, Charles takes to be due to the Vulgate, not to the text of Jubilees.[17] In view of the evidence for the Jewish understanding of Ex 19:6 which we are now to consider, we wholeheartedly agree with R. H. Charles that the original reading of Jubilees 16:18 is that of the Ethiopic version.

2 Maccabees 2:18

At the conclusion of the second of the two letters prefixed to the Second Book of Maccabees (written in its present form in 124 B.C. or shortly afterwards), a final appeal is made to the Jews of Egypt to attend the feast of the Dedication of the Temple in Jerusalem:

Since therefore we are about to celebrate the purification, we write to you. Will you therefore please keep the days? It is God who has saved all his people, and has returned the inheritance to all, and *the kingship and the priesthood and the consecration* [*to basileion kai to hierateuma kai ton hagiasmon*], as he promised through the Law. For we have hope in God that he will soon have mercy upon us and gather us from everywhere under heaven into his holy place, for he has rescued us from great evils and has purified the place (2 Mac 2:16–18).

The passage in the Law referred to is evidently Ex 19:6: 'Now therefore, if you obey my voice and keep my covenant, you shall be my own possession among all peoples; for all the

15. *The Apocrypha and Pseudepigrapha of the Old Testament*, vol. II, p. 38.
16. Vol. II, p. 69.
17. *Loc. cit.*

earth is mine, and *you shall be to me a kingdom of priests and a holy nation*' (Ex 19:5–6, Masoretic text).

The rededication of the Temple was for the author of 2 Maccabees proof that God was being faithful to his promises. Only with the ingathering of the exiles, however, would the promise made to Moses be really fulfilled.

Unlike the accepted understanding of the Masoretic text, the tradition on which the author of 2 Maccabees depends sees three distinct privileges conferred on Israel at Sinai. They are a kingdom *and* a priesthood *and* a holy nation. In this the work is at one with the Book of Jubilees.

Philo's reading of Ex 19:6

Twice Philo cites Ex 19:6 in Greek and on each occasion sees two distinct privileges in the 'kingdom' and 'priesthood'. In *De Abrahamo* 56 he cites it as 'a kingdom [or 'a royal house'] and a priesthood and a holy nation' (*basileion kai hierateuma kai ethnos hagion*). In *De Sobrietate* 66 he speaks of *basileion kai hierateuma Theou* ['*basileion* and priesthood of God'] and goes on to explain *basileion* as 'the king's house'. He, too, evidently saw three privileges, not two, conferred on Israel in Ex 19:6.

The Septuagint rendering

As is well known, the Septuagint translators rendered the relevant passage of Ex 19:6 as *basileion hierateuma kai ethnos hagion*, a text reproduced verbatim in 1 Pet 2:9. This Greek is generally understood to mean 'a royal priesthood and a holy nation'. *Basileion* is taken to be a neuter adjective, not a substantive. The prerogatives of Israel would then be two, not three.

The question immediately arises whether the author of 2 Mac 2:17 and Philo knew of a Greek translation different from our present Septuagint text or whether they took *basileion* of our present Septuagint text as a substantive and understood the passage to speak of three privileges. A further question that arises is the original meaning of the Septuagint Ex 19:6.

That *basileion* can be used as a substantive is quite clear. It is found occasionally in the singular but more commonly in the plural in profane Greek in the sense of 'kingly dwelling', 'palace'. It is also found with the meaning of 'seat of empire', 'capital', and that of 'tiara', 'diadem'.[18] In the Septuagint it is also used in the sense of 'sovereignty' or 'kingship' (1 Kgs 14:8; 1 Chr 28:4; Dan 4:32; 7:22 and, of course, 2 Mac 2:17). To these texts, noted by F. J. A. Hort[19] and E. G. Selwyn,[20] we could add the 'Septuagint' rendering of Dan 5:30 ('and the *basileion* was taken from the Chaldaeans and given to the Medes [6:1] and Artaxerxes of the Medes received the kingdom—*ten basileian*'). This text shows that *basileion* and *basileia* could be almost interchangeable terms. In the Fathers and occasionally in Plutarch, *basileion* also denotes kingship.[21]

In view of the evidence from 2 Maccabees and Philo, such eminent scholars as F. J. A. Hort,[22] H. B. Swete[23] and E. F. Selwyn[24] believe that *basileion hierateuma* of Septuagint Ex 19:6 is to be understood as two substantives: 'a royalty, a priesthood', and not as 'a royal priesthood'. This, too, is the view of A. H. McNeile in his commentary on Exodus.[25]

The Aramaic renderings

All the Aramaic renderings of Ex 19:6 see three distinct privileges conferred on Israel at Sinai. The Palestinian Targum as found in Codex Neofiti, the Fragment Targum and in MS. F of the Cairo Geniza, render: 'You shall be to my name *kings and priests* [*mlkyn wkhnyn*] and a holy nation.' The Targum of Pseudo-Jonathan translates: 'You shall be before me *kings* bearing the crown *and ministering priests* and a holy people.' The Targum of Onkelos has: 'You shall be before me *kings and priests* and a holy people.' The Syriac Peshitta rendering is in the same tradition: 'You shall be to me a *kingdom and priests* (*mlkwt' wkhn'*) and a holy people.' What connection the Peshitta Pentateuch has with the Aramaic targums is a matter of debate.[26] In the present instance the Peshitta may well depend on Apoc 1:6; 5:10 rather than on the targums.

18. Liddel-Scott-Jones, *A Greek-English Lexicon*, new, ninth ed. (Oxford: Clarendon Press, 1940), p. 309.
19. *The First Epistle of St. Peter I.1–II.17* (London 1898), p. 125.
20. *The First Epistle of St. Peter* (London, 1955), p. 165.
21. Cf. Hort, *loc. cit.*, and Selwyn, *op. cit.*, p. 166.
22. *Loc. cit.*
23. *The Apocalypse of St. John* (2nd ed., London, 1907), p. 8.
24. *Op. cit.*, p. 165: 'That this is so is rendered almost certain by 2 Mac 2:17.'
25. *The Book of Exodus*, p. 111.
26. For views and bibliography on this point, see M. McNamara, *The New Testament and the Palestinian Targum . . .*, p. 51, note 34; above, pp. 66–68.

To sum up the evidence: in the Old Testament and in later Judaism there was the belief that at the covenant at Sinai God made the entire people of Israel a kingdom, a priesthood and a holy nation. This priesthood did not mean merely that the nation was provided with priests. The entire nation was a priesthood in virtue of its election by God from among all the nations of the earth.

How this universal priesthood of all Israel was related to the ministering priesthood of the sons of Aaron was a matter that did not exercise the Jewish mind. In no sense did it exclude this other priesthood nor was the Aaronid priesthood found incompatible with it.

The privileges bestowed on Israel at the Covenant (Ex 19:6) are connected in 2 Mac 2:18 with the fulfilment of the promises, a fulfilment to be brought about by the ingathering of the exiles and the reconstitution of the True Israel.

The New Testament evidence

In view of the fact that the early Church considered itself the true Israel, the new people of God, the New Covenant in the Blood of Christ, one is not surprised to see it consider the privileges of the Israel of old transferred to itself. The New Testament gives us ample evidence of the thorough fashion in which it did this. Among other things it saw itself as the People of God described in Ex 19:6.

The Apocalypse

The Apocalypse refers to our text on two occasions. In his opening address to the seven churches the author writes (1:5-6): 'To him who loves us and has freed us from our sins by his blood, *and made us a kingdom, priests* [*basileian hiereis*] to his God and Father, to him be glory and dominion for ever and ever. Amen.' As Israel was spared through the blood of the paschal lamb, was redeemed from Egypt and made a kingdom and a priesthood at the covenant of Sinai, so now by the redemption in the blood of Christ Christians are made a kingdom, priests to God. They are his new chosen people. This kingdom and priests they are already here on earth.

The second reference in the Apocalypse to Ex 19:6 is found in the hymn in praise of the redemption sung by the four living creatures and the twenty-four elders:

> Worthy art thou to take the scroll and to open its seals, for thou wast slain and by thy blood didst ransom men for God from every tribe and tongue and people and nation, and hast made them a kingdom and priests [*basileian kai hiereis*] to our God and they [shall] reign on earth (5:9f).

Whether the proper rendering is 'they shall reign' (*basileusousin*) or 'they reign' (*basileousin*) is uncertain. If the future tense is intended, the text probably refers to the millennium and those who participate in the first resurrection. 'Over such, the second death shall have no power, but they shall be priests of Christ and shall reign with him a thousand years' (Apoc 20:5). In any event, Christians already on earth are a kingdom and priests. They shall be more fully so after the resurrection.

In these texts John is dependent on the tradition which sees in Ex 19:6 three privileges conferred on Israel. The exact words he employs ('kingdom [and] priests') are those of the Peshitta. This, however, as we have said, may be dependent on John. His expression 'a kingdom and priests' is a combination of the Septuagint rendering and that of the targums—'kingdom' being attested in the former and 'priests' in the latter.

I Peter 2:9[27]

As is well known, 1 Pet 2:9f reproduces the exact words of the Septuagint rendering of Ex 19:6:

> But you are a chosen race, *a royal priesthood, a holy nation* [*basileion hierateuma ethnos hagion*], God's own people, that you may declare the wonderful deeds of him who called you out of darkness into his marvellous light. Once you were no people, but now you are God's people; once you had not God's mercy but now you have received mercy.

A preliminary question to be considered here is whether in

27. See J. Coppens, 'Le sacerdoce royal des fidèles. Un commentaire de la 1 Petr. II, 4–10' in *Au service de la Parole de Dieu. Mélanges offerts à Mgr André-Marie Charue* (Gambloux: Editions J. Duculot, 1969), pp. 61–75.

view of the meaning of the Septuagint Ex 19:6 we should take *basileion* as a substantive or an adjective; whether, in other words, we should render 1 Pet 2:9 as 'a kingdom (or 'royalty'), a priesthood and a holy nation', or (as all translations do) as 'a royal priesthood and a holy nation'. After a careful consideration of the evidence for the understanding of Ex 19:6 in the Septuagint and other sources and granting that the Septuagint translators apparently meant *basileion* as a substantive, Hort believes that the author of 1 Peter intended it as an adjective. This conclusion he draws from the careful parallelism of the four clauses of the passage.[28] There is force in this argument. Selwyn, on the other hand, believes that *basileion* in 1 Peter, as in the Septuagint text, is intended as a substantive.[29] He puts a comma between it and *hierateuma* and understands it as 'a king's house'. By the term the author would then have meant the same thing as the 'spiritual house' mentioned in verse 5. Selwyn strengthens his position by noting that as the author of 1 Peter in 2:4 anticipates and interprets certain words in the Old Testament passages which he will quote in verses 6–7, so he appears to be doing in verse 5 in relation to Old Testament passages to be quoted in verses 9 and 10.[30]

Whatever of the exact understanding of *basileion* and of Dr. Selwyn's view, verses 5 and 9 must be taken in conjunction in a consideration of 1 Peter's teaching on the priesthood of all Christians. In the former texts he tells his readers to draw near to Christ, the living stone, 'and like living stones be yourselves built into a spiritual house, to be *a holy priesthood*, to offer spiritual sacrifices acceptable to God through Jesus Christ'.

Verse 9 clearly recalls the Exodus in which, according to the words of the Jewish hymn conserved in the Mishnah tractate *Pesaḥim* (10:5)[31] God wrought wonders 'for our fathers and for us. He brought us out from bondage to freedom, from sorrow to gladness . . . and from gladness to great light.' By the new exodus of salvation Christians are now a chosen people, a royal priesthood. They proclaim God's greatness by the virtuous life of which the passage following on 2:9f speaks.

28. *Op. cit.*, p. 125.
29. *Op. cit.*, p. 166.
30. *Ibid.*, p. 280.
31. In Danby's translation, p. 151.

Christians as a royal priesthood (2:9), a holy priesthood (2:4) must offer spiritual sacrifices acceptable to God. These spiritual sacrifices are spoken of at length by St. Paul in Rom ch. 12:

> I appeal to you, therefore, brethren, by the mercies of God, to present your bodies as a *living sacrifice, holy and acceptable to God, which is your spiritual worship.* Do not be conformed to this world but be transformed by the renewal of your mind, that you may prove what is the will of God, what is acceptable and perfect.

In other words it consists in having the mind of Christ in oneself and practising one's faith in charity according to the gifts received from God, as the continuation of the chapter goes on to show. See also Eph 5:1f; Phil 4:18; Heb 13:15.[32] For the author of 1 Peter this means the imitation of Christ (2:21ff; 3:18ff) and the practice of brotherly love (1:13ff). Whether the author of 1 Peter included the Eucharist in this spiritual worship is debated.[33]

The priesthood of the faithful and the hierarchical priesthood

The universal priesthood of Israel in the Old Testament originated on the analogy of the priesthood of the children of Aaron. These were consecrated and set aside to be mediators between God and men. So too by the covenant had Israel been consecrated and set apart from among the nations, as a people to proclaim God's great deeds to the Gentiles. This universal priesthood was in no wise incompatible with that of the house of Aaron, nor did it render it unnecessary. The object of each was different.

The New Testament teaching on the universal priesthood of believers is based on the teaching of the Old Testament and of later Judaism. It applies to Christians what these predicated of Israel. The basis of this New Testament priesthood is the New Covenant in the blood of Christ. The blood of the Lamb has redeemed Christians and made them a kingdom and priests to his God and Father. It in no wise dispenses with the hierarchical priesthood nor is it in any way incompatible with it.

---

32. See further, Selwyn, *op. cit.*, pp. 294ff.
33. See Selwyn, *op. cit.*, pp. 294–98.

The objects of both are different; both however, come from the same source and tend towards the same goal. The object of the one is to perform sacred acts in the name of, and for the benefit of, the Christian community. The spiritual sacrifices offered by the other is the testimony of a good life in imitation of Christ. Both are founded on the New Covenant and serve the people of God (cf. Vatican ii, *Lumen Gentium* §10). Further specification of the relation of the ministerial priesthood and the priesthood of the faithful appertains to dogmatic theology.

16

Other Passages

I. The New Testament

What we have given in the preceding chapters are but a few of the many ways in which the Palestinian Targum to the Pentateuch throws light on the New Testament. In this concluding chapter we give a few further examples.

Gustav Dalman maintained that the phrase 'answered and said', found so frequently in the Gospels, was due to the Greek authors of our canonical Gospels who in this were dependent on the translation Greek of the Septuagint.[1] Taking Onkelos and some other texts as his criterion for the Aramaic of Christ's day, and ignoring or rejecting the evidence of the Palestinian Targum to the Pentateuch, he concluded that the phrase did not exist in the Aramaic of first-century Palestine. 'Answered and said' is of very frequent occurrence in the Palestinian paraphrases to the Pentateuch, *especially in free paraphrase and midrashic passages where no influence from the Hebrew text can be suspected.*

'He (etc.) opened his mouth and said' is another good idiom of the same paraphrase. So are such other New Testament expressions as 'he thought in his heart and said' (e.g. Gen 15:1); 'he kept these things in his heart'.

In the Gospels we read of great multitudes (*ochlos polys, ochloi polloi*) following Christ. The Greek word *ochlos* has passed over into Aramaic as a loan-word and is encountered occasionally in the Palestinian Targum to the Pentateuch and in other targums also. God says to Cain that the blood of the just multitudes (*'ôchlôsîn*) that were to arise from Abel was crying out against him from the earth (Gen 4:10). God tells Moses to keep the people away from Mount Sinai lest his anger

---

1. *The Words of Jesus*, pp. 24f.

be enkindled against them and numerous multitudes (*'ôchlôsîn sagyan*) of them should fall (Ex 19:21).

We often read in the Gospels of things happening 'at that hour'. This is the manner in which 'at that time' (cf. Irish: *an uair sin*) is expressed in Palestinian Aramaic. It is the invariable targumic rendering of 'at that time' of the Hebrew text.

R. Le Déaut has shown the significance of the expression 'to taste the cup of death' (a phrase found only in the Palestinian Targum to the Pentateuch) for Christ's reference to his passion.[2] In the Palestinian Targum on Gen 49:25 we find the very words used by the Palestinian woman when addressing Christ, but in reverse order: 'Blessed are the breasts from which you have sucked and the womb in which you lay', i.e. the womb that bore you.[3] Finally, in this connection we may remark that in the Palestinian Targum, particularly in Neofiti, *bar nash*, *bar nasha*—'a son of man', 'the son of man'— is very often found in the sense of 'man', 'anyone', 'whoever'. It is evidence to be borne in mind in any discussion of the New Testament Son of Man problem.[4]

Into the extremely difficult question of the bearing of the Aramaic of the Palestinian Targum on the Aramaic substratum of the New Testament we have not entered. That such an Aramaic substratum has to be reckoned with, at least as far as the Gospels and parts of the Acts of the Apostles are concerned, seems clear. Aramaic was most probably, if not certainly, the

2. *Biblica* 43 (1962) 82–86.
3. Cf. *The New Testament and the Palestinian Targum . . .*, pp. 131–33.
4. The use of *bar nash(a)* in Aramaic (in both targums and midrashim) has been treated of extensively by G. Vermes in an appendix to the third edition of Matthew Black's *An Aramaic Approach to the Gospels and Acts* (Oxford, 1967), pp. 310–28. From the evidence for the use of the expression in extra-targumic texts he concludes that, like the other Aramaic expression *hahû gabra* (literally: 'that man'; cf. English 'yours truly') *bar nash(a)* is also used as a circumlocution for the first person singular pronoun: 'I' (pp. 320–27). M. Black considers the evidence put forward by Vermes for the use of *barnash* as a surrogate for the first person pronoun clear and convincing (p. 328). J. Fitzmyer (*Catholic Biblical Quarterly* 30 [1968] 427f) admits that some of the examples Vermes cites in evidence for *bar nash(a)* used as a circumlocution for 'I' seem convincing, but naturally objects to the use of 'later' Aramaic in this discussion of New Testament texts (*ibid.*, pp. 426f). See also R. Le Déaut's detailed discussion in *Biblica* 49 (1968) 397–99. Here we may note that there is basic agreement in Fitzmyer's and Le Déaut's criticism of the third edition of Black's *Aramaic Approach*, apart from the use of targumic material in New Testament studies, of course.

language used at least normally by Christ. It was also that of his first listeners and followers. His words were transmitted in Aramaic for some time within the Aramaic period of the nascent Church. The first stage in the formation of the gospel tradition can, then, be presumed to have been Aramaic. That this early stage of the tradition should show through in our present Greek texts of the Gospels and Acts is to be expected. We must further recall that other writers of the New Testament, even when using the Greek language, were in mental make-up Semites, with Aramaic or Hebrew as their mother tongue. It is but natural to expect that their Semitic thought-patterns should occasionally show through the Greek they use. It has for long been the preoccupation of certain scholars of Aramaic and Hebrew to determine the Aramaic or Hebrew equivalents, or originals, of New Testament expressions, to reproduce the sayings of Christ in their 'original' Aramaic form, to determine the influence of one or other of these languages on the grammar of the New Testament.

The quest for the Aramaic substratum is altogether praise-worthy. The determination of it is, however, an extremely delicate task, and in a consideration of the problem the entire formation of the gospel tradition must be borne in mind. First we have the life and teaching of Jesus. Then we must consider how these words and deeds of Christ were transmitted in the early Church, in both its initial Aramaic and later Greek phases. It was not merely a question of passing on the record of the words and works of Christ unchanged from generation to generation. The early Church was very much a living community animated by the teaching and example of Christ. There was, in other words, an intensive evolution of doctrine during the nascent period of the Christian Church, in both its Aramaic and Greek phases. This means that not everything in the Gospels need represent an Aramaic (or Hebrew) original.

The period of which we have just spoken is studied by the science of Form Criticism. Redaction Criticism has made us aware that the authors of the Gospels as we now have them have impressed their own personalities on the tradition in consigning it to writing. All this means that in our quest for the Aramaic substratum we must ask ourselves whether a given expression is due to an Aramaic background, to the language spoken by Christ or the early Christians, or whether it really is occasioned by the theological viewpoint of the evangelist, or of the theological tradition on which he depends. To give an example of this difficulty: elsewhere[5] the present writer has put forward the view that behind the Greek word *hypsôthênai* ('to be lifted up', 'exalted') of John 12:32–34 (see also John 3:14; 8:28) there lies the Aramaic word *'istallaq, 'ist^elaq*, which literally means 'to be lifted up', then 'to depart', 'to die'. The ambiguities, or polyvalence, would then be there in the (presumed) Aramaic original as well as in the Greek word used to render the Aramaic. The Aramaic word, I argued, is more apt than the Greek, because it has a direct connotation of death, absent from the Greek. In John, however, one has to reckon not merely with the possibility of translation from Aramaic. There is also the problem of johannine theology, which makes it quite possible that the use of *hypsôthênai* is due not to any Aramaic background or substratum, but solely to the author's intention of presenting Christ's death as his glorification or exaltation, or at least as one component part of this exaltation.

While conscious of problems such as this, there still remain many passages where an Aramaic substratum can be presumed. But in seeking the Aramaic behind a given Greek text of the New Testament we must still reckon with the nature of New Testament Greek, i.e. the *Koinè* or common Greek, which itself had already undergone a certain Semitic influence, or at least presents peculiarities found also in the Semitic languages. What this adds up to is that what at first sight might look like a Semitism (i.e. a peculiarity of a Semitic language, such as Hebrew and Aramaic), may really be normal in *Koinè* Greek.

When *Koinè* influence is ruled out, there remains the task of determining what is specifically an Aramaism (i.e., a peculiarity of Aramaic) and what is a Hebraism. Being Semitic languages, they have very many features in common. And more so as regards the forms of these languages as spoken in Palestine, where, apart from their family relationship, each

5. *The New Testament and the Palestinian Targum* . . ., pp. 145–49; 'The Ascension and the Exaltation of Christ in the Fourth Gospel' in *Scripture* 19 (1967) 65–73; above p. 130.

language had to a certain extent contaminated the other. This difficulty leads a number of scholars to speak of Semitisms in the New Testament, rather than deal with a specific Hebrew or Aramaic influence.[6]

Now we come to the final difficulty in this field. When we speak of an Aramaic substratum, what form of Aramaic can we legitimately take as representing the language of first-century Palestine? J. Fitzmyer, as we have seen, says it must be Aramaic which is clearly of the first century, i.e. the Aramaic of Qumrân and of first-century inscriptions. The Aramaic found in the Palestinian Targum(s) he considers to be a later development.[7] While recognizing the great importance of Qumrân Aramaic, we should be conscious of its limitations in our particular field.

To begin with, Qumrân Aramaic must be looked on as literary Aramaic. We cannot without further ado take it to represent the spoken language of the people. We have evidence of a difference between the literary mishnaic Hebrew of the Qumrân scribes and the spoken Mishnaic of the same period.[8] There is every likelihood that the same holds true for Aramaic. But even if the Aramaic of Qumrân were shown to be practically the same as the spoken language, there remains the further difficulty that literary texts reveal the trained, learned mind. The syntax and manner of expression of the learned differ from those of the common people. It is much more likely that from this point of view the Palestinian Targum is much closer to the language of the common people in New Testament times than are the Aramaic texts from Qumrân. In this aspect, it is of less importance whether the spoken language of Palestine in Christ's day was typically of the Palestinian form found in the Palestinian Targum or not. The probabilities are that the language used by Christ and by the Aramaic-speaking nascent Church was the language of the common people rather than that of the learned. From this it would seem to follow that the Palestinian Targum retains its importance in the study of the

---

6. Cf. the title of K. Beyer's important work, *Semitische Syntax im Neuen Testament*, Band I, Satzlehre, Teil I (Göttingen: Vandenhoeck & Ruprecht, 2nd revised edition, 1968).

7. See above, p. 14.

8. See above, p. 60.

Aramaic substratum of the Gospels, the Acts and other writings of the New Testament.

II. Jewish Christianity

Targumic studies are not without relevance for a study of Jewish Christianity, to which our attention has been drawn in recent years, particularly by the researches of Jean Daniélou and H. J. Schoeps.[9] In his work *Théologie du Judéo-Christianisme*[10] Daniélou devotes a chapter to 'Judaeo-Christian Exegesis' in which he treats of 'Judaeo-Christian targumim' and 'Christian midrashim'. Here he occasionally attributes too. great a creative activity to the authors he studies, believing their paraphrases come from the Judaeo-Christian communities in an effort to christianize the text of the Old Testament. Targumic and other Jewish evidence shows that at times the 'Christian' element in the paraphrase is minimal, at other times nil.

Thus, for instance, Num 21:8–9 cited in *The Epistle of Barnabas* (12,7) as: '[Moses has said]: When one of you shall be bitten, if he turns towards the serpent placed upon the wood [*xylon*] and hopes, believing that although without life, this [serpent] can give life, he will be cured.'[11] With this we should compare the targumic rendering of Numbers already cited. The only typical Christian addition is the reference to the tree.

Barnabas (12,9) cites Ex 17:14 as follows: 'Moses said to Jesus, son of Nave: Write this which the Lord has said: The son of God will exterminate the house of Amalek to the very root in the last days.' This Daniélou takes as 'a resumé which christianizes the text'.[12] Actually it is a resumé rather of the text of Pseudo-Jonathan on Ex 17:14,16:

> And the Lord said to Moses: Write this memorial in the book of the ancients of yore and place these words in the hearing of Joshua because I shall utterly destroy the memory

---

9. *Theologie und Geschichte des Judenchristentums*, 1949; *Das Judenchristentum* (Berne: Francke, 1964).
10. *The Theology of Jewish Christianity* (London: Darton, Longman & Todd, 1964); original title, and that followed here: *Théologie du Judéo-Christianisme* (Tournai: Desclée, 1958).
11. *Théologie* . . ., p. 106.
12. *Théologie* . . ., p. 111.

of Amalek from under the heavens . . . And he said: Because the Word [*Memra*] of the Lord has sworn by the Throne of his Glory that he in his Word [*Memra*] will wage war on those of the house of Amalek and blot them out for three generations, from the generation of this world, and from the generation of the Messiah and from the generation of the world to come.

The only Christian addition, if addition it be, is the reference to the Son of God. But even this may be merely a christianization of the *Memra* of the targumic text.

In 7,3 *Barnabas* cites Lev 23:29 as: 'The commandment has been given: He who does not observe [literally: 'fast'] the fast shall be punished by death.'[13] In the biblical text, both HT and Septuagint, however, there is question of 'humiliation', not fasting ('For whoever is not afflicted on this same day shall be cut off from his people'). In Neofiti (and in Pseudo-Jonathan but not in Onkelos) this becomes: 'For whoever eats on the *fast*, and does not fast at the time of the fast of the atonement, shall be blotted out from the midst of the people.'

We may note in passing that G. A. Allon[14] has found quite a resemblance between the halakah of *Barnabas* and that of Pseudo-Jonathan. Research in this field will benefit both Jewish-Christian and targumic studies, showing how deeply rooted Jewish Christianity was in the traditions of its people and how old targumic traditions are.

R. Le Déaut has given an indication of how targumic studies may benefit liturgical research by showing that in the Targum to Gen 14:18 Melchisedech is designated a 'high priest', as he is in the Canon of the Mass.[15] The biblical text merely calls him a priest of the Most High God.

The work that has been done on the Palestinian Targum to the Pentateuch over the past decades shows that here we have a vein as yet ill-explored which can enrich many branches of study, particularly that of the New Testament.

13. *Théologie* . . ., p. 113.
14. 'The Halacha in "Barnabae epistula"' in *Tarbiz* 11 (1939–40) 23–38; 'A Note to "The Halacha in *Barnabae epistula*"', *ibid.*, p. 223; both in Hebrew.
15. *Recherches de science religieuse* 50 (1962) 222–29. In the new English translation of the Canon of the Mass, however, Melchisedech is called simply a priest, no longer a high priest.

Conclusion

We come now to cast a glance backwards on the material we have considered in the course of this work. We have seen something of the development that went on over the period covered by the writings of the Old Testament and even later. One of the manifestations of this later development is the tradition enshrined in the Palestinian Targum to the Pentateuch, which tradition we consider to have been basically formed by the time of Christ.

The targumic tradition was a sacred tradition, originating in the liturgy. The Palestinian Targum, being recited every Sabbath in the synagogues, would have been well known to Christ and his Apostles, as well as to the Jewish converts to Christianity. That Christ should have made use of the religious traditions of his people when addressing his message to them is altogether natural. He came not to destroy the Law but to fulfil it, to bring it to perfection. The task which he completed was being prepared right through the Old Testament period. This preparation included the progress in the understanding of revelation found in the targumic paraphrases. Jesus was a Jew of the Jews. His language and mental make-up were theirs. It is, then, not surprising that the manner in which he, and later the Apostles, presented the gospel to the Jews was that already known to them.

Form Criticism sets itself the task of studying the formation of the gospel tradition during the period prior to the writing of the Gospels, a period in which the gospel message was, in the main, transmitted orally. This new science seeks to find the life situation, the *Sitz im Leben*, of each particular literary form of the Gospel narrative. In the light of this life situation within the Church, the *Sitz im Leben Ecclesiae*, Form Criticism sets itself the task of determining the origin and development of each particular literary form. One may legitimately ask whether this is too narrow a perspective. The early Church lived within a Jewish milieu. Surely the formation of the Gospel tradition must have been influenced by the tradition of Judaism. The Christians of the nascent period of the Church in Palestine were, after all, Jews. A knowledge of the targumic tradition, then, may well benefit Form Criticism in its studies of the Gospels.

The synoptic problem is well known to students of the New Testament. It arises from the fact that by and large the first three evangelists—Matthew, Mark and Luke—record the same episodes, the same miracles, the same parables, the same discussions and the same major events of the life of Jesus. A comparison with the Fourth Gospel shows how much the first three evangelists have in common. Yet despite this similarity, there are also very evident differences in the manner in which they report the words of Christ and episodes from his life. How explain this unity in diversity and diversity in unity? Perhaps the synoptic problem of the Palestinian Targum to the Pentateuch has something to contribute. For in this targum we do have a synoptic problem. No two texts of this targum in different manuscripts are altogether the same. There never was, it would appear, a fixed text. What we have is a fixed tradition of exegesis, found in basically identical fashion in the texts of Neofiti, Pseudo-Jonathan, the Fragment Targum and the Geniza fragments. Yet within this tradition there are differences in the manner in which it is expressed. We can presume that already in New Testament times this variety existed. Could not this variety within Judaism have influenced the formation of the gospel tradition, allowing various regions to formulate the basic Christian tradition in slightly divergent ways?

Redaction Criticism studies the editorial work of the evangelists. It seeks to determine how each of the evangelists moulded the tradition and set it forth in accord with his own theological viewpoint. It is not always easy to determine whether differences between the synoptics are due to the evangelist or to the tradition on which he depends, and redaction critics tend to attribute too great a creative activity to the evangelists, to consider them outside their tradition. Targumic studies may be of help here. From what we have already said we see that apart from an individual text there was the larger Jewish tradition permitting a given concept to be expressed in a number of ways. For instance, God, when communicating with his people, could be referred to as *Dibbêra* ('the Word'), 'the Holy Spirit', 'the Spirit', the 'Voice from heaven' (*Bath Qôl*). One Jewish text chooses one of these words, another text uses another. The same holds true for 'Father in heaven'. There does not appear to have been any hard and fast rule for the use of these terms. Were a student of the targums to seek to determine which of these expressions, when variants occur, is 'original' in the Palestinian Targum, he would very probably be setting himself an impossible task.

Might not the same be true for the New Testament? Some scholars are unduly preoccupied with determining the exact words used by Christ—the *ipsissima verba Jesu*. Are such expressions as 'the Father in Heaven', 'this world—the world to come', 'the Son of Man', the *ipsissima verba Jesu* or are they due to the activity of the early Church? Why does the New Testament show such lack of concern for the exact form of Christ's words? For the early Christians there probably was no problem. The evidence of the Palestinian Targum, and of rabbinic Judaism, seems to indicate that it was a matter of indifference whether one used one or other of the synonyms to which we have referred above. When viewed in the light of its origins within Judaism, we more readily understand the manner in which the words of Jesus are transmitted in the Gospels.

It would be a mistake to attempt to explain everything in the New Testament through the targums. Pan-Targumism is no more a solution than Pan-Babylonianism, Pan-Hellenism or any of the many other '*Pan's*' which at one time or another have been put forward as explanations of the New Testament. The evidence seems to indicate, however, that in the Palestinian Targum to the Pentateuch we have a very ancient paraphrase which has not yet yielded up all its secrets. It is a rich corpus to which students of the New Testament can turn with profit.

APPENDIX:

Introduction to all Extant Targums

With the exception of Ezra-Nehemiah and Daniel, targums to all books of the Hebrew Bible are known to exist. These targums differ quite a bit among themselves. From the point of view of language they fall into two groups: the Babylonian and the Palestinian. The latter are composed in Palestinian Aramaic while the former are in what is now often referred to as scholastic Aramaic. The Babylonian Targum (i.e. Onkelos to the Pentateuch and Jonathan to the Prophets) was edited in the Jewish academies of Babylon, and came to the West towards the end of the first millennium. All the other targums originated at various times in western Jewry. Since each group of targums presents us with its own peculiar problems, we shall now treat of each separately, concentrating mainly, however, on the targums to the Pentateuch. For the other targums the reader is referred to the classic introductions, the most complete and most recent of which is R. Le Déaut's *Introduction à la littérature targumique*, Rome, 1966.

17

Targums to the Pentateuch

To the Pentateuch we possess the Targum of Onkelos and the Palestinian Targum, this latter preserved in the texts of Pseudo-Jonathan, the Fragment Targum, the Cairo Geniza fragments, and in Codex Neofiti 1. All these require separate treatment. We have already treated of the Syriac Peshitta, written in Oriental Aramaic, which is in some way related to the Palestinian Targum.

I. The Targum of Onkelos

This targum covers the entire Pentateuch. Its connection with the person of Onkelos is due to a text (*Meg.* 3a) of the Babylonian Talmud:

> R. Jeremiah, or as some say, R. Hiyya bar Abba, said: 'The Targum to the Torah, Onkelos the Proselyte composed [literally: 'said'] it from the mouths of R. Eliezer and R. Joshua. The Targum to the Prophets, Jonathan ben Uzziel composed it from the mouths of Haggai, Zechariah and Malachi.'

R. Jeremiah was a disciple of R. Hiyya bar Abba (*ca.* A.D. 320). R. Eliezer and R. Joshua lived about A.D. 120. If this tradition were correct the Targum of Onkelos would have been composed sometime in the early second century A.D. A difficulty with the tradition is that while Onkelos the Proselyte is mentioned a number of times in the Tosephta and in the Babylonian Talmud, nowhere, apart from the text given above, is a translation of the Scriptures associated with his name. A parallel text from the Palestinian Talmud (*Meg.* 1,9,71c) throws light on that of the Babylonian. The text from the Palestinian Talmud reads:

R. Jeremiah, in the name of R. Hiyya bar Ba [i.e. bar Abba] [said]: '*Akylos the Proselyte* translated the Torah before [i.e. in the presence of] R. Eliezer and before R. Joshua, and they praised him.'

The person mentioned here is Aquilas the Proselyte, whose Greek rendering is well known. The translation of which the text of the Palestinian Talmud speaks must, then, be the Greek one of Aquilas, not an Aramaic targum. What has happened, apparently, is that the passage of the Babylonian Talmud mentioning Onkelos is interpolated from the Palestinian. 'Onkelos' of that text is merely a Hebrew form of the Greek Aquilas and the rendering attributed to Onkelos is a Greek version, not an Aramaic targum. In like manner, 'Jonathan' of the text of the Babylonian Talmud is merely a Hebrew form of the Greek name Theodotion, the other noted translator of the Bible into Greek. This understanding of the talmudic texts is now becoming generally accepted.[1]

It follows that we have no tradition on the rendering associated with Onkelos. The place of origin of this targum seems to have been Palestine. This commonly accepted view was challenged in 1902 by Hommel and in more recent times by Paul Kahle.[2] Both of these scholars believed that Onkelos was composed in Babylon, not in Palestine. Kahle's chief argument is that Onkelos is nowhere cited in Palestinian sources during the mishnaic or talmudic period. It makes its presence felt only at a later date, together with other products of Babylonian Judaism.

The traditional view on the origin of Onkelos has been championed against Kahle by E. Y. Kutscher[3] and P. Wernberg-Møller[4] and, it would appear, justly. Babylonian Jewry, which took its traditions fundamentally from Palestine,

---

1. See P. Kahle, *The Cairo Geniza*, 2nd ed. (Oxford: Blackwells, 1959), pp. 191f; D. Barthélemy, *Les devanciers d'Aquila* (*Vetus Testamentum, Supplement*, vol. 10, Leiden, 1963, pp. 152f; 148ff).
2. *Op. cit.*, pp. 194f.
3. *Scripta Hierosolymitana*, vol. 4 (Jerusalem, 1958), pp. 9ff.
4. *Studia Theologica* 15 (1961) 126–82, esp. 178ff; *Journal of Semitic Studies* 7 (1962) 253–66.

can be expected to have also got its targum from there.[5] Together with this, Onkelos seems to bear a relation to the Palestinian Targum. W. Bacher, in the early part of the century, noted that the paraphrase of Onkelos appears to be a curtailed form of an earlier and longer one, one still found in its entirety in the Palestinian Targum.[6] As instances he gives Gen 4:7,10; 49:3,22; Ex 14:15; Num 24:4 and Deut 29:17.

Whatever of its place of origin, Onkelos is justly called 'the Babylonian Targum', being that cited by the Babylonian Talmud as the official rendering for Babylonian Judaism, and called there 'our targum'. It was edited in the Jewish academies of Babylonia and, being an official text, its rendering was made to reflect the official teaching of Babylonian Judaism. P. Kahle thus describes it: 'It has a fixed text; it is an authorized version. It existed in two editions which show slight variations and were connected respectively with the Jewish academies of Sura and Nehardea in Babylonia; with these academies were also connected distinctive readings in Babylonian biblical MSS.'[7]

Onkelos in general is a rather literal rendering of the Hebrew text with, however, occasional paraphrase, and indications of curtailed paraphrase. Paraphrase is most noticeable in the poetic sections. We have already remarked how Onkelos has been seen to be related to the Palestinian Targum to the Pentateuch. Points of contact between the two are in fact innumerable,[8] indicating the Palestinian origin of Onkelos. There is an especially close relationship between Onkelos and Neofiti, but it is not easy to determine whether this is to be explained by a common origin or by the influence of the former on the latter.

Texts, versions and concordances — The Aramaic text of Onkelos

---

5. There are other indications, too, of Palestinian origin, e.g. the presence of loan-words from Greek. A full list of these is given by G. Dalman, *Grammatik des jüdisch-palästinischen Aramäisch*, 2nd ed. (Leipzig, 1905; reprinted, Darmstadt, 1960), §37, pp. 182–87. They are also noted in A. E. Silverstone, *Aquila and Onkelos* (Manchester: University Press, 1931), pp. 148–52. 'The eastern element in the T. O. can easily be explained . . . by the fact of its transmission in Babylonia. But it would be difficult to account for the presence of western elements if it had originated in the east': E. Y. Kutscher, *art. cit.*, p. 10.

6. In his article 'Targum' in *The Jewish Encyclopedia*, vol. 12 (New York, 1906), p. 59.

7. *The Cairo Geniza* (The Schweich Lectures, 1941), London, 1947, p. 119; in a modified form in 2nd ed., pp. 194ff.

8. Cf. R. Le Déaut, *Introduction . . .*, pp. 85f.

was first printed in Bologna in 1482, and later in the Polyglots and in the Rabbinic Bibles. A. Berliner re-edited the work in 1884 (*Targum Onkelos*, Berlin) in two volumes, one containing an excellent introduction. The most recent critical edition is that of A. Sperber: *The Bible in Aramaic; I, Targum Onkelos*, Leiden, 1959. A. Díez Macho is preparing a new edition from MS. *Ebr. Vat. 448* to be printed in the Madrid Polyglot. This manuscript is of exceptional importance, provided, as it is, with a very early form of vowel-points.

There are two concordances to the work, that of E. Brederek, *Konkordanz zum Targum Onkelos* (*Beihefte, Zeitschrift für alttest. Wissenschaft*, IX, Giessen, 1906), and that of C. J. Kasowski, *A Concordance to the Targum of Onkelos* (Jerusalem, 1940). All the words of Onkelos are reproduced in G. Dalman's *Aramäisch-neuhebräisches Wörterbuch*, 1897–1901.

A Latin rendering of Onkelos can be found in Walton's London Polyglot and also in the earlier Polyglot Bibles. An English rendering of Onkelos and of the Palestinian Targums was made by J. W. Etheridge: *The Targums of Onkelos and of Jonathan ben Uzziel on the Pentateuch with the Fragments of the Jerusalem Targum*, 2 vols., London, 1862–65. This rendering is not perfect, but is the only one available. It was reprinted in 1968 (New York: K.T.A.V. Publishing House).

II. Pseudo-Jonathan: Targum Jerushalmi I (TJ 1)

The first reference to a paraphrase of the Pentateuch by Jonathan ben Uzziel (the reputed author of the Targum to the Prophets) is found in the writings of Menahem Recanati, a fourteenth-century Italian kabbalistic writer. About 1540, Elias Levita says in the introduction to his targumic lexicon (the *Meturgeman*) that he had read in Recanati's writings that Jonathan ben Uzziel had compiled a targum to the Pentateuch as well as to the Prophets. Elias tells us that he himself had not seen this work and expresses surprise that it should have so quickly perished. The work had not been lost. In fact, it could still be found in Italy, even if not known to Elias. Some thirty-five years after Levita had written his introduction, Asaria de Rossi noted in his work *Me'or 'Enayim* (1573–75) that he had seen two complete and verbally identical copies of a targum to the Pentateuch. One was in the possession of the Foa family at Reggio and bore the title 'The Targum of Jonathan ben Uzziel'. The other was in the possession of R. Samuel Kasi at Mantua and bore the title 'Targum Yerushalmi'. De Rossi further notes that both targums began with the same words, which were not *bḥmt'* (*bᵉḥokmᵉta*: 'in wisdom') but *mn 'wwl' br' h* (*min 'awla bᵉra' h*: 'from the beginning God created'). Since the Targum Yerushalmi proper was, it would seem, known to begin with the words 'in wisdom',[9] and that of Pseudo-Jonathan with *min 'awla*, de Rossi had actually seen two complete copies of Pseudo-Jonathan, one falsely titled (or classed as) 'Targum Yerushalmi'.

The copy de Rossi had seen in the possession of the Foa family must have been the Foa MS. which we know was shortly afterwards (1591) published as the *editio princeps* of this targum. What happened to the other copy of the targum we cannot say. For long it looked as if no other copy of this work existed. Then in 1896 G. Dalman drew attention to an extant copy of the work in MS. Add. 27031 of the British Museum. This MS. was further described by H. Barnstein in 1899 and published in its entirety by M. Ginsburger in 1903.[10] This MS., according to Ginsburger, is in a sixteenth-century Italian hand.[11] At the end of Deuteronomy it bears the signature of the censor Domenico Gierosolomitano with the date 1593.[12] The work was therefore in Rome towards the end of the sixteenth century, where, like other Jewish works, it was subjected to ecclesiastical censorship.

The *editio princeps* lacks the following verses: Gen 5:5–7; 6:15; 10:23; 18:4 (save two words); 20:15; 24:28; 41:49; 44:30–31; Ex 4:8; Lev 24:4; Num 22:18; 30:20b–21a; 36:8–9. Gen 18:4 and 20:15, but not the other verses, are in the London MS. A blank space is left in the London MS. where Gen 24:28 and 44:30f should have been written. The Rabbinic

9. As still does the Paris MS. 110 of the Fragment Targum, but in the absolute form: *bᵉḥokma*. Other texts of the Fragment Targum have: 'In the beginning in wisdom' (*bᵉreshît bᵉḥukma*), where *bᵉreshît* may have originally been merely intended to indicate the opening word of the Hebrew text (in the usual targumic fashion). The margin of the Paris MS. adds: 'Varia lectio: in (literally: from) the beginning' (*mn lqdmyn*). These are the opening words of Neofiti.

10. *Pseudo-Jonathan* (*Thargum Jonathan Ben Usiël zum Pentateuch*) *nach der Londoner Handschrift Brit. Mus. Add. 27031 herausgegeben* (Berlin, 1903).

11. Cf. *op. cit.*, p. iii.

12. On Domenico see R. Le Déaut, *Biblica* 48 (1967) 522, note 2.

Bible of 1794 (Vienna) carries the targum to Gen 44:30f. According to Ginsburger[13] the following verses, found in the *editio princeps*, are missing in the London ms.: Gen 16:9; 37:31; Ex 14:6; Lev 7:26,36,37; 23:41; 25:19; Num 2:21; 4:31-32; 9:4; Deut 23:12; 24:21.

The work probably came to be called 'Targum of Jonathan (ben Uzziel)' through a false understanding of the abbreviation 'T.Y.' This, which really stood for 'Targum Yerushalmi'— the Palestinian Targum—was taken to mean 'Targum Yehonathán'—the Targum of Jonathan. The composition had nothing to do with Jonathan and is now generally designated as the Targum of Pseudo-Jonathan.

Characteristics of Pseudo-Jonathan—Ps.-Jon. contains an Aramaic rendering of the entire Pentateuch, with the exception of the verses already noted. Unlike Onkelos and the Palestinian Targum proper (e.g. Neofiti), Ps.-Jon. is a composite and complex work. In some passages it reproduces Onkelos, even verbatim. In other passages its paraphrase is that of the Palestinian Targum. But even here the Aramaic it employs, while Palestinian, is not that of the Palestinian Targum as known from our other texts. This is especially noticeable in the form of the pronominal suffixes.

A much more distinctive feature of Ps.-Jon., however, are the numerous paraphrases and midrashim proper to itself, i.e. found in no other text of the Palestinian Targum. These again are of various kinds. Some of them are demonstrably interpolated into the text from Jewish midrash. We have a clear example of this at Ex 14:2 (from the Mekilta to the same passage), where the language betrays the interpolation. It has some recent references, such as the names Adisha and Fatima, the wife and daughter of Mohammed (Gen 21:21); of the six orders of the Mishnah (Ex 26:9): and of Constantinople (Num 24:24). The first two examples can be taken as interpolations, while the third example appears to be merely a rewriting of an earlier text to bring it up to date. The parallel text of the Fragment Targum has 'in the Great City' instead of Constantinople.

Other paraphrases of Ps.-Jon. are of a rather lascivious

13. *Ibid.*, p. iii.

character, and, to our minds at least, quite improper in a liturgical rendering. They, too, may conceivably be later interpolations into the text. But this should not be too readily affirmed. The antiquity of at least one of these paraphrases (Gen 37:36) is vouched for by Jerome (*Heb. quaest. in Gen.* 37:36).

But apart from these there are many other paraphrases proper to Ps.-Jon. which are demonstrably very old. Thus, e.g., the reference to the angels who fell from heaven (Gen 6:2,4). Others have been shown to represent very early Jewish haggadah. A. Marmorstein made a special study of the halakah of the work and found it similar to that of Philo and the Karaites, surmising that it may have been contemporaneous with Philo and a source for the Karaites.

Pseudo-Jonathan and the New Testament[14]—Some of the paraphrases proper to Ps.-Jon. illustrate certain texts of the New Testament. The paraphrase of Lev 22:28 reads: 'My people, children of Israel, as our Father is [or: 'as we are'?] merciful in heaven, so shall you be merciful on earth.' This is practically the text of Lk 6:36 (parallel Mt 5:48). This text is now found only in Ps.-Jon., but there is good evidence that it once stood in all texts of the Palestinian Targum. The midrash on Jannes and Jambres, found only in Ps.-Jon. Ex 7:11f, gives us the tradition referred to in 2 Tim 3:8, while the midrash on the veil of Moses, with the assertion that 'the Lord is the Spirit', of 2 Cor 3:17; 4:4, follows a midrash preserved in the main only in Ps.-Jon. The relation of the paraphrase proper to Ps.-Jon. with the Apocalypse is especially close. In this paraphrase we find parallels to the divine name 'who was and who is and who is to come', and to other passages of the Apocalypse as well.

Origin and date of Pseudo-Jonathan—The paraphrase proper to Ps.-Jon., then, deserves special attention. It has a special unity within itself, at least at times. One passage often presupposes another. To take but one example: Ps.-Jon. Gen 3:25 supposes that Adam and Eve had a special glory, lost by the fall; 4:21 again refers to this.

How explain this combination of ancient and recent elements? When did the oldest portions of Ps.-Jon. come into being? Ps.-Jon. Deut 33:11 contains a prayer for Johanan the

14. On this point see *The New Testament and the Palestinian Targum* . . ., pp. 258f for summary of the evidence.

High Priest, who can scarcely be any other than John Hyrcanus
(135–105 B.C.). A. Geiger, T. Nöldeke, P. Kahle and others
take it that this passage dates from his reign.[15] This view,
although it has been objected to, has much in its favour. We
may indeed date this passage and the older portions of Ps.-Jon.
to the pre-Christian age. In fact the conquests of John Hyrcanus
and of Alexander Janneus (103–76 B.C.) may possibly be
reflected in the geographical terms of the Palestinian Targum
in general.

It is by no means easy to explain how our present composite
text of Ps.-Jon. came into being. Some scholars (G. Dalman,
P. Kahle, P. Grelot, *et al.*) believe it is merely Onkelos completed by texts borrowed from older forms of the Palestinian
Targum. Others (e.g. W. Bacher, R. Bloch, A. Díez Macho)
believe that Ps.-Jon. is fundamentally a text of the Palestinian
Targum which was later influenced by Onkelos. Finally G.
Vermes is of the view that Onkelos depends, either directly
or indirectly, on Ps.-Jon.[16]

Text and versions—We have already spoken of the MSS. of
Ps.-Jon.[17] The text of the 1591 edition can be found in the
London Polyglot and in the Rabbinic Bibles. As far as Genesis
is concerned, the differences between the London MS. and that
printed in 1591 are minimal and where significant are noted
in a new translation to be published soon. In other books (e.g.
Lev 22:28) there are occasional significant differences.
Ginsburger's edition of the London MS. is accompanied by a
very useful introduction and notes giving midrashic parallels
to the text. His edition of the Aramaic text itself is very inferior,
and abounds in misreadings. The Aramaic text will be reprinted directly from the London MS. in the forthcoming
Madrid Polyglot.[18]

A Latin rendering, not always faithful, accompanies the
Aramaic text in the London Polyglot. The only English render-
ing made is that by J. W. Etheridge, noted above under
Onkelos. His translation is far from perfect.

---

15. See *ibid.*, pp. 60–62; 112–17; for argument from the Aramaic of sections of Ps.-Jon.
see above, pp. 82f.
16. For greater detail, see R. Le Déaut, *Introduction* . . ., p. 100.
17. See *The New Testament and the Palestinian Targum* . . ., p. 135.
18. On this see *Scripture* 18 (1966) 47–55, ≐ *Irish Ecclesiastical Record* 109 (1968) 158–65.

III.   The Fragment Targum: Targum Yerushalmi 2 (TJ 2)

In 1517 the Jewish convert Felix Pratensis published a MS. bearing portions of the Palestinian Targum. This work is now aptly described as the Fragment Targum. Being a second recension of this Targum it is also called Targum Yerushalmi 2 (TJ 2). Four MSS. of the work have for long been known to exist: one at Rome, the MS. Ebr. Vaticanus 440; another at Nuremberg (Cod. Nor. 1); the third at Leipzig (Cod. Lip. 1); and the fourth that of the Bibliotèque Nationale of Paris (MS. Hebr. 110), published by M. Ginsburger in 1899. To these we must now add a further MS., that in the Sassoon Library, Letchworth, England. This MS. has not yet been fully examined. Some scholars—P. de Lagarde, G. Dalman and A. Díez Macho—are of the opinion that the Leipzig MS. is that nearest the text published by Felix Pratensis.

The Fragment Targum has portions of the Targum to sections of all five books of the Pentateuch. L. Zunz has calculated that it covers about one-third of Genesis, three-twentieths of Exodus, one-fourth of Leviticus, one-fifth of Numbers and one-fourth of Deuteronomy. Sometimes the paraphrase reproduced may cover entire chapters, but this is very much the exception. Often the paraphrase reproduces a long midrash to a given verse; sometimes it has merely a few words, on occasion even a single word.

Since all known MSS. of the work have, by and large, the same text, they must all come from a single original. It is not easy to say how or why this original work came into being. From our present knowledge we can safely say that the fragments were drawn from some entire text or texts of the Palestinian Targum. Zunz surmised that the fragments are really variants which someone collected to supplement an entire text of the Palestinian Targum in his possession (Ps.-Jon. for Zunz). A. Geiger held the view that they were glosses inserted into the margin of an entire text of the Palestinian Targum. H. Seligsohn took the Fragment Targum to originate in glosses intended to compensate the literal rendering of Onkelos. G. Vermes, on the other hand, takes the Fragment Targum to be an *aide memoire* for preachers, to help them recall the interpretative traditions which they would be presumed to know.

It is indeed hard to say how these fragments came together to form a single work. The Aramaic in which they are written is generally of a corrupt kind, being influenced by the Aramaic of the Babylonian Talmud. This is more evident in some MSS. (e.g. Paris 110) than in others. The midrash contained in them is also occasionally affected by later Jewish tradition. Be this as it may, the texts represent a genuine Palestinian targum and are of no small value for the study of it, the paraphrase of TJ 2 being, at times, older and purer than that conserved in the other texts of the Palestinian Targum.

Texts and versions—As we have seen, the text of TJ 2 was first published in 1517 in the first Rabbinic Bible. This text, later corrected, was reproduced in later Rabbinic Bibles and in the Polyglot Bibles, inserted at the appropiate places in the text of Pseudo-Jonathan. The Paris MS. was published by M. Ginsburger in 1899 (*Das Fragmententhargum*, Berlin), accompanied by variant readings from the other MSS., and by an invaluable list of citations from the Palestinian Targum found in Jewish writings. His reproduction of the Paris MS. is, unfortunately, badly done, and his readings from the other MSS. are worse still! A new edition of all extant TJ 2 texts is being prepared by A. Díez Macho for the Madrid Polyglot.

Walton's London Polyglot has a Latin rendering of the Fragment Targum. J. W. Etheridge published an English rendering in the work referred to above under Onkelos.

IV. *The Cairo Fragments of the Palestinian Targum*

In 1930 Paul Kahle published portions of six MSS. of the Palestinian Targum from the Cairo Geniza.[19] MS. A with Ex 21:1; 22:27; MS. B with Gen 4:4–16; MS. C with Gen 31:38–54; 32:13–30; 34:9–25; 35:7–15; MS. D with Gen 7:17; 8:8; 37:20–34; 38:16–26; 43:7; 44:23 (fragments); 48:11–20; Ex 5:20; 6:10; 7:10–22; 9:21–33; Deut 5:19–26; 26:18; 27:11; 28:15–18, 27–29; MS. F with Ex 19:1–20,23; Lev 22:26; 23:44; Num 28:16–31; MS. G with poetic rendition of Ex 15 and 20. Later A. Díez Macho found and published four additional fragments

---

19. In *Masoreten des Westens* II, *Das palästinische Pentateuch-Targum, die Palästinische Punktuation, der Bibeltext des Ben Naftali* (Stuttgart: Kohlhammer).

of MS. E with the Targum to Gen 37:15–44; 40:5–18; 40:43–53; 42:34; 43:10.[20]

These new texts revolutionized the study of this ancient targum. Kahle dated MS. A to the late seventh or early eighth century A.D.; MS. E to A.D. 750–800; MSS. B, C and D to the latter half of ninth century; and MSS. F and G to the tenth or eleventh century. This would mean that already in the seventh century MSS. of the Palestinian Targum were being made in Palestine. We may legitimately presume that the Palestinian targumic tradition was being consigned to writing before this. What we have in the Cairo Geniza are merely the fragments which, owing to an accident of history, have escaped destruction.

While the early dates ascribed by Kahle to these earlier targum texts of the Geniza are not quite certain and may require revision,[21] the fact remains that in them we have MSS. some seven hundred years older than the other extant MSS. of this work, most of which are from the sixteenth century. A comparison of these MSS. among themselves (e.g. MSS. E and D Gen 38:16–26) and with other texts of the Palestinian Targum shows that various recensions of the targum were current, all carrying substantially the same paraphrase, but expressing it in different ways.

V. Tosefta Targumica

Some MSS. contain *toseftas* (additions) drawn from the Palestinian Targum, but written in Babylonian, not Palestinian, Aramaic. These *toseftas* are probably texts of the Palestinian Targum rendered into Babylonian Aramaic for the benefit of Jews who did not understand the Aramaic of Palestine.

VI. Codex Neofiti 1

Until A. Díez Macho identified Codex Neofiti as a complete text of the Palestinian Targum, it was known only partially in the text of Pseudo-Jonathan, in that of the Fragment Targum and in the fragments from the Cairo Geniza published by P. Kahle in 1930.

20. *Sefarad* 15 (1955) 31–39.
21. J. L. Teicher, for instance, does not agree with the early dating of Kahle. Cf. *Vetus Testamentum* 1 (1951) 125–29; *Journal of Jewish Studies* 1 (1949) 156–58; cf. also A. Díez Macho, *Vetus Testamentum* 8 (1958) 116; G. Widengren, *Numen* 10 (1963) 67.

Work on the Targum of Onkelos brought Professor Díez Macho to the Vatican Library in 1949. Among the works listed in the catalogue as Onkelos was one numbered Codex Neofiti 1. A rapid glance at the MS. raised doubts in Díez Macho's mind. Not being particularly interested in the Palestinian Targum at the time, he let matters rest there. When, however, he came to study the Targum of Palestine, his thoughts returned to Neofiti 1. He contacted Juan Arias, a young confrère of his studying for the priesthood in Rome, and asked him to copy for him the opening chapter of the MS. On examination it was seen that Neofiti 1 was not Onkelos but a genuine text of the Palestinian Targum.

This Codex contains the entire Palestinian Targum to the Pentateuch—apart from a number of verses omitted through homoiteleuton. It is written in a very clear, square hand, and has innumerable marginal and occasional interlinear glosses. The text is divided into liturgical parashoth such as one finds in the MSS. and editions of the Hebrew Bible. Certain words and passages of the text have been erased, evidently by a censor. These are, in the main, texts referring to idols (images), or ones which could be seen in the sixteenth century as derogatory to Christians.

The colophon tells us that the transcription of the text was completed at Rome for Maestro Egidio (written *'yydyw*)[22] 'in the glorious [*hnhdr*] month of Adar'. In accord with an accepted Jewish practice, the date of composition is to be found in the numerical value of the Hebrew letters *h, n, h, d, r*; i.e. $5 + 50 + 5 + 4 + 200$. This gives us 264, i.e. the year 5264 of Jewish chronology, which corresponds to A.D. 1504.

The Maestro Egidio for whom the work was written was most probably the noted humanist Giles (Egidio) of Viterbo.[23] He had a keen interest in Judaism, particularly in the Kabbala, and from 1517–27 had with him in Rome the Jewish scholar Elias Levita. A difficulty immediately faces us here: if the MS. in question was made for Giles of Viterbo, how is it that no influence from it is found in later writings of his, even where

22. In MS. Pluteus 1, Codex 22 (vol. I, p. 15 of A. M. Biscioni's catalogue) the name of Giles (Egidio) is transcribed in Hebrew letters as *'yydy'ws* and (fol. 8) as *'y'ydy'w*.

23. On Giles see now F. X. Martin O.S.A., *The Problem of Giles of Viterbo. A Historiographical Survey* (Heverlé-Louvain: Augustinian Historical Institute, 1960).

one would expect it? And why does the MS. appear to have been totally unknown to Elias? He compiled a lexicon of the Targum (the *Meturgeman*). Although there is evidence that he used a complete MS. of the Palestinian Targum to the Pentateuch now lost or unknown, an examination of the citations from the Palestinian Targum found in his *Meturgeman* reveals that he scarcely could have known Codex Neofiti I. Some of the citations found in the printed edition of the *Meturgeman* are found in Neofiti. This, however, does not invalidate the general conclusion drawn from the many differences between the other citations. A check of the citations in the first part of the MS. of the *Meturgeman* in the Angelica Library, Rome, has confirmed the present writer in this conclusion. Then again, many of the marginal glosses of Neofiti come from Pseudo-Jonathan, a work Elias said he did not know. These glosses must have originated in circles other than those of Levita; nor do the glosses appear to have been known to him.

Early history of Neofiti—The researches of R. Le Déaut have thrown light on the early history of Codex Neofiti I.[24] It gets its name from the fact that it is listed as No. 1 of the Neofiti MSS. of the Vatican Library. This lot of MSS. came to the Vatican from the Pia Domus Neophytorum in Rome, and in fact bears the seal of this college on the title-page together with the name of Ludovicus Canonicus Schüller, the last rector of the Domus. In 1543 Paul III founded a Domus Catechumenorum in Rome for converts from Judaism. In 1577 Gregory XIII founded the Pia Domus Neophytorum, or to give it its original name, the Collegium Ecclesiasticum Neophytorum. The last rector of the house entered office in 1886. During his tenure of office its books and MSS. were sold to the Vatican Library. The archives of the Pia Domus are now in the Vicariate of Rome. It is from these and other sources that R. Le Déaut has succeeded in throwing new light on the early history of Neofiti.

From the archives we learn of a list of eighty-two works donated to the college by Ugo Boncampagni in 1602. No. 20 of these is described as *fogli scritti a mano dove vi è el targumio hieroslomi*, probably a text of the Fragment Targum. No. 39 is *Aparafasi [= Una parafrasi] Caldea sopra al Pentateuco scritta a*

24. 'Jalons pour une histoire d'un manscrit du Targum Palestinien (Neofiti 1)' in *Biblica* 48 (1967) 509-33.

mano in carta pecora, i.e. a Chaldaic (Aramaic) paraphrase on the Pentateuch written by hand on sheepskin, = Codex Neofiti 1.

This, and others of these works, were bequeathed to Ugo by the renowned convert Rabbi Andrea de Monte (21 September 1587) who is known from other documents as having acted as official ecclesiastical censor of Jewish works. He saw anti-Christian polemic in such terms as idols, idolators, etc. It is doubtless he who has censored the present text of Neofiti. We may presume that some time after its completion for Giles of Viterbo, it passed into his hands for censorship. This explains how it remained unknown to Elias Levita. It was probably in Andrea's possession even before 1517.

Characteristics of Neofiti—The paraphrase of Neofiti is in general rather sober, and lacks some paraphrases found in other texts of the Palestinian Targum. The Aramaic is generally of a purer type than that of other texts of this targum, though somewhat more recent than that of the Geniza fragments of this targum. In certain sections of the work, nonetheless, the language and paraphrase appear to have been influenced by Onkelos. Here, however, a certain caution is indicated: in such matters it is not easy to say on which side the influence lies.

Neofiti lacks those recent references found in Pseudo-Jonathan. What date we should ascribe to the form of the Palestinian Targum as preserved in Neofiti is less certain. A. Díez Macho read a paper on the MS. at Oxford in 1959, after which W. F. Albright informed him that the geographical data of the targum pointed towards the second century A.D. as the date of the final recension of Neofiti. Díez Macho himself considers this targum to be, on the whole, a pre-Christian version. Rabbi Menahem Kasher, a specialist in rabbinic studies, goes further and considers Neofiti to be older than all the halakic midrashim and earlier than the Mishnah; in fact he takes it to have originated some centuries before the Christian era. The validity of these claims must yet be tested. Astounding though they look, they will probably prove substantially correct. Below we will study the geographical names of Neofiti and see how the evidence from them tends to corroborate these claims.

Transmission of Neofiti—The text of the Targum conserved in

Codex Neofiti appears to have been faithfully transmitted, notwithstanding some interpolations and scribal errors. It may have been a semi-official text in Palestinian Judaism: it abides faithfully by the Mishnah and later rubrics on targumic renderings. It leaves untranslated those texts which the Mishnah (*Meg.* 4:10) says are to be read in Hebrew but not translated.[25] Palestinian rabbis from the second to the fourth century A.D. occasionally cite Aramaic renderings of the Bible. A study of these citations shows that they are in the main very similar to—when not identical with—the text of Neofiti.[26]

Neofiti and the Arûk—At the beginning of the twelfth century R. Nathan ben Yehiel († 1106) compiled his lexicon, known as the *Arûk*, in which there are numerous citations from the Palestinian Targum to the Pentateuch. Probably more than one text of this work was available to him. A study of his citations reveals that his main work must have been a text identical, or almost identical, with our present Codex Neofiti 1.[27] Before Neofiti became known the targumic lexica had certain Aramaic words marked as being attested only in the *Arûk* (e.g. *p^egaš*) but which are now found also in Neofiti. Occasionally where a lexicographer corrects an *Arûk* form of a word, we find that Neofiti supports the *Arûk* reading; thus e.g. *srd'* (*s^erada*) of Gen 36:39 which Jastrow (p. 1023) emends to *ṭrd'* (*ṭirda*) of the Fragment Targum.

Of 158 citations from the Palestinian Targum to Genesis found in the *Arûk*, all but 48 are verbatim as in Neofiti. Of these 48, the difference between the text of Neofiti and the *Arûk* are often only minimal, and real differences could be reduced to about 30. The picture is the same in the citations from Exodus: 52 of the 87 citations are identical with the text of Neofiti; a further 14 are practically identical. Major differences are no more than 11. The *Arûk* has some 69 citations from the Palestinian Targum on Leviticus. Of these, 44 are identical with Neofiti (not reckoning 13 cases of differences in *matres lectionis*); there are 7 insignificant differences and 6 real

25. We have already noted above (p. 37) the relation of Mishnah, *Ta'anith* 4,3 to Neofiti Gen ch. 1.

26. On these see *The New Testament and the Palestinian Targum* . . ., pp. 45–56.

27. The question is now being studied in detail by S. Speier, 'The Relationship between *Aruk* and Targum Neofiti 1' in *Leshônenû* 31, fasc. 1 (October 1966) 23–32; fasc. 3 (April 1967) 189–98, to be continued; in Hebrew. The *Arûk* citations are printed in full.

differences of text. Of the 53 *Arûk* citations from Numbers, 31 are identical with Neofiti; there are a number of minor differences, but only 11 real ones. Neofiti's text for Deuteronomy is noted for the brevity of its paraphrase. It might appear that in it we have an abbreviated form of the Palestinian Targum to this book. Yet, our text appears to be identical with, or very similar to, that used by Nathan ben Yehiel. Of the 54 *Arûk* citations from the Palestinian Targum to Deuteronomy given by M. Ginsburger, 25 are identical with the text of Neofiti. There are only 4 real differences; the others are minor ones: one case of a different suffix; one of singular/plural; one of a different grammatical form; five with differences of only one word; five of very slight difference in spelling; two cases where the rendering is partly identical, partly different; eight with other forms of very slight difference.

A logical conclusion from this evidence is that the principal text of the Palestinian Targum used by R. Nathan ben Yehiel of Rome at the end of the eleventh century was identical with, or very similar to, Codex Neofiti 1.

The glosses to Neofiti—A feature of Codex Neofiti 1 are the numerous marginal glosses and occasional interlinear ones it contains.[28] The marginal glosses are by several hands; one series of them is by the author of the colophon, who by means of an acrostic even introduces his name (Menahem) in glosses to Ex 35:30.[29]

These marginal glosses occasionally contain corrections of the text, but more often are variant readings from other targumic renderings. Menahem Kasher believes they are drawn from at least three different recensions. Many of them carry the text of Pseudo-Jonathan; occasionally they agree with Onkelos and occasionally, especially for Genesis, they agree with the fragments of the Cairo Geniza. Some of them agree with the Fragment Targum. The marginal glosses occasionally have a more or less extended paraphrase; more often they consist of a few words, even of a single word, giving a synonymous variant

---

28. On these glosses see *The New Testament and the Palestinian Targum* . . ., pp. 46f, note 26, and now A. Díez Macho, *Neophyti 1. Targum Palestinense* (Madrid-Barcelona, 1968), pp. 24–28; 43–48; 53–56.
29. As noted by R. Le Déaut, *Introduction* . . ., p. 116.

to the text of Neofiti. In our rendering,[30] an attempt has been
made to reproduce these synonyms in English, keeping the
rendering of Ps.-Jon. in mind when the Aramaic word of the
gloss is that found in Ps.-Jon. The interlinear glosses are mainly
grammatical.

These numerous variants must have been drawn from MSS.
of the Palestinian Targum extant in the sixteenth century
and now, in part at least, apparently lost. They give us a vivid
picture of variety to be found in this rendering and of the
Palestinian Targum synoptic question. There was a well-
formed tradition expressed in varying ways. Neofiti and its
glosses can be compared to a Greek MS. of one of the Synoptic
Gospels with marginal glosses giving parallel readings from
the other two.

Editio princeps of Neofiti—The *editio princeps* is being brought
out by the Spanish Consejo Superior de Investigaciones
Científicas, under the editorship of Alejandro Díez Macho.
The first volume has appeared: *Neophyti 1. Targum Palestinense.
MS de la Biblioteca Vaticana. Tomo I. Genesis*, Madrid-Barcelona,
1968; 643 pages, plus 137 pages of introduction. It carries
the Aramaic text and glosses of Neofiti, together with a Spanish
translation by the editor, a French translation by R. Le Déaut,
and an English translation by the present writer and M. Maher
M.S.C. The long introduction contains a detailed account of
the MS., its name and provenance; the copyists and glossators;
the nature of the glosses; the date of copying and date of
composition of Neofiti; its relation to other targums; date of
its form of Aramaic, etc. etc.

30. Made for the *editio princeps* of Codex Neofiti, noted in n. 28 above. It is intended
to publish a revised text of this rendering together with a translation of the text of
Pseudo-Jonathan.

18

Geography of Neofiti

In view of the importance of the geographical terms used for ascribing a date to the composition of Neofiti, we treat here in some detail of the non-biblical names of places and peoples found in the codex.[1] The study has been made as comprehensive as possible; it is regretted that it has proved impossible to make it exhaustive.

Adiabene: *hdyp (Hadyeph)*, Gen 10:11–12, rendering Calah of HT. By New Testament times it embraced most of the territory of ancient Assyria east of the Tigris (see Pliny, *Nat. Hist.* 5,13,66). In the early first century it was ruled by native kings under some kind of dependence on Parthia. In the early first century Izates II († *ca.* A.D. 55), king of Adiabene, and his sister Helena embraced the Jewish faith (see Josephus, *Antiquities* 20:2–4; *Jewish War* 2,19,2; 5,2,2; 3,3; 4,2; 6,1; 6,6,3f). This dynasty ended in A.D. 116 when Trajan conquered Adiabene and made it the province of Assyria. There must have been strong Aramaic-speaking Jewish communities in Adiabene before the Christian era. Josephus wrote the first edition of the *Jewish War* in Aramaic and sent it to 'the Upper Barbarians' whom he describes as 'the Parthians, Babylonians, the remotest Arabians and those of our nation beyond the Euphrates, with the Adiabenes' (Prooemium to *Jewish War* 1,2). No town

1. On the importance of geographical identifications in early Judaism see above, p. 34. An argument in favour of the early formation of the targumic tradition on geographical identifications may be drawn from the Peshitta which on this point often coincides with the Palestinian Targum to the Pentateuch. See C. Peters, 'Peschitta und Targum des Pentateuchs' in *Le Muséon* 48 (1935) 1–54; e.g., p. 20. See also A. Díez Macho, *Neophyti 1. Targum Palestinense*, Madrid-Barcelona, 1968, pp. 72*–73*. Rudolph Cortes is doing a doctoral dissertation on the geography of Neofiti under the direction of Díez Macho. 'The impression of Cortes agrees with that of Albright [see above, p. 186 . . .: there is question of a toponomy of the Roman period; there are many names which are much older; there are names which continued in use during much later centuries; on the whole, however, the geography appears to be the geography of that period' (*ibid.*, p. 72*).

bearing the name Adiabene is known. The capital of the region was Arbela.

Africa: *'prq'*, Gen 10:2. See Phrygia.

Ain Gedi of the Palm Trees: Gen 14:7; Num 34:15. Identified with Hazazon-tamar of HT, an identification known to Jerome (*Hebr. quaest in Gen.* 14:7).

'Aion, Fortress of (*krk' d'ywn; karka di-'ayôn*). According to an additional paraphrase of Num 34:15, this lay to the east of Beth Yerah, on the boundary of the two and a half eastern tribes. Not found in the Fragment Targum. Identification unknown.

Amanus (?) of Taurus; see Tauros Menos.

Antioch: *'ntwky' ('Antokya)*, Gen 10:18, rendering Ḥamath of HT. Antioch on the Orontes. Jerome notes (*Hebr. quaest. in Gen.* 10:18) that while most continued to identify Ḥamath with Amath (Epiphania) of Syria, some believed it referred to Antioch: *nonnulli Antiochiam ita appellatam putant.*

Apamea: *'pmyh*, Num 34:10–11. On the northern boundary of Israel, translating Shepham of HT. Perhaps Apamea of Syria is intended; capital of the province of Apamane, it was situated in the valley of the Orontes. The city was destroyed by Pompey (Josephus, *Antiquities* 14,3,2). In the revolt of Syria in 46 B.C. it again plays a major role (Josephus, *War* 1,10,10). Jastrow and Levy (*Wört. über die Targ., s.v.*) believe Paneas in northern Galilee (Caesarea Philippi) is intended, i.e. prosthetic aleph; see Phrygia. The Fragment Targum has *'pmys*.

Asia: *'syh ('Asyah)*, Gen 10:3. The region or Roman province around Ephesus. Identification of Ashkenaz of HT.

Atadah: Gen 50:10. Aramaic form of Atad of HT.

Avlas of Cilicia (?): *'wwls dqylqy*, Num 24:8. In HT: Zedad. A town on the northern border of Israel. Levy (*op. cit.*) renders Aulon of Cilicia and refers to Josephus, *Antiquities* 13,21(23). Jastrow surmises that the Cilician Gates (*Pylae*) may be intended. Could the place intended be Abila, chief town of Abilene, or Abilene itself, between Damascus and Heliopolis? Perhaps we should render as 'Abila of Chalcis'. There is also a town by the name of Abila between Damascus and Paneas mentioned by Eusebius in his *Onomasticon*. It was for a time in Jewish hands. See Schürer, *History of the Jewish People* I, II, pp. 335–39.

'Ayna *('yynh)*, Num 34:10. Renders Ain of HT.

Barbaria: *brbry' (Barbarya)*, Gen 10:3. HT: Togarmah. A foreign (non-Roman) country. The exact place intended varies from text to text (in the midrash). Here, apparently, it refers to a region of Asia Minor, probably the Commogene near the borders of Cappadocia. In the targum to Ezek 27:14; 38:6, 'the house of Togarmah' is rendered as 'the province of Germania', probably Germanicia in the Commogene. *Gen. rabba* 37 identifies Togarmah of 10:3 as Germania *(q.v.)* or Germanicia. Jerome *(Hebr. quaest. in Gen.* 10:3), following Josephus, identifies Togarmah with the Phrygians. On the word 'Barbaria' in rabbinic literature see Strack-Billerbeck, *Kommentar* III, pp. 27–29.

Barbôi (?) or **Barkevi** (?): *brb[k?]wy*, Gen 10:3. HT: Riphath. Probably an error for Parkewi, the reading found in Levita's *Meturgeman*, i.e. a country in northern Ariana (see Jastrow). *Gen. rabba* has Adiabene.

Batanea: *bwtnyyn (Botneyin)*, Num 21:33; 32:33; 34:15; Deut 3:1,3,11; 4:10,13f,43,47; 29:6; 32:14; 33:22; *Mtnyn (Matnîn)*, Deut 1:4: HT: Bashan. The area known as Batanea in Roman times. The form Botneyin is proper to the Palestinian Targum. In the other targums Bashan is rendered as *Matnan*.

Beth Yeraḥ and **Yeraḥ.**[2] According to the paraphrase of Neofiti Num 34:15, the border of the two and a half eastern tribes went to the fortress of Ayôn *(Karka di-Ayôn)* which is east of Beth Yeraḥ, and from the east of the Sea of Beth Yeraḥ (i.e. of Genesereth) it went to Yadyoqita (?). Yeraḥ was at the most southerly point of Lake Tiberias. Beth Yeraḥ (near Yeraḥ) was a twin town of Sennaberis (texts in Jastrow, pp. 595f). In *Gen. rabba* 98:17, to Gen 49:21, explaining Kinnereth of Deut 3:17, R. Eleazar *(ca.* A.D. 270) says that it is Genesereth; R. Samuel ben Nachman *(ca.* 260) that it is Beth Yeraḥ, while R. Judah

---

2. See also W. F. Albright's words in A. Díez Macho, *Neophyti 1*, pp. 71*–72*.

ben Simon (*ca.* 320) says that it is Sennaberis and Beth Yeraḥ. According to Josephus (*War* 3,9,7) Sennaberis was about 30 stadia (¾ mile) from (the town of) Tiberias. See also Strack-Billerbeck, *Kommentar* I, pp. 101, 108. The name Beth Yeraḥ does not occur in other texts of the Palestinian Targum.

Bithynia: *bytny'*, Gen 10:2. In Asia Minor. Identification of Jubal of ht.

Caesarea (Philippi): *qsrywn* (Caesareon), Gen 14:14. ht: Dan. *Tarnegal* (or *Watchtower*) *of Caesarea* (*trngwl dqsrywn*): Num 34:15. (Also in Ps.-Jon. Num 34:8.) Called 'Upper Tarnegala which is above [or near] Caesarea' in Tosefta, *Shebi.* 4,10.

Callirrhoe: *qlrhy (Qalrahî)*, Gen 10:19. ht: Lesha. The renowned hot springs east of the Dead Sea.

Cappadocia(ns): *kpwdqyy'* (Gen 10:14); *kpwtqyy'*, *kpwqdyy'* (Deut 2:23). ht: Caphtorim.

Cilicia. See Avlas (of Cilicia).

Ctesiphon: *qtyspyyn*, Gen 10:10. ht: Kalneh. A large city in the southern part of Assyria, on the eastern bank of the Tigris; first mentioned by Polybius (5,45; second century b.c.). Pliny (*Nat. Hist.* 5,44) states that Ctesiphon was in Chalonitis (cf. also Polybius 5,44). The identification is probably a very old one.

Damascus. Always written as *drmšq* in Neofiti. *The Springs of Damascus* (*'yynwwtyh ddrmšq*) are mentioned in free paraphrase of Num 34:15.

Daphne: *dpny*, Num 34:11. ht: Riblah. Septuagint: Arbela; elsewhere the Septuagint renders Riblah as Dibletha. On the northern boundary of Israel: 'Their boundary went from Apamea (?, *q.v.*) to Daphne.' The identification of Riblah with Daphne is general in rabbinic tradition; texts in Strack-Billerbeck, *Kommentar* I, 33; II, 682; IV, 905,998.

Dardania: *drdny*[*'*], Gen 10:4 (identifying Dodonim of the ht). A territory of Mysia in Asia Minor, mentioned already by Homer. Cf. also Strabo 7, p. 596; Ptol. 3,29; Pliny, *Nat. Hist.* 3,9,2.

Edessa: *hds (Hadas)*, Gen 10:9–10. HT: Erech. Ancient capital
of Osrhoene peoples, called Ruhu by Assyrians (eighth century
B.C.). Its name was changed to Edessa under Seleucus I (312–
280 B.C.). In 132 B.C. it was capital of the Osrhoene. Its
identification with biblical Erech is also found in St. Ephrem.

Ford of the Passes: *mgzwt ʿbryyh.* Num 33:44; probably a mere
interpretative rendering of Iye-abarim of HT.

Fort Tarnegolah: *krk trngwlh* (literally: 'the fortress of the cock'),
Deut 2:8. HT: Ezion-geber. Since this place-name does not
occur elsewhere, it is possible that in Neofiti Deut 2:8 we have
merely an interpretative rendering of the Hebrew; *geber*
(Hebrew) = cock.

Gabla: *gbl', gblh*, Gen 14:6; 32:4; 33:14; Deut 1:2,44; 2:1,5,8,
12,22. HT: (Mount) Seir. The home of Esau. Thus also the
Fragment Targum and Ps.-Jon. The identification of Seir with
Gabla (Gebal) is found in the *Genesis Apocryphon XXI*, 11,29,
first century B.C.: 'the Hurrians who [were] in the mountains
of Gebal [HT: 'in Seir', Gen 14:6] until they reached El-Paran
which is in the desert'. It is the *Gobolitis* or *Gebalene* which
according to Josephus (*Antiquities* 2,1,2, §6; 'These [the sons
of Esau] occupied the region of Idumaea termed Gobolitis';
3,2,1, §40; 9,9,1, §188) formed part of Idumaea. Cf. J. A.
Fitzmyer, *The Genesis Apocryphon of Qumran Cave 1. A Commentary*,
Rome, 1966, pp. 132f, 147f). The Samaritan Targum, too,
renders Seir by Gabla. In Deut 32:2 'the *mountain of Gablah*'
(ṭwrh dgblh) renders Mount Paran of the HT. Tradition apparently considered it located in Gabla; cf. Gen 14:6.

Gennesar (Gennesareth), Sea of: *ym' dgnysr*, Num 34:11;
Deut 3:17. HT: Sea of Chinnereth. The name Gennesareth is
first attested in 1 Mac 11:67; then in the New Testament and
in Josephus.

Gerarah, Gen 20:1. Aramaic form of the biblical Gerar. The
Aramaic form is found also in Josephus, *Antiquities* 1,12,1, §207.

Germania: *grmnyh*, Gen 10:2; identifying Magog of HT. This is
best located in Asia Minor, probably Germanicia of the
Commogene. In fact, the original form of the name may well
have been Germanicia, with which a tradition conserved in

the Palestinian Talmud (*Meg.* 1,71 bot.), Babylonian Talmud (*Yoma* 10a) and *Gen. rabba* (37) identifies Togarmah. Historical events could have brought about the change. In Jerome's day some took Gog and Magog of Genesis and Ezekiel as referring to the Goths (*Hebr. quaest. in Gen.* 10:2), evidently a change in the understanding of an earlier view.

Gileadah, Gen 31:21,23; Deut 2:46. Aramaic form of biblical Gilead.

Ḥaluṣa: *ḥlwṣh,* Gen 16:17; 20:1; Ex 15:22. ht: Shur; Gen 16:14. ht: Bered. Ancient Halasa. The Idumaean city Elousa of Ptolemy (*Geog.* 16,10, second century A.D.) and Elousa of the early Christian Church. It was a Nabataean emporium on the Petra-Avdat-Gaza route, about 45 miles southeast of Gaza. A Nabataean inscription (possibly of the third century B.C.) has been found there. The Israelis have restored the ancient name Halutsa to the site. Onkelos renders Shur and Bered as Ḥagra, probably in the district of Petra (cf. Mishnah, *Gittin* 1,1). *Genesis rabba* 45,6 (on Gen 16:7) explains 'on the road of Shur' by two Aramaic words ('on the road of Ḥaluṣa') found in, and probably borrowed from, the Palestinian Targum. Here, as apparently elsewhere, the Palestinian Targum appears to underlie the midrash.

Hauranite(s): *ḥwrnyyh,* Gen 36:20f (vv. 22–30a missing in Neofiti); Deut 2:12,22. In these passages the ht speaks of the Horite(s) who dwelt in Seir. This in Neofiti becomes 'the Hauranite(s) who dwelt in Gabla'. I have not been able to find this word in the lexica of Jastrow, Levy or Buxtorf. The Fragment Targum, where extant, renders as Horites and so does Onkelos. In Neofiti Gen 14:6 they are called Haurites (*ḥwwryy'*). Hauranitis or Auranitis is Hauran of Ezek 17:16,18. It was part of the territory of Herod's son Philip.

Hellas (?): *'ls,* Gen 10:4. Identification of Elisha of the ht. Jastrow (p. 72) believes *Magna Graecia* in Italy is meant; Levy understands it as a district in Asia Minor: Aeolis, Aeolia, probably Elis.

Ḥirata, Taverns of. See Taverns.

India (Greek: *Indikê*): *hndqy,* Gen 2:11. ht: Havilah. Current

Jewish interpretation in Jerome's day (cf. *Hebr. quaest. in Gen* 2:11).

Italy: *'ytly'*, Gen 10:4 (Num 24:24). Identification of Kittim of HT. Kittim occurs again in Num 24:24 in an oracle of Balaam: 'But ships shall come from Kittim and shall afflict Asshur and Eber; and he also shall come to destruction.' This in the Fragment Targum becomes: 'And great multitudes shall come in Liburnian ships from the great city [or 'province'] and many legions from among the Romans shall be allied with them and they shall enslave Assyria and shall afflict all the sons of Mesopotamia [Abarnahara] but the end of both one and the other of these is that they be destroyed, and the destruction is for eternity.' The scribe of Neofiti wisely left blank the space where 'Romans' should fit. Yet the censor erased from both text and marginal glosses any conceivably offensive word. Among these there probably stood 'Liburnian ships' (*l^ebarnayya*) i.e. light, fast-moving vessels. Mention of them is made by Plutarch (first to second century A.D.) and Strabo (first century B.C. to first century A.D.) among Greek writers, and by Caesar, Horace, Tacitus and others among the Romans.

Jabboka: *ybq'*, Deut 2:37; 32:23. The Aramaic form of the Hebrew Jabbok.

Kardun: *qrdwn*, Gen 8:48. HT: Ararat. The mountain in Armenia on which the ark rested. It is 'the mountain of the Cordyaeans [*Korduaiôn*]' on which, according to a passage of Berossus (*ca.* 330–250 B.C.),·cited by Josephus (*Antiquities* 1,3,6, §93), one tradition believed part of the ark could still be found. The Peshitta, too, renders Ararat by Kardun.

Lehayyath Moab: *lḥyt, lḥyyt* (i.e. Fort of Moab), Deut 2:9,29 (HT: Ar Moab); Deut 2:36; 4:48 (HT: Aroer); Num 21:15,28 (poetic text) *lḥwwt* (HT: Ar). This latter writing (*Leḥawwat* ?), not found in lexica, may be due to a scribal error.

Lydia: *lydy'*, Gen 10:13. HT: Ludim. Lydia in Asia Minor.

Macedonia: *mqdwny'*, Gen 10:2. Identification of Javan of HT.

Media: *mdy*, Gen 10:2. Identification of Madai (*mdy*) of HT.

Mount of Iron: *ṭwr przl'* (*Ṭûr Parzela*), Num 34:4. HT: Zin. The HT reads: 'and your boundary shall . . . cross to Zin, and the end shall be south of Kadesh-barnea.' In Neofiti 'the Mount of Iron' replaces Zin, and 'Reqem' (i.e. Petra) replaces Kadesh-barnea. This is the only place where Zin occurs alone in the Pentateuch. In Num 13:21; 20:1; 27:14 (twice); 33:36; 34:3; Deut 32:51 we read of the wilderness of Zin, identified as Kadesh in Num 33:36. In all these cases Neofiti reproduces the Hebrew form 'wilderness of Zin', which it naturally identifies as Reqem in Num 33:36. Pseudo-Jonathan on the other hand inserts a reference to the Mount of Iron in Num 33:36: 'in the wilderness of Zinai (*ṣyny*) the Mount of Iron, that is Reqem'. The Mount of Iron is described by Josephus in the *Jewish War* (4,8,2, §454). Describing the Transjordan he tells how a second range of mountains beginning at Julias 'extends itself southward as far as Somora, which borders on Petra in Arabia. *In this ridge of mountains there is one called the Iron Mountain, that runs in length as far as Moab.*'

Mount of Snow: *ṭwr tlgh* (*Ṭûr Talgah*), Deut 3:8; 4:8. HT: Mount Hermon. In the free paraphrase of Num 34:15 the Mount of Snow (*ṭwr tlg'*) is given with Lebanon as the northern boundary. Here, too, Hermon must be intended.

Mysia: *mwsy'* (*Mûsia*). A district in Asia Minor, Gen 10:2 identifying Meshech of the HT. The reading of Neofiti is supported by the *Arûk*.

Nile of the Egyptians: *nylws dmṣryy*, Num 34:5. HT: the Brook of Egypt. 'The Nile of Egypt', Gen 15:18. HT: The River of Egypt.

Nisibin: *nṣybyn*, Gen 10:10. HT: Calneh (RSV: Calah). A town between Edessa and Mosul; modern Nusaybin in Turkey on the Syrian border. It is referred to in Assyrian inscriptions from the beginning of the first millennium as Nesibina. In the third century B.C. it was the capital of a rich province under the Seleucids. In 68 B.C. it was taken by Pompey, but fell to the Persians later and was recaptured by Trajan in A.D. 115.

Orthosia *(Orthosites)*: *'rtwsy'*, Gen 10:17. HT: Sinites. Orthosia was a Phoenician seaport, north of Tripoli, mentioned in 1 Mac 15:37.

Paneás, in Northern Galilee. See Apamea.

Pardesayya, Plain of; see Plain of the Gardens.

Pelusium: *pylwsyn (Pêlûsin;* Greek: *Pêlousion),* Ex 12:37; Num
33:3 (Num 33:5, *Pylûsypîn,* presumably a scribal error). HT:
Rameses. Place of residence of the Israelites in Egypt.

Phrygia: *'pryqy (Aphrîqî),* Gen 10:2. Region in Asia Minor.
Identification of Gomer of HT. That Africa is not meant follows
from the fact that Gomer is a son of Japheth and that almost all
the other peoples of the verse are located in Asia Minor.
Josephus (*Antiquities* 1,61, §123) identifies the Gomarites with
the Galatians. The prefixed aleph is typical of Palestinian
Aramaic. For other examples in place-names see *Reqem*
(Josephus: *Arekem*) and *Trachon* (also written *'Atrachôn*).

Plain (or Valleys) **of the Gardens** (or of Pardesayya): *myšr*
prdsy': mêšar pardesayya, Gen 14:17. HT: Valley of Shaveh;
Gen 14:3,8,10. HT: Valley of Siddim. The area in Gen 14:17
is one near Jerusalem where Melchisedech comes out to meet
Abram. This must be the same as the Phordisia mentioned in
a fifth-century Christian text, and the Phordesa (*Phordêsân*)
found in a fifth/sixth-century processional cross; see J. T.
Milik, 'Saint-Thomas de Phordesa et Gen 14:17' in *Biblica* 42
(1961) 77–84. Milik suggests that Pardesayya as a rendering of
Siddim (HT: sdym) in 14:3,8,10 in Neofiti and other Palestinian
Targum texts comes from reading the Hebrew *sdym* as *sādîm—*
'fields' instead of Siddim as in the pointed Masoretic text. We
cannot really say when this area was first called 'The Plain of
Pardesayya'. In the *Genesis Apocryphon* 22:13 it is identified as
'the Valley of the King, the Valley of Beth-haccherem' (i.e. of
'the House of the Vineyard').

Plains (or Valleys) **of the Vision:** *myšry ḥzwh (mêšre ḥezwah),*
Gen 12:6. HT: 'the oak of Moreh'; Gen 13:18; 14:13; 18:1.
HT: 'the oaks of Mamre'. The rendering may be a purely
interpretative one, there being no place bearing that name.

Pontus: *pwnṭws,* the kingdom of Arioch according to Gen 14:9.
HT: Ellasar (here and in 14:1; in 14:1 Neofiti reproduces HT).
Pontus is on the Euxine Sea in northeastern Asia Minor. The
Genesis Apocryphon (21:23), making Arioch king of Cappadocia,

also places his kingdom in Asia Minor. Symmachus and the Vulgate also identify Ellasar as Pontus. See further, J. F. Fitzmyer, *The Genesis Apocryphon*, p. 142.

Pundaqê Ḥirata: see Taverns of Licentiousness ('the Horn of Projection'; 'the Horn of the Corner'?).

Qeren-Zavve: *qrn zwwy*, Num 34:15. A point on the eastern boundary of the two and a half tribes, given in a free paraphrase of Num 34:15 and found only in Neofiti: 'And from the Great River, the River Euphrates, their boundary went to Qeren-Zavve which is behind it, and all Tarchon . . .' The Fragment Targum has *qrwn zkt'* (= 'the innocent towns' ?). Both texts may be corruptions.

Qesem: *qsm*, Num 34:4f. HT: Azmon. The Targum to Josh 15:4 reproduces the Hebrew word. The name is probably preserved in present day '*Ain Quṣeimeh* where some exegetes locate Azamon (see D. Baldi, *Giosue*, Rome, 1952, p. 118).

Ramatha: *rmth* ('height'), Num 21:20; 23:14; Deut 3:17,27; 4:49; 34:1. Renders Pisgah of the Hebrew Text.

Raphion: *rpywn*, Num 34:15. A border-town in the territory of the two and a half tribes, mentioned between Batanea and Shuq Mazai—Ain Gedi. Probably Raphana of Pliny (*Nat. Hist.* 5,16,74), and Raphôn of 1 Mac 5:37 (= Josephus, *Antiquities* 12,8,4). See Schürer, *History of the Jewish People II*, 1, pp. 105f.

Reqem: *rqm*, Gen 14:7; 16:14; 20:1; Num 13:26; 20:1,14,16,22; 33:36f; Deut 1:46. HT: Kadesh. Reqem was the Semitic name for Petra; see Josephus, *Antiquities* 4,4,7, §82: 'a place in Arabia which the Arabs have deemed their metropolis, formerly called Arce [perhaps error for Arekem] today named Petra'; 4,7,1, §161 (on the death of Rekem [Septuagint: Rokom], the Midianite king, Num 31:8): 'the fifth Rekem; the city which bears his name ranks highest in the land of the Arabs and to this day is called by the whole Arabian nation, after the name of its royal founder, Rekeme: it is the Petra of the Greeks.' The Semitic form of the name has recently been found in a Nabataean inscription; see J. Starcky, *Revue biblique* 72 (1965) 96–97. See further, *idem,* in *Dictionnaire de la Bible, Supplément,* vol. 7 (fasc. 39, 1964) cols. 896–98.

Reqem de-Gaya: *Rqm dgyʿh* (so too TJ 1 and 2; Onkelos: *rqm gyʾh*—with *aleph* where others have *ain*), Num 32:8; 34:4; Deut 1:2,19; 2:14; 9:23. The constant rendering of Kadesh-barnea of the Hebrew Text in Neofiti. So also in Peshitta. The town of Gaya is situated by Eusebius (*Onomasticon*) near Petra. The name is already attested in three Nabataean inscriptions in the forms *gyʾʾ, gyʾ* and *gʾyʾ,* i.e. 'the valley' (hence Starcky [*loc. cit.,* col. 897] believes the best form is that of Onkelos) and is retained in the present-day *el-Ği,* better known as the Wadi Musa, a mile and a quarter east of Petra.

Ṣapit(a): *ṣpyt(ʾ),* Gen 31:49. Perhaps merely an Aramaic rendering of Mizpah of the HT.

Saracens: *srqʿyn, srqyn,* Gen 37:25,27f; 39:1. HT: Ishmaelites. By the fifth century A.D. the Saracens are well known. At the time Jerome wrote his commentary on Isaiah (*ca.* A.D. 408–10) they had been known for a sufficient time in Palestine to give their name to a region: 'Cedar is a region beyond *Arabia of the Saracens*' (on Is 42:11). See also *idem, In Ezech.* VIII, c. xxv. As in Neofiti, the Ishmaelites of the Bible were identified with them: 'Cedar is a region of the Saracens who are called Ishmaelites in Scripture' (on Is 60:7). Augustine (*Questiones in Numeros* IV, q. 20, on Num 12:1) says that the Midianites of Ethiopia were in his day called Saracens. The Saracens are mentioned about A.D. 380 by Ammianus (*Hist.* 14,4). About A.D. 300 R. Levi says one of the three angels appeared to Abraham in the form of a Saracen (*Gen. rabba* 49:8, on Gen 18:2). In the second century Ptolemy (*Geogr.* 6,7,21) gives the Saracens (*Sarakênoi*) as a people of Arabia Felix and in *Geogr.* 5,17,3 he gives *Sarakênê* as a region of *Arabia Petraea* near Egypt. They must, then, have been known in the area long before. They were probably nomads who were accustomed to migrate from the northeast towards Egypt. They are probably the people mentioned by Pliny (first century A.D.) in *Nat. Hist.* (6: 28[32] 157); the reading of the text, however, is uncertain. In the Palestinian Talmud (*Bab. Met.* 2,8c) a Saracen is mentioned in an episode narrated of R. Simeon ben

Shetah of *ca.* 90 B.C. It is quite probable that they were known in Palestine before the Christian era. Once known, the identification with the Ishmaelites of the Bible could easily be made.

Segûlah, Valley of: *nḥl sgwlh*, Deut 1:24. HT: Valley of Eshcol.

Seleucia: *sylywqyh* (written:´*syl ywqyh*), Deut 3:10. HT: Salecah. Town in northeastern Palestine. Probably the Seleucia mentioned by Josephus among the conquests of Alexander Janneus (see *Antiquities* 15,15,4; *Jewish War* 2,20,6; 4,1,1; *Life* 37).

Shuq Masai: *šwq msyy*, Num 34:4. Given as the extreme western end of Israel's southern border: 'and it shall pass at the boundary of Shuq Masai at Qesem.' Nothing corresponding in HT, and not found in other targumic texts.

Shuq Mazai (?): *šwq mzyy*, Num 34:15. Given in a free paraphrase as a locality on the boundary of the two and a half tribes: '[Their border] went to Raphion and to Shuq Mazai and to the Cave of Ain Gedi until it reached the coast of the Sea of Salt.' Fragment Targum writes as one word: Shuqmezê. Not recorded in lexica.

Sukkatha: *skth*, Num 33:17. Aramaic form of Sukkoth of HT.

Tanis: Ex 1:11. Pithom of HT.

Tarnegola: see Fort Tarnegolah.

Tarsus (?, Greek: Tarsos): *ṭrss (Tarsas)*, Gen 10:4. Identification of Tarshish of HT. Josephus (*Antiquities* 1,6,2, §127) sees the name in Tarsus of Cilicia. Jastrow gives *Tarentum*.

Ṭauros Menos (?): *ṭwwrws mynws*, Num 34:8; *hwmyns ṭwwrws*, Num 34:7. A town or region on the northern boundary of Israel. HT: *hor ha har*: Mount Hor. The other Mount Hor, on the borders of Edom, where Aaron died (Num 20:22,23,25,27; 21:4,33–41; Deut 32:50) retains the name Mount Hor (*hr ṭwrh, hr ṭwr'*) in Neofiti. There was a town by the name of Tauromenos or Tauromenon on the eastern coast of Sicily. There may have been another of that name in northern Palestine. The varying forms of the name in Neofiti, however, indicate a corruption in one or other form, perhaps in both of them. The reading *Ṭauros Menos* is supported by the Fragment Targum which has *ṭwwrs mwnos*, and perhaps by the Arûk (*ṭwry ysmys*) and Elias Levita (*ṭwry ysmynyn*). The true reading is probably *Ṭauros Amanus*, practically that of Ps.-Jon., which has *ṭwwros 'wmnws: Ṭauros Omanus*. Taurus Amanus is given in Tosefta, *Halla* 2:11(99) as the northern extremity of Israel: 'What is Israel and what is foreign territory? Everything lying from the Taurus downwards . . . is the land of Israel; from the Taurus Amanus and beyond is foreign territory' (text in Strack-Billerbeck, *Kommentar I*, p. 91). The corresponding text in the Mishnah (*Halla* 4:8, *Shebi* 6:1; words of Rabban Gamaliel *ca.* A.D. 90) reads: [the river] Amana.

Taverns of Hirata (or 'of Licentiousness'?): *pwndqy ḥyrth, ḥyrt'* (*Pûndeqê Ḥîrata*), Ex 14:2,9; Num 33:7f. HT: *Pi hahiroth*. The *Mekilta* (on Ex 14:2) interprets *ḥrwt* of the Hebrew text to mean the licentiousness (*ḥerût*) of the Egyptians. This tradition, apparently, has influenced some texts of Ps.-Jon. and Frag. Targ. which for Ex 14:2 write *ḥerûta*, not *ḥyrth*. See Levy, *Wört. über die Targ.*, p. 271.

Telassar: *tl'sr*, Gen 10:12. HT: Resen. 'Telassar between Nineveh and Adiabene'. It may be Telassar of Is 37:12; cf. 2 Kgs 19:12. Other Palestinian Targum texts on Gen 10:12 have Talsar (*tlsr*).

Thracia (Greek: *Thrakê*): *trq'* (*Tarqa* or *Tarqê*). In northern Greece—Gen 10:2. HT: Tiras.

Ṭirat 'Addarayya: *ṭyrt 'dryyh*, Num 34:4. HT: Hazar-addar. The Fragment Targum has *dîrat 'addarayya*, 'the shed of the flocks'.

Ṭirat 'Anvatah: *ṭyrt 'nbth*, Num 34:9; *ṭyrt 'nwwth*, Num 34:10. HT: Hazar-enam. The other Palestinian Targum texts have *dîrat 'anvata*.

Trachona, Trachonitis: *ṭrkwnh* (Deut 3:4); *trkwnh* (Deut 3:13f). HT: Argob; *ṭrkwn*, Num 34:15, free paraphrase. In a gloss to Neofiti 3:4 the name is written as *'ṭrgwn'* (*'Aṭargôna*); in Frag. Targ. Deut 3:14 as *'ṭrkwn'* (*'Aṭarkôna*); cf. Reqem-Arekem. *Tarchôna* of the targums is the *Tracho* (*ho Trachôn*) of Josephus (*Antiquities* 13,16,5; 15,10,1; *War* 2,6,3); *Trachonitis* of Luke 3:1. In the days of John Hyrcanus (134–104 B.C.), Aristobulus raised an army from Libanus and Trachon (*Antiquities* 13,16,5). See Schürer, *History of the Jewish People* I, II, p. 11, note.

Valley of Acquisition: *Naḥal Segûlah*; see *Segûlah*.

Valley of the Vision; see Plains of.

Valleys of the Gardens; see Plain of.

Villages of Jair: *Kuphranê dᵉyaʾîr*: Num 32:41 (*kwprny dyʾyr*); Deut 3:14 (*kwprnwy dyʾyr*). ʜᴛ: Havvoth-jair.

Yadyoqiṭa, Yadyoqiṭôs: *ydwqyṭʾ*, *ydywqyṭws*: A town near Caesaraea Philippi. Num 34:15 in free paraphrase: 'And from the east of the sea of Beth Yeraḥ their boundary went to Yadyoqiṭa and from Yadyoqiṭôs Tarnegol Caesariôn which is east of the Cave of Dan their boundary went to the Mount of Snow.' The text may be corrupt. The Fragment Targum had *Diôqyanôs* and *Yoqyanôs*: 'And from Hoba, which is to the north of the Springs of Damascus, their boundary went to *Diôqyanôs* the Mount of Snow [*ṭur tagla;* read: Turnagla] of Caesarion which is to the east of the Cave of Dan; and from Yôqyanôs Turnagla of Caesarion which is east of the Cave of Dan their boundary went to the Great River, the river Euphrates.'

Interpretative renderings·

There are some names of people and places which Neofiti (as other texts of the Palestinian Targum) paraphrases rather than reproduces or identifies.

Bela, a town identified with Zoar in Gen 14:2,8. This place-name is rendered in Neofiti as 'the city which swallowed up [*dblʿt*] its inhabitants'; *balaʿ* (*bᵉlaʿ*) in Hebrew and Aramaic means 'to devour'.

'The **Emim** in Shaveh-kiriathaim' (*ha-êmîm bᵉšaweh qiryatayim*) of Gen 14:5 becomes 'the awe-inspiring ones (*ʾmtnyh*) who were dwelling in the midst of the city' (*bgwwh dqrth*). The proper name Emim is interpreted from the root *ʾêmah*—'dread'. So also in the other occurrences of the word in Deut 2:10f. In Gen 14:5 the Septuagint reproduces Emim as *ommaioi*, but renders *Shaveh-kiriathaim* as 'Save the City'. In Deut 2:10f the Septuagint reproduces Emim as *Ommin*. In Deut 2:10f Neofiti has the form *ʾwmtnyyh*, not *ʾmtnyh* as in Gen 14:5.

Hormah. In Num 14:45 and Deut 1:49 we read of Israel pursuing their enemies 'to Hormah', i.e. as far as the place Hormah. Hormah in Hebrew means 'destruction' (cf. Num 21:3). In Num 14:45 and Deut 1:49 'to Hormah' (*'d ḥrmh*) is rendered in Neofiti as 'to destruction' (*šyṣyw—shêṣayû*) unless *Shêṣayû* is intended as a place-name. In Num 21:3 Neofiti reproduces Hormah of the HT.

Mount Sirion. Sirion according to Deut 3:9 was the Sidonian name for Mount Hermon. Neofiti (and other texts of the Palestinian Targum), instead of reproducing the word, interprets through the root *šerê*, 'to decay', as 'the mount which corrupts its fruit', i.e. which produces tasteless fruits. So also in Targ. Ps 29:6 and 1 Chr 5:23.

Ur of the Chaldees, Gen 11:28,31; 15:7. This name is always rendered as 'the furnace of fire of the Chaldaeans', *Ur* in Hebrew meaning 'light', 'flame', 'fire'. The interpretation is connected with the ancient tradition (found partly in *Jubilees* 12:12–15, second century B.C.) that an attempt was made to burn Abraham in a furnace of fire in the land of his birth. Ignorance of the fact that Ur was a city may also have contributed. The Septuagint interprets Ur as 'region' (*chôra*).

Zuzim, Gen 14:5. In his invasion, Chedorlaomer 'subdued the Zuzim in Ham' (*hzwzym bhm = haz-zuzîm bᵉham*). Failing to recognize that *zwzym* and *hm* were both proper names, the Septuagint renders: 'the strong people together with them' (= *bahem*). Neofiti (and the other texts of the Palestinian Targum) render in a similar fashion: 'the noblest who were among them'. This Aramaic rendering is reproduced by *Gen. rabba* s. 42 on this verse. The *Zamzummim* of Deut 2:20 are probably the same as the *Zumim* of Gen 14:5. In Neofiti the word is rendered as *Zamthanayya* (*zmtnyyh*), probably intended as a proper name. The Septuagint reproduces the name as *Zamzommin*.

Conclusion

There is nothing in the geographical names used in Neofiti which necessitates a date of composition after the beginning of the Christian era. With one or two exceptions, the names used are all attested before the time of Christ or in the early centuries of our era. And these names first attested in Christian times can be supposed to have existed earlier.

More detailed study may reveal what traditions are represented in the geography of Neofiti and of the Palestinian Targum in general. They may be liturgical and halakic, i.e. precise identifications of places which were connected with Jewish liturgical halakah.

19

Targum to the Prophets

I.   Babylonian Targum to the Prophets

The Targum to the Earlier and Later Prophets has traditionally been attributed to Jonathan ben Uzziel, the disciple of
Hillel (*ca.* A.D. 50). This is due to the Babylonian Talmud,
Meg. 3a. It is now becoming generally recognized, however,
that the 'Jonathan' mentioned in this text is a Hebrew form of
Theodotion, just as 'Onkelos' of the same text is but a Hebrew
form of Aquila. The translation connected with the name of
Jonathan (i.e. Theodotion) in the text of the Talmud is most
probably a Greek, rather than an Aramaic, targum. Elsewhere in the Babylonian Talmud the Targum to the Prophets
is associated with the name R. Joseph bar Hiyya, not with
that of Jonathan. But this association does not amount to a
tradition on the authorship of the targum. It follows that we
know nothing on the author of the Targum to the Prophets.
This, of course, is in keeping with the origins of the targums
in general.

The Targum to the Prophets as we now have it has come to
us as redacted in the Jewish schools of Babylon. It must, however, have come originally to Babylon from Palestine. This
means that it is basically a Palestinian work. We cannot really
say how much the Babylonian redaction has affected the
original work. We can presume that no small amount of
paraphrase was removed to bring the text nearer the original
Hebrew. The redaction, however, has been less thorough-
going than was the case with Onkelos, the result being that
the Targum Jonathan to the Prophets retains more paraphrases
than does the Babylonian Targum on Genesis.

In its present form, the Targum to the Prophets dates from
the third to fifth century A.D. It must have been widely known

in Babylon at an earlier date because it is cited at the beginning of the fourth century as authoritative (Babylonian Talmud, *San*. 94b).

In view of its Palestinian origin, it merits study for a knowledge of the early teaching of Palestinian Judaism on certain points. The extent of the paraphrase varies from one book to another. The book that has retained the most is probably the Targum on Isaiah. P. Grelot has shown how some of its paraphrase is very old and related to the Palestinian Targum to the Pentateuch.[1] Other texts of this targum throw light on passages of the New Testament. The messianic interpretation we find in Targum Micah 5:1: 'And you Bethlehem . . . from you shall the Messiah come forth before me' (cf. Ps.-Jon. Gen 35:21) is probably pre-Christian. Such an interpretation of the text was less likely to originate later, when there appears to have been a tendency among the Jews to play down this particular prophecy (cf. Origen, *Contra Celsum*, i, 51).[2]

Editions and translations

The Targum to the Prophets was first printed at Leiria in 1494; then at Venice in 1518, and later in the Polyglots and in the Rabbinic Bibles. It was re-edited by P. de Lagarde (*Prophetae Chaldaice*, Leipzig, 1872). The most recent critical edition of the Aramaic text is that of A. Sperber: *The Bible in Aramaic II— The Former Prophets according to Targum Jonathan*, Leiden, 1959; *The Bible in Aramaic III—The Later Prophets according to Targum Jonathan*, Leiden, 1962.

A Latin rendering of the entire Targum to the Prophets can be found in Brian Walton's *London Polyglot*. There is no English rendering of the entire work. C. W. H. Pauli published an English translation of the Targum to Isaiah in 1871 (*The Chaldaic paraphrase on the Prophet Isaiah*, London). In 1949 J. F. Stenning published the Aramaic text and an English rendering of the Targum of Isaiah (*The Targum of Isaiah*, Oxford). This edition is accompanied by an excellent introduction on the nature of targumic renderings and the bearing of this on the Targum to Isaiah.

1. *Revue biblique* 70 (1963) 371–80; cf. *The New Testament and the Palestinian Targum* . . ., pp. 230–33.
2. For what rabbinic texts there are on Micah 5:1 see P. Billerbeck, *Kommentar* I, p. 83.

II. *Palestinian Targum to the Prophets*

The targum from which the rendering of Jonathan to the Prophets is derived can be called a Palestinian targum to the Prophets. What the nature or fate of this targum was we cannot say. We may legitimately presume that while the Babylonian academies were using and editing the targum now bearing the name of Jonathan, there continued to exist in Palestine a Palestinian targum, composed in the Aramaic of Palestine. Such a work would be needed for the rendering of the passages from the Prophets (the *Haftarôth*) read in the synagogue.

No complete text of the Palestinian Targum to the Prophets is now known to exist. Occasional citations from this targum, however, are found in Rashi, Kimhi and in the *Arûk* of R. Nathan ben Yeḥiel. Some MSS. of the targum have 'additions' (*tosephtas*) which agree with the citations of the medieval Jewish writers just mentioned. Occasionally (e.g. Codex 116 of King's College, London) these additions are given as 'tosephtas of the Land of Israel', i.e. of Palestine; in the *Codex Reuchlinianus* they are often introduced as 'the Targum of Jerusalem'. These texts led L. Zunz to conclude that there once existed an entire Palestinian targum to the Prophets, different from that of Jonathan. The same author notes that what we now have in extant fragments appears to correspond to the *Haftarôth*. Apparently the sections of the targum recited in the liturgy were the last portions to be lost, not however without bequeathing to us a few small fragments. Other fragments of this targum are probably to be seen in renderings of short prophetic texts found in the Palestinian Targum to the Pentateuch.

A greater knowledge of this Palestinian Targum to the Prophets would be of extreme importance for New Testament studies. What remains, however, is very meagre indeed. And even this has to be used with caution. The Aramaic in which it is written is influenced by that of Onkelos, and its midrash may conceivably be later too.

20

Targums to the Hagiographa

Unlike the Law and the Prophets, the Hagiographa did not form part of the synagogue liturgy. No Aramaic rendering was then required for synagogue use. Yet we possess targums to all these works, with the exception of Ezra-Nehemiah and Daniel. All these targums, with the possible exception of that on Proverbs, are basically in Palestinian Aramaic. Relatively little study has been done on them. Each presents its own peculiar problems. According to what general view there is on the subject, these works are held: 1) to have originated not before the talmudic period, and are perhaps later; 2) to be the works of individuals, unlike Jonathan and Onkelos; 3) not to have been destined for the use of school or synagogue. More detailed study would probably introduce many nuances.

I. Job and Psalms

Because of the nature of their language these two renderings are taken to be the work of a single individual. A feature of both targums is that for some passages they give variant readings from other targumic texts. Palestine must have known more than one current rendering of these books, as it did for the Pentateuch. There are probably recent and ancient elements in both these targums. The rendering of Ps 68(69):19 may well be reproduced, or presupposed, in Eph 4:8.[1] The Targum on Job is quite distinct in language and character from the fragments of the Targum on Job found in Qumrân.[2]

II. Proverbs

The Targum on Proverbs is similar in character to the others

---

1. Cf. *The New Testament and the Palestinian Targum* . . ., pp. 78–81.
2. See above, p. 63.

of the Hagiographa, but presents a curious feature in being
very similar in language to the Syriac rendering of this book.
A third or so of the work, in fact, corresponds word for word
to the Peshitta rendering, thus giving us typical Syriac forms
of Aramaic. This phenomenon is explained by assuming that
the Targum to Proverbs is based on the Syriac, or that both
are based on an early rendering made for Syriac-speaking
Jews. Despite its mixed character, the work is acknowledged
as containing some old traditions.

III.   The Five Megilloth

The targum to the Five Megilloth (Canticles, Esther, Lamen-
tations, Ruth, Qoheleth) is characterized by its developed
paraphrase and many midrashic additions. It is a recent,
post-talmudic composition, its language being a mixture of
Western Aramaic and of that of the Babylonian Talmud.
Strictly, we should not speak of *a* targum to the Megilloth.
The paraphrase of each book presents its own peculiar
problems, to be studied separately. Each of these targums contains older material. The Targum on Lam 2:20 may throw
light on Mt 23:35.[3]

IV.   Chronicles

The Polyglot Bibles carry no targum to Chronicles, the reason
being that none was known to exist when these works were
published. The targum of 1 Chronicles was first published in
1680; that of 2 Chronicles in 1683, both accompanied by a
Latin translation. Another text of this targum from a Cambridge
MS. was published in 1715. P. de Lagarde published a critical
edition in *Hagiographa Chaldaice*, Leipzig, 1873.[4] W. Bacher
believes the work dates from the third to fourth century A.D.
It is written in Palestinian Aramaic and has many points of
contact with the Palestinian Targum to the Pentateuch. In the
Table of Nation the targum to Chronicles seems to follow the
same tradition as Pseudo-Jonathan, which in this particular
point is different from the other texts of the Palestinian Targum.

---

3. Cf. *The New Testament and the Palestinian Targum* . . ., pp. 160–63.
4. For another inidentified MS. in the Vatican Library, see Le Déaut, *Introduction* . . .,
p. 145, n. 1.

Index to Authors

Van der Ploeg, J. 63 f., 65
Van der Woude, A. 63
Vermes, G. 129, 161 n., 180 f.
Vööbus, A. 66

Walton, B. 176, 207
Weingreen, J. 29, 30, 31, 36
Wernberg-Møller, P. 67, 174
Wilson, R. McL. 130 n.

Winter, P. 65 f.
Wohl, S. 66
Wolfson, H. A. 101
Wright, A. G. 9 n., 50 n., 53 n., 69 n., 77n.

Zuckermandel, M. S. 35 n.
Zunz, L. 82, 181, 208

Index to Citations and References

OLD TESTAMENT

Index to Subjects and Persons